Philosophical Counselling
& The Unconscious

Requests for permission to reproduce material from this work
should be sent to Permissions, Trivium Publications, P. O. Box 1259
Amherst, NY 14226

ISBN: 978-0-9713671-2-8

0 0 1 2 3 4 5 6 7 8 9 0 0

Philosophical Counselling & The Unconscious

Edited by

Peter B. Raabe

Volume I:
Philosophical Psychology Series

Editor: Brent Dean Robbins

"We'll call the part of the soul with which it reckons and reasons the rational part, and the part with which it lusts, hungers, thirsts, and gets excited by other desires the irrational appetitive part... The spirited part is a third thing in the soul that is by nature the helper of the rational part, provided that it hasn't been corrupted by bad upbringing."

—Plato. Philosopher. 428–347 BC

"The power of the id expresses the true purpose of the individual organism's life. This consists in the satisfaction of its innate needs.... The task of the ego is to discover the most favorable and least perilous method of obtaining satisfaction, taking the external world into account. The super-ego may bring fresh needs to the fore, but its main function remains the limitation of satisfaction."

—Sigmund Freud. Psychoanalyst. 1856–1939

"What distinguishes psychoanalysis is that it would disappear if the hypothesis of the unconscious were to be abandoned."

—Serge Lebovici. Emeritus Professor of Psychiatry. 1999

CONTENTS

CONTRIBUTORS

LYDIA B. AMIR is an Associate Professor of Philosophy and Head of Humanities at the School of Media Studies, The College of Management, Academic Studies, in Tel-Aviv, Israel, and an adjunct associate professor at the Department of Business Administration in Tel-Aviv University. Along-side her academic work, she has been working for more than ten years as a philosophical and ethical consultant for individuals and organizations. She has published various articles on the relevance of philosophy for non-phi-losophers, bearing both on their personal life (love) and on their working environment (ethics), on the possibility of dialogue, on the method she uses within her philosophical practice and on the importance of humor. Her first book *Philosophy as Redemption: Comparing Spinoza and Nietzsche* is being currently reviewed by Nijhoff Press. Her second book, *Tragic Laughter, Comic Vision: The Story of Humor and Philosophy*, is published by SUNY Press. E-mail: lydamir@colman.ac.il.

SYLVIA BURROW is currently Visiting Assistant Professor at the University of Utah. Her areas of specialty include Moral Psychology, the History of Ethics, Feminist Ethics, and Emotion Theory. She recently graduated from the University of Western Ontario in London, Ontario. Her Doctoral dissertation (2002) is entitled *Showing Some Humean Sympathy: The Role of Emotion in Moral Theory*. E-mail: sylvia.burrow@mic.ul.ie.

DANIEL BURSTON is an Associate Professor of Psychology at Duquesne University in Pittsburgh, an Adjunct Faculty Member of the C. G. Jung Analyst Training Program of Pittsburgh, and an Associate of the Center for Philosophy of Science at the University of Pittsburgh. He is the author of four books, *The Legacy of Erich Fromm* (Harvard University Press, 1991), *The Wing of Madness: The Life and Work of R. D. Laing* (Harvard University Press, 1996), *The Crucible of Experience: R.D. Laing and the Crisis of Psycho-therapy* (Harvard University Press, 2000), and *Fromm's Legacy Reconsidered* (Trivium Publications, forthcoming), and Editor, with Victor Barbetti and

Brent Dean Robbins, of *The Legacy of R.D. Laing* (Trivium Publications, forthcoming). He is the Founding Director of The Society for Laingian Studies. E-mail: burston@duq.edu.

ELLIOT D. COHEN is principal founder of philosophical counselling in the United States; co-founder and Executive Director of the Society for Philosophy, Counseling, and Psychotherapy; Ethics Editor for *Free Inquiry Magazine*; Editor-in-Chief and founder of *International Journal of Applied Philosophy* and *International Journal of Philosophical Practice*; and author or editor of thirteen books including *What Would Aristotle Do? Self-Control through the Power of Reason* (Prometheus, 2004).

ELI EILON teaches philosophy at Haifa University and at the Hebrew University of Jerusalem, Israel. His fields of specialty include Nietzsche, 19th century European philosophy, and philosophy of education. E-mail: Eli.Eilon@huji.ac.il.

ANDRIES GOUWS studied art in Cape Town, Düsseldorf and Amsterdam, and philosophy in Utrecht (Netherlands). He teaches in the School for Philosophy and Ethics at the University of KwaZulu-Natal, Durban 4041, South Africa. E-mail: gouwsa@ukzn.ac.za. Website: www.andriesgouws.com.

ORA GRUENGARD has a Ph.D. in philosophy from the Hebrew University in Jerusalem, and has studied economics, cognitive psychology, and family therapy in Israel, France and the USA. Gruengard's dissertation and later studies are concerned mainly with self and others' knowledge and understanding and therefore with the epistemological problems of the human condition and the social sciences, including an exploration of psychotherapeutic and in particular psychoanalytic, notions and presuppositions. After many years of teaching and research, mostly at Tel Aviv university, Gruengard has made a partial shift towards the practical application of philosophy, and has been practicing philosophical counseling since 1992. E-mail: Orag@mail.shenkar.ac.il

PIERRE GRIMES, the founder-president of the Noetic Society, Inc., For the Study and Exploration of Platonic and Neo-Platonic Works, of

Dialogue and the Dialectic, in 1968, introduced its Philosophical Midwife Program in 1978. He is certified in client counseling, a faculty member and a board member of the American Philosophical Practice Association. His articles on philosophy, philosophical counseling, and a computer program "To Artemis: The challenge to know thyself," which is designed to explore personal problems, can be accessed on his web site, openingmind. com. For over fifteen years he has conducted philosophical workshops at Esalen Institute, at Big Sur, California and in 2004 will offer a philosophical counseling workshop based upon his book, *Philosophical Midwifery: A New Paradigm for Understanding Human Problems With its Validation*. E-mail: pierre@openingmind.com.

MARTIN HUNT is an artist and writer whose work focuses on the concepts and imagery of science. Early in his career he studied physics and mathematics. He has been a computer programmer for 20 years and has developed many computer simulations of physical processes as an aid to his ongoing research. The goal of this research has been a personal understanding of how life and mind could arise in a purely physical universe. His thinking has been deeply influenced by chaos theory and by the theory of evolution. E-mail: simulat@shaw.ca.

FIONA JENKINS teaches and researches philosophy at the Australian National University. She worked for several years as a volunteer counseller at a rape crisis center and recently took a course on philosophical counseling, though she has never formally practiced as a philosophical counselor. The importance of drawing philosophy into an engagement with life beyond the academy as well as the importance of reconceiving philosophy in terms true to its history, as the attempt to grapple with life's most pressing questions, both shape her interest in philosophical counseling. She has previously published articles on the relevance of Foucault for philosophical counseling as well as articles on Nietzsche, feminist philosophy, ethics, and contemporary French philosophy. E-mail: Fiona.Jenkins@anu.edu.au.

ALEXANDER KEALEY maintains a private philosophical practice in Mt. Shasta, California. He has taught at Towson University, College of the Siskiyous, and University of Phoenix. He is author of *Revisioning Envionmental Ethics*. E-mail: kealey@siskiyous.edu or dakealey@email.uophx.edu.

RAN LAHAV teaches part time philosophy and philosophical counseling at Haifa University in Israel. During the rest of the year he lives in his rural home in Vermont, USA. He has practiced philosophical counseling for more than ten years, and has given numerous workshops and lectures on the topic. He has published articles in various journals and edited *Essays On Philosophical Counseling* (UPS: Lanham, 1994). In 1995 he co-organized the First International Conference on Philosophical Counseling held in Canada. E-mail: lahavr@construct.haifa.ac.il.

DAVID O'DONAGHUE has doctoral training in both clinical psychology and philosophy. His eighteen years of clinical experience working within the psychoanalytic/Jungian framework has provided a rich ground for the development of his practice of philosophical counseling in which he uses the resources of philosophy in working with individual and group dilemmas. He is the founder and director of the Lyceum, a school of culture and values, located in New Orleans. The school seeks to integrate personal and collective experience in the exploration of meaning. E-mail: druben2@hotmail. com.

DENNIS POLIS is a non-academic philosopher with a doctorate in theoretical physics from the University of Notre Dame (1970). He has published articles and book reviews on Aristotle, projective realism, mysticism and the philosophy of science, as well as writings on the fundamental nature of the human mind. He has been engaged in philosophical counseling since the early 1990s. He is also the founder and moderator of the Christian Philosophy internet discussion group xianphil@yahoo.com. E-mail: dfpolis@ktb.net.

PETER RAABE received his Doctorate from the University of British Columbia (UBC) for his research and work in philosophical counselling. He is a member of the International Editorial Board of the British peer-reviewed journal *Practical Philosophy: Journal of the Society for Philosophy in Practice*, Certified Practitioner and Associate Member of The American Society for Philosophy, Counseling and Psychotherapy (ASPCP), and Certified Practitioner and Fellow of The American Philosophical Practitioners Association (APPA). He is the author of the books: *Philosophical Counseling: Theory and Practice* (Praeger, 2000) and *Issues in Philosophical Counselling* (Praeger, 2001). He has an active private practice in philosophical counselling, he facilitates a regular monthly philosophy café in North Vancouver, and he teaches philosophy at the University College of the Fraser Valley. E-mail: raabe@interchange.ubc.ca. Web site: www.interchange.ubc.ca/raabe/

BERNARD ROY was born in Paris, France. He moved to the United States in his twenties. His first career was in the hospitality industry. He received his Ph.D. in philosophy from the Graduate School of The City University of New York. He is presently on the guest faculty in philosophy of Sarah Lawrence College where he has added Modern Socratic Dialogues to the requirements of some of his seminars. Bernard has published in the fields of history of philosophy and logic, as well as in those of practical philosophy. For the past five years Bernard has hosted a biweekly "café philo" in New York City. He also frequently animates a similar café in France where he has made it a sort of specialty to hold them in nursing homes. E-mail: broy@mail.slc.edu

CAMERON TSOI-A-SUE is studying both philosophy and philosophical counselling with Dr. Peter Raabe at the University College of the Fraser Valley. He attends a local philosophers café. This is his first published work. E-mail: zog14@hotmail.com.

PREFACE & ACKNOWLEDGEMENTS

This book addresses the topic of the unconscious from three different perspectives: philosophy, clinical psychology, and personal mental health. It is therefore relevant to a variety of individuals, such as students and philosophers studying philosophy of psychology and philosophy of mind, and students and practitioners in the field of mental health for whom the formal definition and description of the unconscious has undergone radical changes. In addition, it is informative and helpful in a practical way to individuals for whom a consideration of the unconscious has played a role in dealing with their own mental health.

As the title suggests, this book is also meant as a resource for practitioners in the field of philosophical counselling. Philosophical counselling consists of a trained philosopher helping an individual deal with a personal problem or an issue that is of concern to that individual. The topic of the unconscious has been largely ignored in the philosophical counselling literature because the unconscious has been so strongly associated with psychology. But philosophical counsellors often find themselves seeing individuals who have previously undergone some form of psychotherapy. This means that not only must the philosophical counsellor be prepared to offer the client a perspective on personal problems that is removed from the psychotherapeutic medical model of distress as 'mental illness,' but the counsellor must also be able to offer assistance free from the influence of the popular misconception that the unconscious is a controlling but ultimately incomprehensible entity buried deep within the mind. The chapters in this book are intended to help the philosophical counsellor achieve those ends.

While the writers of these essays discuss complex issues in significant depth, they have attempted to keep the use of clinical language and technical jargon to a minimum. This makes the contents readily accessible not only to academics but to lay individuals, students, and practitioners interested in acquiring new perspectives on the unconscious.

I wish to thank all the authors whose writings are found in these pages for their effort and cooperation.

Peter Raabe

INTRODUCTION

There is an enormous gulf between the contemporary clinical and academic definitions of the unconscious and its conception in popular culture. The popular conception is in fact the most powerful force in society, shaping not only the way human thinking and motivation is portrayed in the media, but strongly influencing the way individuals imagine how their own mind works, what determines their reasoning, emotions, and actions, and what it is they are ultimately made of. While the clinical and academic world has moved a considerable distance beyond the antiquated Freudian description of the unconscious, popular culture is still promoting the idea of an unconscious whose secret wishes and unsatisfied desires force us to act against our better judgement, and whose hidden agenda determines who we are meant to be, even against our will. The popular conception of the unconscious leads logically to the conclusion that the thing we call "me" is nothing more than the physical machine under the control of a driver, the "real me," we call the unconscious. In other words, the freely acting individuals we imagine ourselves to be are merely an illusion, nothing more than the fantasy of the slave who believes he is the master. Over the years this has raised considerable controversy in regards to the question of whether a person can be held responsible for his or her actions, especially in criminal justice cases. The question of whether the accused can be blamed for what the unconscious "made" him or her do still surfaces often in legal cases, although the courts have become increasingly reluctant to dismiss criminal charges attributed to unconscious forces.

But, despite what judges are saying, the question remains: is there an unconscious that is in fact in control behind each person's actions? If there is, what exactly is it? And if there is no unconscious how can we explain the motivation behind odd behaviour, or worse, criminal actions? Furthermore, was Freud completely wrong about what constitutes the unconscious, or was he simply mistaken about some of the minor details? In other words, is criticizing Freud's conception of the unconscious merely trivial, or perhaps even malicious? And since this book is addressed to those counsellors and therapists whose interest lies in cognitive and philosophical methodology, is a discussion of the unconscious necessary or even useful?

The authors of this volume stand on several sides of the issue: some defend a concrete conception of the unconscious that "drives" the physical mechanism, similar to the one developed by Sigmund Freud, and argue that it must be taken into account in any form of counselling or therapy. Others claim that any conception of a substantive unconscious is ultimately logically and scientifically indefensible, or worse nonsensical, and that counselling and therapy cannot claim to be concerned with an unconscious because there is simply nothing to be concerned about. Still others maintain the more moderate view that, in order for therapy and counselling to be genuinely helpful and effective, it must at least acknowledge the popular conception of unconscious forces acting within each mind as the starting point for any meaningful self-examination.

Below is a short description by each of the authors themselves of the contents of each of their chapters. As with any philosophical text, the authors in this volume don't aspire to solve the problem and end the controversial discussion surrounding the unconscious. Quite the opposite is true. The authors offer you, the reader, their particular perspectives in the hopes that these discussions will allow you to come to your own conscious decision about to what to think and believe.

Lydia B. Amir

The Unconscious: Sartre versus Freud

This chapter addresses Freud's and Sartre's controversial views of the unconscious. This controversy is important because Sartre's criticism of Freud's theory of the unconscious occupies a unique place within the history of philosophers' attitudes towards this concept. Amir recalls, therefore, the reception of psychoanalysis by philosophers in order to assess the importance of Sartre's criticism within the philosophical tradition. Freud's theory of the unconscious is then presented as continuous yet innovative in relation to previous views of the unconscious. Sartre's criticism of the unconscious and his own proposal for explaining self-deception or bad faith, follow. Amir then lists some similarities and differences in both of these thinkers' views and their respective therapeutic practices. Drawing on Sebastian Gardner's view of Sartre as committed to an "impossible" picture of the mind, she suggests that we pay a price for adhering to Sartre's view of irrationality. Finally, she derives from the Freud-Sartre controversy some consequences for the issue of philosophical counseling and the unconscious.

Andries Gouws

"Mankind Cannot Bear Too Much Reality": Wishful Thinking and the Unconscious

This chapter gives a sketch for a reconstruction of the Freudian unconscious and an argument for its existence. The strategy follows attempts to side-step the extended debates about the validity of Freud's methods and conclusions by basing itself on desire/belief schema for understanding and explaining human behavior—a schema neither folk psychology nor scientific psychology can do without.

People are argued to have, as ideal types, two fundamental modes of fulfilling their desires: engaging with reality and wishful thinking. The first mode tries to acknowledge the constraints reality imposes on the satisfaction of desires, while the second mode tries to ignore, deny, or disguise these constraints, inasmuch as they threaten to make such satisfaction impossible or unfeasible. Crucially, wishful thinking can be used to ignore or deny any desire that is incompatible with other strong desires. Thus we end up unaware of the existence or nature of some of our desires, of the fact that they are influencing our thought and behavior, and of the process our own mind has used to thwart awareness of them. Once we acknowledge this possibility, we are already seriously entertaining the possibility of the Freudian unconscious, or something fairly close to it.

The more aware the subject is that her wishful thinking is just that, the less effective it becomes. Wishful thinking thus requires an unconscious; it is inimical to a clear, complete and unambiguous acknowledgement of its own status.

Next, Gouws emphasizes various aspects of his account (and Freud's) that allow a conception of the unconscious in non-Cartesian terms: the unconscious is largely constituted by *semantic* phenomena of a particular type: forms of representation which would conceal their meaning even if the full light of 'attention', Cartesian 'consciousness' or 'introspection' were cast upon them.

If wishful thinking is an integral part of mental life, philosophers and others wishing to "educate humanity" will have to proceed differently from what would have been appropriate had rational thought and action been the only available option for satisfying desires.

Gouws admits that it is not entirely clear to him what conclusions philosophical counsellors should draw from his account of the unconscious. If this account appeals to the philosophical counsellor, reading Freud and trying out the experience of undergoing psychoanalysis would be ways of further exploring this line of thought and practice, with a view to seeing how philosophical counseling can benefit from it.

He suggests that the more everyday manifestations of wishful thinking may fit within the ambit of philosophical counselling (especially Raabe's Phase 1) without further ado, but that it is doubtful that philosophical counselling is the right context for dealing with those manifestations of wishful thinking which more clearly show the features of the unconscious. He maintains that philosophical counselling quite legitimately strives to adhere to norms of rationality and evaluate behavior from an ethical point of view. This is inimical to accessing and working with unconscious material, which basically requires the 'bracketing' of such norms so as to allow for an associationist approach. Moreover, if the unconscious is unleashed in philosophical counselling, the time, setting and skills needed to manage phenomena typical for the unconscious—like regression, transference and acting out—probably won't be available.

But Gouws points out that he does not wish to exclude the possibility that, with sufficient insight into the different nature and demands of rational conversation and working with the unconscious, individual therapists may find effective ways of moving between these modes, and even be able to formalize their method and teach it to others.

Daniel Burston

Divided Loyalties: Cultural "Weltanschauungen" and the Psychology of the Unconscious

Various explanations have been put forward to account for the schism between Sigmund Freud and Carl Jung, varying from Jung's rejection of Freud's libido theory and Oedipal monism, to the fact that both men inadvertently became privy to the other's sexual secrets. Both explanations have merit, as far as they go. Nevertheless, their intellectual differences and personal animosity could have been overcome, or at least reconciled, up to a point, had their cultural and intellectual affinities been more closely aligned. Though he leaned heavily on Romantic thought, Freud was basically a rationalist and an Enlightenment thinker, whose reflections on the collective unconscious bespeak a secularized monotheistic sensibility quite consistent with his Jewish origins. Jung, by contrast, was fundamentally a Romantic with irrationalist leanings, whose concept of the collective unconscious evinces strong neo-pagan and Gnostic sensibilities that are completely at variance with Freud's on many essential points. In the wake of their parting, which seems inevitable, in retrospect, it appears that neither Freud nor Jung had a monopoly on truth, though in recent years, Freudian analysts have been far less open and conciliatory than Jungians, by and large.

Sylvia Burrow

Hume and Character Revision

This chapter argues that moral agents can voluntarily engage in character revision through self-reflection incorporating sympathy with others. Burrow extends Hume's account of how the emotional responses of pride and humility arise in response to self-reflection to argue that those emotions reveal whether or not one is maintaining integrity. Since we want to be able to bear our own survey, we are motivated to avoid doing that which brings about humility and to do that which brings about pride. Her claim is that mature moral agents will bring in an awareness of the effect of their characters on others as part of self-reflection by engaging sympathetically with them. Philosophical counselors who bring persons to consider their emotional responses to their own motives in the way Burrow has outlined encourage those persons to take responsibility for their character traits. But those counselors who endorse a view of *unconscious* motivation cast the issue of moral motivation as a matter of observing one's own externally influenced motives just as any other observer would. This latter approach, she argues, neither advances responsibility for one's own motives nor for one's very own character.

Cameron Tsoi-A-Sue

Sometimes a Cigar is Just a Cigar

Tsoi-A-Sue argues that forms of therapy focusing on Freudian or psychodynamic therapies are not therapeutic. This chapter further claims that Freudian therapy is also dehumanizing. These points are defended using a philosophical rather than psychological base. The chapter follows John, the universal client, and the processes involved in John's decision-making process if John were a "Freudian person" and compares how John's decision-making process would change if he were a "philosophical person."

David O'Donaghue

Nietzsche and the Unconscious

This chapter describes Friedrich Nietzsche's conceptualization of the unconscious that predated Freud by twenty years and offers a different model of a possible positive relationship between conscious experience and the deep instinctual life that lies underneath it. Nietzsche had a well-developed theory of drives and organismic energies that threaten to disrupt the conscious rational processes and therefore are repressed. Unlike Freud, however, Nietzsche did not view the necessity of such repression, but rather claimed that a fuller expression of instinctual energies would provide crucial healing for the constricted modern psyche. He thus anticipated much of the revision of classical psychoanalysis in the work of C.G. Jung, Norman O. Brown, Herbert Marcuse, Wilhelm Reich, and James Hillman. This chapter offers a homage to the legacy of Nietzsche's thought that has greatly influenced contemporary psychology.

Fiona Jenkins

Addressing the Crisis of Meaning: Towards a 'Psychotheological' Reading of the Unconscious

In this chapter Jenkins first develops an account of a certain type of crisis of meaning, one she links to what Nietzsche called 'nihilism' and which she suggests we think of as an experience of life as lacking ultimate purpose or intelligibility. She then outlines an account of the unconscious which allows viewing unconscious life as similarly located at the limits of intelligibility and purpose, and thus as presenting opportunities and problems that parallel those of the nihilistic crisis. By focussing on Judge Daniel Schreber's famous breakdown—a case discussed by Freud—Jenkins tries to draw out some contrasts between a psycho-pathological account of breakdown and a more philosophical one, but concludes that philosophical counsellors may have much to learn from psychoanalytic approaches about the importance of engaging unconscious life. This possibility of engagement is one she links in turn to a Wittgensteinian sense of the 'enigmatic' life of language and of a philosophic 'therapy' that holds open, rather than closing off, a sense of the ungraspable. Philosophy, she argues, cannot claim to 'know' the unconscious mind. Philosophical counselling must, however, learn ways to 'acknowledge' the uncanny pressure and desire of unconscious life.

Pierre Grimes

The Pathologos: the Unsuspected Underlying Belief

This chapter is based upon Grimes' study of the dialogues he has had with subjects who desired to explore their problems through a Socratic method called philosophical midwifery, later called Dialectical Philosophical Practice (DPP). This philosophical movement presents itself as a new paradigm for understanding human problems and as such it is essential to distinguish it from psychotherapy. It is from this experience that Grimes sees the fundamental roots of human problems as not having their origin in the unconscious but instead in unarticulated false beliefs about oneself, which he calls the 'pathologos.' These beliefs were learned in one's youth, but until they are surfaced they are unacknowledged by the believer. Further, he argues that the pathologs-beliefs do surface and their function becomes clear with the commitment to pursue one's most meaningful goals. The formidable power of such beliefs as the pathologs are clearly detailed, their transmission is described, their function as a model for one's life is set forth, and, most importantly, how the belief was made believable is presented. The insights subjects gain into the causes and power of the pathologos are tested and refined through the continued interplay between their understanding gained through DPP talks and the everyday manifestation of their pathologos as problematic behavior.

Alexander Kealey

Dialogue and the Unconscious

In this chapter Alexander Kealey argues that philosophical counseling involves both conscious and unconscious aspects. The unconscious provides certain contextual influences to the dialogue. These are not limited to psycho-analytical interpretations which are focused on pathology, but are an impetus to inspiration and problem solving. While most discussion of the unconscious focuses on the patient or client, Kealey argues that the philosophical counselor can use his or her own unconscious to nurture positive growth in the client.

Bernard Roy

Hidden Kantian Full Thoughts in Modern Socratic Dialogues

Modern Socratic Dialogues (MSD), a species of philosophical counselling, have been structured and developed by the German philosopher, Leonard Nelson (1882-1927). A successful dialogue will have participants leave with a feeling of "owning" (having made their own) the knowledge of the concept discussed during the dialogue. Today, businesses seeking to comply with ethical standards, universities which offer seminars on single topics such as beauty, justice, friendship, etc., and private groups use the MSD to bring to consciousness metaphysical or useful knowledge. Metaphysical knowledge may be illustrated by a question like, "What is symmetry?" Useful knowledge would be an answer to questions of the form, "What is integrity?" In this chapter, Roy wants to suggest that a fruitful source of metaphysical knowledge may be found in G. W. Leibniz's (1646-1716) theory of innatism, and a source of useful knowledge could be found in I. Kant's (1724-1804) concept of reproductive imagination. Thus memory and imagination are the faculties of which philosophical counselling makes the most use. A corollary of this thesis is that philosophical counselling can be distinguished from other forms of counselling, e.g., psychological or pastoral, because it makes no use of entities such as the unconscious or the soul.

Dennis Polis

Unconscious and Philosophical Counselling

This chapter applies the author's projection paradigm (mappings of multidimensional reality into restricted cognitive spaces) to the problem of unconscious contents in philosophical counselling. A model of the unconscious is constructed from various projections of mind including Augustine's "imago dei," the Hindu concept of "avidya," psychoanalytic repression, cognitive association, and neural net representations. The resultant model allows us to conclude that illumination of unconscious contents is a proper part of philosophical counselling.

Ora Gruengard

Can Philosophers Deal with the Unconscious?

The so-called discovery of the unconscious means for many the replacement of philosophical self-search and dialogues by means of psychological treatment. Psychologists are supposed to know how to get deeper, to access unconscious secrets whch are ignored by philosophers, and to help people change through "the unconscious." This chapter examines the presuppositions of that approach and purports to show, first, that there are many kinds of "scientific" non-conscious entities, most of which have philosophical, religious, or otherwise mystic sources, and none are scientific discoveries. Second, the chapter argues that only some of those notions have an epistemologically justifiable cognitive status, while others are mostly laden with social, cultural, and moral preferences and myths. A critical philosophical counsellor, for which such preferences are a matter of exploration and reasonable choice rather than unconscious indoctrination may therefore stick to the old philosophical way: the exploration of non-conscious ideas, concepts, wishes and emotions by the analysis of the conflicting or otherwise problematic opinions, values, principles, criteria, etc., what are presupposed by the "stuck" person or group. She can thereby do consciously and critically what psychotherapists, presenting to do something else, are actually but uncritically and non-consciously doing.

Martin Hunt and Peter B. Raabe

Causal Nets and the Disappearance of the Unconscious

The theories of the mind devised by Freud, Jung, and others have long been overshadowed by modern research and clinical practice. But the idea of a dark and sinister unconscious, in which experiences and even separate personalities dwell, and which causes irresistible thoughts and troublesome behaviour, is still very powerful and pervasive in our modern Western culture. This conception of the human mind relies on a simple linear model of cause and effect that is similar to the medical disease model in which a physical pathology is diagnosed, by means of "reductionism," to its simple cause, and that cause is then treated in order to bring about a cure. In many forms of psychotherapy a patient's mental suffering is handled in a similar manner:

it is assumed to be a pathology, diagnosed by means of reductionism to its simple cause, and that cause is then treated in order to bring about a cure. But, unlike psychotherapy, philosophical counselling recognizes that the cause of a person's mental distress is not a pathology resulting from a simple cause. It almost always consists of a multitude of overlapping and interlocking factors. These factors form what may be termed a 'causal net' whose explanatory power removes the need for a theory of the unconscious.

Eli Eilon and Ran Lahav

Transcending the Unconscious: Philosophical Counseling Sessions with Arthur Schopenhauer

Eilon and Lahav argue that philosophical counselling need not deal with the counsellee's unconscious, but should rather transcend it. The authors use an imaginary case study with Schopenhauer to demonstrate that philosophical counseling should not attempt to expose, analyze, or meddle with hidden psychological forces. Rather, it should help counsellees to overcome their predicament by going beyond their narrow, self-regarding needs towards a broader attitude about life.

Chapter 1

The Unconscious:
Sartre versus Freud

Lydia B. Amir

Why would philosophers assume that the self is coherent or "transparent" to itself? Indeed, the devoted practice of philosophy itself would seem to be a prime example of how one set of virtues can wreak havoc with another, more mundane set of virtues. (Philosophers who refuse to recognize the usual social reaction to the continuous skepticism, logic-chopping, and overly critical examination of every casual thesis, and the literal construal of even the most hackneyed idiom, may miss this point). It is not only the familiar fact of self-deception that prompts us to think of the self as far more labyrinthine than the Cartesian *cogito* would suggest. It is also the familiar fact that we recognize in ourselves not just one identity but several, some of them conveniently sorted according to the circumstance and social surroundings and others, particularly in a time of crisis, in full-blown confrontation. One does not need to invoke "split brain" phenomena or other extreme psychiatric disorders in order to raise fascinating philosophical questions about the fragmented and partially hidden self (Cf., for example, Nagel, 1979; Graham, 1994). (R. B. Solomon, *The Joy of Philosophy*, 1999, p. 188, and p. 256, n. 33.)

Sartre's criticism of Freud's theory of the unconscious has a unique importance in the history of philosophers' attitude towards this concept. This is why I have chosen the Freud-Sartre controversy as the topic of this chapter. In the introduction, I would like to recall the reception of psychoanalysis by philosophers so that we can appreciate the importance of Sartre's criticism within the philosophical tradition. I will then present Freud's theory of the unconscious as continuous yet innovative in relation to previous views of the unconscious (section one), followed by Sartre's criticism of the unconscious (section two). I will then present Sartre's own proposal for explaining self-deception or bad faith (section three). The similarities and differences between both thinkers' views and in the practice of Freudian psychoanalysis and Sartreian existential psychoanalysis will be presented in the following section (section four). The price we have to pay for adhering to Sartre's view of irrationality will be explained afterwards (section five). According to Sebastian Gardner, for example, Sartre's view is to be rejected because it leads us to an "impossible" picture of the mind, of the sort to which Sartre is committed. Finally, I will draw from the Freud-Sartre controversy some consequences for philosophical counselling and the unconscious (section six). Let's begin, then, with a brief summary of Freud's position among the philosophers.

Introduction: Freud and the Philosophers

In order to appreciate the importance of Sartre's criticism, I propose to summarize briefly the reception of psychoanalysis by philosophers. Psychoanalysis gained some support from within the philosophical community during Freud's lifetime—two examples are Hugo Friedman, a German philosopher who publicly defended Freud's view of the unconscious (Decker, 1977) and Israel Levine, a British philosopher (1923). It seems, however, that these were exceptions, if we trust Donald Levy's first statement in his book *Freud Among the Philosophers*: "For as long as psychoanalysis has existed, its central concept, that of unconscious mental activity, has been the object of hostile scrutiny by philosophers" (Levy, 1996, p. 1).

Although a few philosophers published work dealing with or touching on psychoanalytic topics in the 1920s (e.g., Russell, 1921; Field, 1922; Levine, 1923; Broad, 1925), within the analytic tradition serious philosophical attention to Freudian thought seems to have begun in the 1930s with Wittgenstein's lectures at Cambridge. Wittgenstein's criticism of psychoanalysis is in some ways the most complex, including as it does different points to which each of the other critics confine themselves.

For Wittgenstein, psychoanalysis essentially *imposes* interpretations rather than unfolding them as it claims. According to Wittgenstein, a psychoanalytic interpretation essentially involves a myth-like (that is, predetermined) explanation, imposed on a mental state that reduces it to something familiar and common where nevertheless the assent of the person involved is the criterion of the correctness. There is a fundamental tension here, for once the mental state has been identified its correct explanation would seem to be given by the mythology applied, yet the assent or nonassent of the patient is supposed to be dispositive. This is why Donald Levy thinks that for Wittgenstein "psychoanalysis is a kind of crude religion, one that does not even realize that it is what it is" (Levy, 1996, p. 3). It tries too hard to be scientific and so destroys what is individual in us in the process of seeking to reduce mental phenomena to mere law-governed data. In this process, according to Wittgenstein, what is essential about the mind eludes the psychoanalyst's awareness, as well as the patient's.[1]

Wittgenstein inspired a number of philosophers to write about what they took to be Freud's confusion between causal and rational explanations of mental events. This trend culminated in MacIntyre's *The Unconscious* (1958). Yet, there is an important difference between Wittgenstein's view of psychoanalysis and his followers' views. If Wittgenstein objects to psychoanalysis because he thinks it reduces the meaning we can find within ourselves, the main criticism of Freud's central ideas aside from Wittgenstein has been that those ideas are not reductive enough. What is wanted is real scientific knowledge, which, despite Freud's promise, psychoanalysis does not succeed in producing.[2]

William James and Adolph Grumbaum also thought that psychoanalysis is not scientific enough. The former criticizes all proofs of posthypnotic suggestion, one of Freud's main proofs for the existence of unconscious mental phenomena. For James, the very idea of unconscious mental activity is incoherent, that is, self-contradictory (James, 1850). A. Grunbaum's critique of psychoanalysis is that the assent of the subject of the interpretation has no evidentiary status. Therefore, psychoanalytic interpretations are untestable within the confines of the therapeutic situation; only extra-clinical testing can determine their truth, and these tests, on the whole, have not been undertaken (Grunbaum, 1984).

Levy examines the critical views mentioned so far only to conclude: "the critics I examine show basic misunderstandings—not at all obvious ones—of a few psychoanalytic ideas and when these are cleared up, their criticism is neutralized" (Levy, 1996, p. 8).[3] Levy's enterprise may be better appreciated as revelative of a wider context, if we agree with David Livingston Smith's statement that today, "the philosophical climate has never been more congenial to Freudian thinking" (1999, p. 6).

The beginning of the change can be traced to the early 1960s, when David Davidson's groundbreaking work was beginning to undermine the orthodoxy that causal and rational explanations should be sharply demarcated from one another. Simultaneously, in the late 1950s and early 1960s, the groundwork for a new naturalistic consensus was laid by the work of Place (1956), Smart (1959) and others advocating the identity theory of mind-brain relationship, aided and abetted by the rise of cognitive science and the work of Sellars (1956, 1963) and Feyeraband (1963) on the theoretical nature of folk-psychology. Putnam's (1960) functionalism and externalism (1975) completed the picture. By the early 1980s materialism and anti-introspectionism were commonplace, while cognitive scientists such as Marr (1982) were unashamedly offering principled explanations of mental events relying on hypothetical unconscious processes. More recently, philosophers such as Dennett (1987, 1992), Dretske (1995) and Millikan (1984, 1993) have moved in the direction of neo-Darwinian accounts of mental phenomena. Though it might well be that the philosophical climate has never being more congenial to Freudian thinking, only recently did D. L. Smith attempt "a comprehensive reassessment of Freudian thought in the light of the new philosophy of mind." Such a reassessment would, he writes, "at the very least, show Freud to have been a precursor of contemporary philosophical writers and also might reveal that he has something fresh to add to current debates" (Smith, 1999, p. 6).

Jean Paul Sartre, who provides a philosophical term of contrast for Freud, is rarely discussed within the analytic tradition. A notable exception is Sebastien Gardner's *Irrationality and the Philosophy of Psychoanalysis*, where Sartre's view is deemed "the most serious line of objection which it [psychoanalysis] has to face" (Gardner, 1993, p. 227). Sartre's critique of psychoanalytic theory—which highlights its relation to issues of personal identity and which concern the logical shape of psychoanalytic explanations rather than its epistemology—represents, in my view, the most serious challenge to psychoanalytic claims, which need to be met. I have chosen, therefore, the Freud-Sartre controversy as the topic of this chapter. I propose to begin probing this controversy with Freud's theory of the unconscious.

I. Freud and the Unconscious

Sigmund Freud, even late in life, had no idea how extensive attention to the unconscious had been (Whyte, 1960; Ellenberger, 1970). Presenting Freud's theory of the unconscious in historical perspective might help us understand how, in spite of being continuous with previous views, it nevertheless innovates. From L. L. Whyte's detailed survey of Freud's precursors, *The Unconscious Before Freud,* it is clear that some conception or other of the unconscious has been known to man from the beginning of recorded thought. Western recognition, from around A. D. 1600, of unconscious mental drives, at first philosophical but gradually becoming more scientific, may be superficially regarded as the rediscovery of something that was long taken for granted in certain Eastern traditions and also in some Greek and Christian writings. But those early ideas lack an essential feature of the modern concept of the unconscious that became possible only after Western thought had set out on the search for precision and scientific validity and, in doing so, had separated the conscious mind from material processes. That is, this became possible only from 1600 on, or after Descartes. For the ultimate purpose of the concept of unconscious mental processes is to link conscious awareness and behavior with its background—a system of processes of which one is not immediately aware—and to establish this connection without losing the benefits of scientific precision.

It is useful, if oversimplified, to consider that Descartes, by his definition of mind as awareness, provoked as a reaction the Western "rediscovery" of unconscious mental processes. During the two and half centuries between Descartes' *Discourse on Method* (1637) and Freud's first interest in the unconscious, many philosophers, psychologists, biologists, novelists, and poets recognized that mental activity of various kinds occurs without awareness. By the last decades of the nineteenth century it was so widespread in Germany and Britain, and to lesser extent in France, that one can say that by then the existence of the unconscious mind had become a common assumption of educated and psychological discussions.

Between 1750 and 1830 a number of German philosophers and poets (Herder, Goether, Fichte, Hegel and Schelling), increasingly emphasized the emotional and dynamic aspects of the unconscious. Another sequence of German thinkers made the idea of the unconscious a commonplace of European educated circles by about 1880: Arthur Schopenhauer, C. G. Carus, Gustav Fechner, Eduard von Hartmann and Friedrich Nietzsche.

Schopenhauer took the idea of a mainly unconscious will in nature and in man as his central theme. Carus, physician and friend of Goethe, opened his *Psyche* (1846) with the words: "The key to the understanding of the character of the conscious lies in the region of the unconscious" and presented Goethe's favorable view of the unconscious. Fechner, like Freud (who expressed a debt to him), regarded the mind as an iceberg largely below the surface and moved by hidden currents. He used the concept of mental energy, a topography of the mind, an unpleasure-pleasure principle, and a universal tendency toward stability. E. von Hartmann's *Philosophy of the Unconscious* (1869) gave a survey of a vast field of unconscious mental activities, and this book enjoyed a great success in Germany, France and England. He discussed 26 aspects of the unconscious and converted the Goethean ideas of Carus' *Psyche* into a grandiose metaphysical system. Nietzsche, in his penetrating insights into the unconscious, reflected what was already widespread but gave it a new intensity:

> The absurd overvaluation of consciousness . . . Consciousness only touches the surface . . . The great basic activity is unconscious. Every sequence in consciousness is completely atomistic . . . The real continuous process takes place below our consciousness; the series and sequence of feelings, thoughts, and so on, are symptoms of this underlying process . . . All our conscious motives are superficial phenomena; behind them stands the conflict of our instincts and conditions. (Nietzsche, 1974, sec. 354).

Yet L. L. Whyte makes it clear that the conception of the unconscious was nearly always of a state that exists between conscious events, which is very remote from Freud's theory. He points out, moreover, that only in the twentieth century did a theory of unconscious structure arise. But even this comment does not bring out what is required to discriminate

Freud's idea of the unconscious. What characterizes Freud's idea is that in it the unconscious is dynamic and rooted in the emotions and that this gives rise to all the richness of life. For such an idea there are scarcely any precursors, though Whyte mentions Carus (1846), Schopenhauer (1875)[4] and Nietzsche.[5] The insight shown by these thinkers into the nature of unconsciousness was indeed remarkable. They did not, however, develop it into a system, much less into a scientific theory. Freud introduced a radically new theory of the unconscious, unanticipated by practically everyone who preceded him, because of two things: the strictly unconscious (as opposed to the preconscious) nature of the processes he discussed and the dynamic nature of this unconscious.

In order to appreciate Freud's theory of the unconscious, some introduction to his thought is needed. I will address in the following account only those aspects of his ideas that are directly relevant to the theory of the unconscious. For Freud, all mental processes are determined by natural laws, ultimately by those governing chemical and physical phenomena. They are associated with quantities of psychic energy that strive towards release and equilibrium. The primary driving force is instinctual energy (libido, a concept that was first narrowly, then more widely interpreted) expressing an often unconscious wish, and moving from unpleasure to physical pleasure (pleasure principle). The predominant energy is sexual. But other forms are present, and Freud later assumed two basic instincts, sexuality in a broad sense and aggression (Eros and Thanatos). The establishment of civilized life involves restraints on sexual activity, and the unconscious proper (in Freudian theory the accessible unconscious being called the preconscious) consists of instinctual energies, either archaic or repressed during the life of the individual, particularly in childhood (universal incestuous desires of the earliest years, adolescent frustrated dreaming, aggressive impulses, etc.,); these are available only through the use of special techniques. A genetic or developmental approach to mental illness is therefore essential.

Forgetting is an active process in which painful memories are repressed. The Freudian unconscious is a pool of many repressed energies, distorted by frustration and exerting a stress on conscious reason and its shaping of the patterns of daily life. The strain produced by this stress, present in some degrees in all civilized men and women, is seen in neurosis. It is only by exceptional luck in heredity or experience that civilized man can avoid this tragic and potentially universal feature of modern life, the major influence of the unconscious being antagonistic to reason. This doom and neurosis he can escape (wholly, Freud thought at first; later he had doubts) by becoming aware of his situation and gaining insight into the particular traumatic experiences which created his neurosis. Freud began with an unquestioning conviction that insight brought recovery. The interpretation of dreams (which are symptoms and express wish fulfillment) and the process of free association can render accessible the regions of the unconscious producing the neurosis and can make possible a cure. Myths express for communities what dreams do for the individual. Later, Freud developed his ego theory, dividing the mind into three areas: the id, or basic instincts; the ego, or rational part of the mind which deals with reality; and the superego, a differentiated part of the ego which results mainly from the child's self-identification with his parents. This triple division (to which I will refer below as the "structural" point of view) overlaps awkwardly with the unconscious-conscious dichotomy (to which I will refer below as the "topical" point of view), and here the theory becomes obscure. It left Freud unsatisfied—indeed, late in his life he states that understanding of the deepest levels of the mind was not yet possible.

These are, in condensed form, the main ideas that make up the core of the Freudian theory of the unconscious. The theory, in its most characteristic form, is a description of the pathology of civilized man, although for Freud this implied little restriction, since all suffering in some degree results from the neurosis of civilization. The interest of the theory lies in Freud's many applications of it. Self-deception, losses of memory, formation of symptoms, missed acts, and dreams, on which the topical point of view is founded (Freud 1900, 1901, 1915) are part of the consultation room. Following J. O. Wisdom (1956), we can summarize its developed form[6] as follows:

1. There are networks of ideas—attitudes, thoughts, feelings, objects imagined inside a person, and so on—that he cannot realize he possesses, because of the influence of other networks, which he also cannot realize he possesses as long as he relies only on free association. (This is ordinarily described as "unconscious" conflict.)

2. These networks and their conflicts

(a) influence the person's conscious ideas in all situations, reproducing the mutual relationships of the networks, however difficult it might be to recognize them; and

(b) in particular influence him at different times, so that childhood networks and conflicts influence adult ideas.

3. These networks are related in accordance with a large group of theoretical hypotheses, such as the Oedipus complex.

In this summary, (1) might be called the hypothesis of the unconscious, (2a) the guise hypothesis, and (2b) the genetic hypothesis; (3) consists of component theories about specific structures and functions. Together these three hypotheses may be regarded as constituting the theory of the unconscious (Wisdom, 1956, p. 20).

Although psychoanalysts still hold the theory of the unconscious outlined above, some factors amplify the theory significantly. The theory of childhood sexuality, for example, is central to psychoanalysis but strictly speaking it is not relevant to the theory of the unconscious. There are, in Freud's view, other constituents of the unconscious worth mentioning—for example, libido and (at a further level of abstraction) instincts. Interpretation regarded first as an aid to free association and then as an independent tool became operative through the phenomenon of transference.

The theory of transference (which is fundamental to the later development of psychoanalysis) did not affect the theory of the unconscious. For Freud, the interpretation of transference was simply an instrument to bring about a change in the patient. However, there is an overtone of what might be called an object-relational structure in Freud's view of the unconscious, for he does attribute to the same cause the patient's inability to recall and to yield information to the analyst (1914, p. 145 ff). The patient's inability to yield information to the analyst arises because of his object-relationship with the analyst, and Freud's hypothesis here implies that the patient's inability to face his own conflicts has an object-relational basis, although it was W. R. D. Fairbairn (1952), not Freud, who first enunciated this theory.

The theory of repression, however, is an integral part of the theory of the unconscious and deserves therefore some elaboration. Freud's original view was that an idea painful to consciousness is repressed, soon to develop into an unconscious resistance. The later theory of the superego, which is largely an unconscious agent, was the result of an investigation into the nature of the repressing factor (1923, pp. 27ff). Freud's theory is not entirely consistent, since he developed different aspects at different times and never went into the problem of unifying them.[7] What is the bearing of the unconscious superego on the theory of the unconscious? For Freud, the superego acts as both control and defense; it controls the child Oedipal desires and defends him from the anxiety caused by castration fears. It was conceived as operating by means of the mechanism of repression. Is repression a fact or a theory about the facts? To psychoanalysts it is so familiar as to be accepted as a fact. But the facts are simply that people forget things and there is an ascertainable motive for forgetting them. The *theory* of repression conjectures a mechanism by which a force is exerted to produce this result.

We can now take a further step in investigating the theory of the unconscious. To begin with, the term "unconscious" denoted the contents of what was repressed. But as we have seen, it was not long before it was recognized that the repressing factor was also unconscious. At this point the scope of the term "unconscious" was doubled.

Thus, the theory of repression is an integral part of the theory of the unconscious. This should be stressed, since the theory of the unconscious undergoes a modification as a result of subsequent development.[8] Furthermore, the correlation of the concepts of resistance and repression is so central in Sartre's criticism that some further explanation of them is required. As we have seen, they are both essential concepts in psychoanalytic theory:

> The theory of repression is the cornerstone on which the whole structure of psycho-analysis rests ... It may thus be said that the theory of psycho-analysis is an attempt to account for two striking and unexpected facts of observation which emerge whenever an attempt is made to trace the symptoms of a neurotic back to their sources in his past life: the facts of transference and resistance. (Freud, 1914, p. 16; See also 1933, p. 68).

And Freud viewed resistance as a cue for partitive theory, that is, a theory that divides persons in parts[9]:

> His resistance was unconscious too, just as unconscious as the repressed ... We should long ago have asked the question: *from what part of his mind* does an unconscious resistance like this arise? [italics added] (Freud, 1933, p. 68.)

Freud describes resistance and repression as distinct but correlative operations; the strength of resistance is a measure of the strength of repression (Freud, 1926, pp. 157-60). Furthermore, he suggests that resistance is an action, one which is motivated by and undertaken with a view of protecting repression: "This action ['a permanent expenditure of energy'] undertaken to protect repression is observable in analytic treatment as *resistance*" (Freud, 1926, p. 157). Resistance and repression are thus interlocked so as to form a structure of motivated self-misrepresentation.

On Sartre's view, the particular kind of structure exemplified by resistance is self-deceptive. Two issues are now in focus, then. One concerns the object of psychoanalytic interpretation: if Sartre is right, then the immediate clinical datum for psychoanalytic interpretation—its explanandum—is nothing other than self-deception. The other issue concerns the nature of psychoanalytic theory: if Sartre is right, then the concept of the unconscious is, logically, a hypothesis advanced in order to explain self-deception. Before shifting our attention to Sartre's view, an understanding of Freud's justification of the unconscious as partitive or dividing persons in parts, is necessary.

Freud's argument in his "Justification for the concept of the unconscious" is that identifying the part of the person responsible for his irrationality is much like trying to work out what another person is thinking. For if I am irrational, then the cause of my deviation from the norm of rationality must lie–given that I am essentially rational–in some source other than myself. But since this source of my irrationality cannot be external to me in any ordinary sense of "external," it must be "within" me, but only some part of me:

> The assumption of an unconscious is, moreover, a perfectly legitimate one, inasmuch as in postulating it we are not departing a single step

from our customary and generally accepted mode of thinking … that other people, too, possess a consciousness is an inference which we draw by analogy from their observable utterances and actions, in order to make this behavior of theirs intelligible to us. … Psycho-analysis demands nothing more than we should apply this process of inference to ourselves also. … If we do this, we must say: all the acts and manifestations which I notice in myself and do not know how to link up with the rest of my mental life must be judged as if they belonged to someone else: they are to be explained by a mental life ascribed to this other person. (Freud, 1915, p. 169; Cf. 1925, p. 32 and 1933, p. 70)

The problem lies with what seems to be the unpalatable consequence that we bear within our bodies unmanifest pseudo-persons, essentially like us but lacking, for example, access to a voice:

This process of inference … leads logically to the assumption of another, second consciousness which is united in one's self with the consciousness one knows. (Freud, 1915, p. 170)

Presumably things could, in some sense, have been like that—a second, conscious mind is a logical possibility. But introducing a Second Mind into all irrational contexts is self-evidently unwelcome, as Freud recognizes. He therefore says:

We have grounds for modifying our inference about ourselves and saying that what is proved is not the existence of a second consciousness in us, but the existence of psychical acts which lack consciousness. (Freud, 1915, p. 170; Cf. 1925, p. 32)

This interpretation of Freud's concept of the unconscious matches Sartre's understanding of psychoanalysis. It implies that psychoanalytic theory is committed to dividing the person into parts in a very serious way, which goes well beyond the aspectual sense of part involved in Sartre's account of the subject in bad faith as having a "doubling property" (Sartre, 1958, p. 57). He therefore goes on charging psychoanalysis with conceptual confusion, and he attacks the particular kind of structure exemplified by resistance as self-deceptive. Let's turn to Sartre, then.

II. Sartre and the Unconscious

What first strikes us in the Sartreian theory of human reality is that it denies the unconscious. This attitude towards the unconscious lies at the heart of Sartre's philosophy, as the whole of Sartre's ethics depends on the contrast between those who conceal their freedom and those who don't. Frederick Olafson explains this point:

> In the face of freedom, the experience of which is anguish, human be-
> ings can adopt either of two fundamentally different attitudes. They
> can attempt to conceal their freedom from themselves by a variety of
> devices, *the most typical of which is belief in some form of psychological
> determinism.* All of these efforts are doomed to failure, Sartre argues,
> because human beings can try to conceal their freedom only to the
> extent that they recognize it. The attempt succeeds only in producing
> a paradoxical internal duality of consciousness in which consciousness
> thinks of itself as a thing at the same time that it gives covert recognition
> to its freedom. This state, which has to be carefully distinguished both
> from lying to others and from the Freudian conception of a manipu-
> lation of consciousness by subconscious forces, is called "bad faith".
> Its antithesis is an acceptance of one's freedom and a recognition that
> human beings are the absolute origin of, and are solely responsible for,
> their own acts. On the contrast between these two life-attitudes is based
> the whole of Sartre's ethic. (Olafson, 1967, p. 291, my italics.)

It is clear now why more than any other existentialist philosopher, with the possible exception of Karl Jaspers, Sartre showed a profound and sustained interest in psychological theories in general and psychoanalysis in particular. His interest in Freud is pervasive, from his thesis of 1927 (incorporated in *L'imagination*) to a posthumous publication (1984) of two versions from 1958 and 1959 of his scenario to John Huston's biographical movie on Freud. This last text is very sympathetic to Freud; yet Sartre affirmed later, in an interview with Michel Rybalka, that Huston made a mistake "because you do not choose someone who doesn't believe in the unconscious to make a film to glorify of Freud" (Sartre, in Schilpp, 1981, p. 12). He says there that though he later had the opportunity to study Freud's doctrine more profoundly, he was "always separated from him because of his idea of the unconscious." Elsewhere, he says about Freud: "the language that he uses engenders a *mythology* of the unconscious, which I cannot accept. I agree completely on the *facts* of disguise and repression, as facts. But the *words* "repression," "censor," "drive"—which express at one moment some kind of finalism and at the next, some kind of mechanism—, I reject" (Sartre, *Situations* 9, p. 105; my translation)[10]

Two points should be emphasized here. The first is that Sartre rejects the Freudian metatheory or metapsychology, though Freud confers great importance to metapsychology: in 1937, he remarks that one can do nothing without consulting "the sorceress metapsychology . . . Without speculating or theorizing—almost fantasizing—metapsychologically, one cannot advance one step" (Freud, 1937, p. 240). The second point is that, even if Freud referred sometimes to the instincts as "mythological entities" (Freud, 1933, p. 95), he considered the existence of the unconscious as a recognized fact and never as a "mythology," as Sartre deemed it. As we noticed earlier, the phenomena on which the topical point of view is founded (self-deception, losses of memory, formation of symptoms, missed acts and dreams) (Freud, 1900, 1910, 1915) are part of the consultation room. By attributing to the drives the role of the motivating forces of unconscious mental life and its conflicts, Freud used his most suspect theory to explain his "admitted" concepts. Since what first strikes us in the Sartreian theory of human reality is that it denies the unconscious, Sartre's principal challenge will be first to refute the unconscious and second to give another explanation of the phenomena that Freud used in order to justify his hypothesis of the unconscious.

In his critique of the unconscious, Sartre does not distinguish the different forms Freud's theories of the unconscious took. His critique of Freud is stated in such a way as to make the entity which Freud calls the censor mechanism an important part of the theory under attack, whereas this concept had in fact a relatively short life-span in Freud's work.[11]

The challenge that Sartre gives to Freud's view of the unconscious in *Being and Nothingness* is articulated as a philosophical contradiction within Freudian thought (Sartre, 1957, pp. 57-58). What is the meaning of the concept of the censor, which is between consciousness and the unconscious in the topical point of view? Though Sartre does not mention it, there is also a second censor between the unconscious and the preconscious (Freud, 1915). But this proliferation of censors just strengthens Sartre's argument. Is the censor a viable concept? In order to accomplish its function of suppression, the censor must know the unconscious material to be suppressed: actually, it must know it in order not to know it. The censor reintroduces the paradox of the dual unity of the deceiver and the deceived. We are back to the initial problem of self-deception, which the Freudian concept of censor should solve: how can a person (or a censor) deceive herself on the nature of her wishes and desires? It is better to get rid of the censor and explain how a *consciousness* can be divided like this.

In spite of later permutations of Freudian theory, which Sartre does not mention, this problem of the dual unity of the deceiver and the deceived is not resolved from a structural point of view. In *The Ego and the Id* (1923), Freud entrusts the superego with the function of censor instead of a censor located between consciousness and the unconscious. As we shall see later, this view is closer to Sartre's view of the mechanism of self-deception in that the superego can be considered as a critical reflective voice which judges spontaneous experience. But since Freud considers the superego as a discrete entity inside the psyche, it is not clear *how* the superego censor deceives itself about the unconscious material which it recognizes. This objection is valid for Freud's later attribution (1940) about the function of the censor to the ego as the seat of the defenses. A psychological structure (the ego) must both know and not know itself in order to suppress some emotions, ideas and impulses. One may wonder whether the revisions that Freud made to his theory of the censor, which he attributed successively to three different psychological structures, do not reflect the difficulties which he had in understanding this function.

Sartre holds furthermore that the 'ah-ha' of the patient casts doubt on Freudian theory of the unconscious. All the adepts of depth therapy know this phenomenon in which the patient or client is suddenly illuminated by the truth of a certain interpretation: "Ah-ha," says the patient, "this is what's going on all this time; I *see* it now." For Freud, this is the moment in which the unconscious material becomes conscious. But if the patient recognizes herself in the analyst's interpretation, this information was clearly not unconscious before that moment, says Sartre. This feeling of illumination can be explained only if "the subject has never stopped being conscious of his deep tendencies, better yet, only if these drives are not distinguished from his conscious self" (Sartre, 1957, p. 574). Otherwise, if the complex were really unconscious, who would recognize it? The conscious subject would not be capable of that, for only the conscious is accessible to him. And the complex could not recognize itself, for according to Freud, it lacks understanding. Only a subject who both knows and does not know these tendencies and desires could recognize what has been hidden hitherto. Only such a subject could "resist" the analyst's attempts to reveal this material, since only he could know what to resist and what to defend himself against.

Finally, when Freudian psychology refers to drives and to instinctual forces of the profound unconscious, Sartre thinks that it confuses the essential structure of reflective acts and non-reflective acts—that reflection refers to oneself or to another person. A reification of consciousness takes place when "every time that the observed consciousnesses appears non-reflective one superimposes on them a reflective structure which one carelessly pretends to be unconscious" (*La transcendence de l'ego*, p. 39, my translation).[13] Thus Sartre believes that the patient does not become conscious of unconscious tendencies but gets acquainted with his spontaneous experience. The problem is not that these tendencies are too obscure, for:

> [spontaneous consciousness] is penetrated by a great light without being able to express what this light is illuminating. We are not dealing with an unsolved riddle as the Freudians believe; all is there, luminous; ... But this "mystery in broad light" is due to the fact that this possession is deprived of the means which would ordinarily permit *analysis* and *conceptualization*. It grasps everything, all at once, without shading, without relief, without connections of grandeur— not that these shades, these values, these reliefs exist somewhere and are hidden from it, but rather because they must be established by another human attitude and because they can exist only by means *of* and *for* knowledge. (1957, p. 571)

Sartre is describing pre-reflective consciousness without reflective conceptualization. Yet those two are not subdivisions of consciousness.

Contrarily to Freud, Sartre sees consciousness as one piece, without spheres or compartments. Reflective consciousness is but pre-reflective consciousness which turns away from the world and orients itself towards the self, taking for an object its own past actions, emotions and gestures. It is through that turn-around that self-deception becomes possible, for a gap opens between the reflecting consciousness and the reflected consciousness. In order to better understand that, we should examine the Satreian notion of consciousness.

III. Sartre's view of consciousness and bad faith

In contradistinction to the Freudian psyche, Sartreian consciousness does not have a substance or structure. Human reality is not motivated by any underlying drive to satisfy the instincts. Consciousness is transparent rather than opaque. It is an opening towards being, it is *desire* or lack of plenitude yet to come rather than an intra-psychic, autonomous system. Since consciousness creates nothingness or a gap between itself and its objects, it can be conscious of objects in the world. Otherwise, as plenitude, it could not be a presence for the other objects. A human being is not a bundle of drives but rather a stand on Being. Consciousness implies its partner, the world. It is intentional in a Husserlean way, that is, it is always *conscious of* something.

Sartreian consciousness is also *consciousness for*. In other words, it temporizes. It is conscious of a movement out of a past that was its own reality towards a future that is not yet. On this subject, Sartre says that consciousness is doubly "negating" or doubly conscious of itself as *not being* its objects. Consciousness knows that it is *not* its objects and knows that consciousness and its objects are *not* what they are going to be. This movement is perceived both in terms of objects in the world and in terms of a personal project of being, of a way to *pro-ject* itself in the future through those objects. (In French, *pro-jetter* means pro-throwing).

Because consciousness inserts lack at the heart of Being, it can conceive of a future which is different from the present. We all perceive objects in the world according to our project of being. We do not create the world, but to take an example, a mountain is not the same thing for a mountaineer and a geologist. My project also includes all my tastes, all the habits through which I define myself in the world. At the level of pre-reflective consciousness, one discovers a personality in the concrete choices that shed light on its fundamental project. The project is not *behind* this concrete richness but *in* it:

> The value of things, their instrumental role, their proximity and their real distance (which have no relation to their spatial proximity and distance) do nothing more than to outline my image—that is, my choice. My clothing . . . whether neglected or cared for, carefully chosen or arbitrary, my furniture, the street in which I live, the city in which I reside, the books with which I surround myself, the recreation which I enjoy, everything which is mine (that is, finally, the world of which I am perpetually conscious, at least by way of a meaning implied by the object which I look at or use): all this informs me of my choice—that is, of my being. (Ibid., p. 463)

These pre-reflective choices, which include my culinary and clothing tastes as well as my attitude toward the other, may never have been conceived reflectively. It is possible that I do not know, to take an example, why I prefer my steak well done rather than rare or why I prefer to suffer from heat than from cold. According to Sartre, however, all my concrete choices, all my ways of being, doing, and having, are indices for my fundamental project, for the meaning of my being in the world.

The pre-reflective choices might not be better known reflectively than they are in Freudian psychoanalysis. In effect, it is easy to err regarding the meaning of my various manners of doing, being, and having, especially if they are part of the project of deceiving myself. I can, for example, think that I am a generous and warm person, while in fact this warmth is hypocritical and this generosity a simple way of controlling others in making myself likable. But Sartre affirms that my aggressive underlying intentions are not unconscious. One can find them in the manner in which I carry the warm and generous acts and probably also in the way in which I complain when I do not receive the anticipated reactions. According to Sartre, however, to be is to act and to act is to have the intention of acting. In fact, there is no difference between the act and the intention to act, for "our acts . . . inform us of our intentions" (1957, p. 484). If I could study myself while I accomplish those acts which I reflectively designated as "warm and generous," I would discover their true nature. The problem is that I do not want to see this truth because I prefer to maintain the myth of my generosity. If others would doubt my intentions, I will defend myself vehemently, demonstrating thereby that I recognize in a way the truth of their affirmations.

How is self-deception possible, therefore, according to Sartreian concepts? Self-deception is made possible by the gap that exists between pre-reflective consciousness and reflective consciousness. Even if the same person acts spontaneously and conceives of her actions reflectively, these two acts of consciousness are separated by the same nothingness which separates consciousness of its objects in the world. In other words, it is only by not being my spontaneous past self that I can conceive this self reflectively. I am not it, of course, when I reflectively designate it. Bad faith, or the reflective lie to oneself about the nature of reality, is possible essentially because "the reflective attitude . . . involves a thousand possibilities of error . . . in so far that it aims at constituting across that consciousness reflected-on veritable psychic objects which are only probable objects . . . and which can even be false objects" (1957, p. 471). Happily, the basic motivation, in contradistinction to reflective consciousness, "can never be deceived about itself" (Ibid.). It is therefore always possible to liberate oneself by coming back to the pre-reflective level and renaming those objects.

What is the purpose of consciousness when it conceives itself, rightly or falsely, reflectively? In order to answer this question we have to take into consideration the Sartreian idea of the aim of consciousness in its reflective and pre-reflective modes. In contradistinction to Freudian reductionism of meaning to psycho-physiological drives, Sartre affirms that the creation of value is the prime human goal. We try to use the world in order to extract from it our sense of self. Sartre describes this tendency to create a self through objects in the world as a "circuit of selfness" (Ibid. p. 140). Consciousness perceives its "possibilities" in this particular world: for example, consciousness perceives its thirst concretely as this glass-of-water-to drink or its writing project as this-chapter-to-write. While Freud reduces human significance to neuro-physiological forces and evolutionary goals, Sartre attaches an inherent meaning to each concrete human act or movement. It is a teleological signification, which finds interest in the ends to come rather than in past causes, though the past can figure in its designation of ends to come.

Thus, without denying the physiological data of the human condition, one can never say that there is first a drive that finds satisfaction through an object. Consciousness is desire or lack of a plenitude, but this desire is discovered in the world and not in the recesses of the self. This desire is not primarily sexual in nature, even if it can include sexuality among its modes of expression. It is rather a desire to be more than a desire of pleasure or of cessation of tension. Consciousness does not *have* this ontological desire; it *is* it.

But if consciousness is desire, what is this desire? In its concrete mode, the answer varies with every living human being, because each fundamental project is different. Ontologically speaking, however, this is a desire to be a substantial self and nevertheless to remain a free consciousness. This is the meaning of Sartre's phrase, "Man is the being whose project is to be God" (Ibid. p. 566). God, the *ens causa sui* of Aristotelian or Thomist philosophy, is precisely this combination of a substantial being and a transcendent consciousness. Sartre calls this desire which human beings have to become the missing God the "In-itself-For-itself," because it would combine the substantiality of an object ("in-itself," the material world) and human liberty ("for-itself"). Unfortunately, "man is a useless passion" (ibid. p. 615): a human being cannot attain his goal because consciousness projects itself always forward towards the future; it never stops and cannot therefore become a static datum.

Reflectivity is responsible for numerous distortions, whose ontological aim is to create the illusion of a substantive liberty, the In-itself-For-itself. These distortions enable us to avoid liberty and responsibility. Sartre names this escape from reality "bad faith." Although bad faith is *strictu sensu* an ontological category, it is also charged with ethical connotations. For example, Sartre accuses anti-Semites and colonialists of bad faith. A notable exception is the bad faith that manifests itself in mental illnesses: discovering the structures of bad faith in the client's fundamental project does not amount to judging the client, which would clearly be an inadequate description of mental illness. In other words, even if it is always possible to choose the manner in which one lives a given situation, it is not always possible to have a viable choice (Sartre, in Laing and Cooper, 1971, p. 5).

The bad faith to which we all succumb at one moment or the other can take two forms, which correspond to the two aspects of human reality. On one side, one finds facticity, the contingent world which I did not create but which I choose to live in one way or the other. Facticity includes my own past as much as external circumstances. On the other side one finds liberty, my choice of objects in the world as a way of realizing my own fundamental project of being. The full acknowledgement of my liberty includes the recognition that nothing, not me, nor traditional values, nor God, have *a priori* status as value: I create value by bestowing it. I am in bad faith when I adopt a dishonest attitude regarding reality: if I pretend that I am free in a world without facts or that I am a fact in a world without liberty.

If I wish for whatever reason to escape my facticity, I risk being dishonest in proclaiming myself completely free to do or to be whatever I want, free from all connection to my past. The dreamer who always awaits "another day" and the schizophrenic who completely ignores reality are examples of this form of bad faith. The client who refuses to see her past acts as choices or who refuses to accept real present circumstances tries to negate facticity. We can say that the "defense" through denial is exactly the attempt to escape facticity.

The other form of bad faith, escape from freedom, implies a desire to make the world and my past or my character determinant factors for my life. The client who sees the past as caused rather than chosen adopts this form of bad faith, as well as the person who is afraid of change because it implies treason of the past.

This idea that the human being is essentially free within a situation does not imply, nonetheless, a rationalist voluntarism. First, I can choose myself on an emotional, imaginative, or sexual, rational or irrational, mode. Second, choice does not mean "will." Pre-reflective consciousness is the basic motivation. According to Sartre, this motivation cannot in any case be assimilated to the will, which is reflective. Even language can mislead for it originates "for the other" and is more often reflective rather than pre-reflective. Sartre affirms that "voluntary deliberation is always a deception" (ibid. p. 450). "When I deliberate, the chips are down," because I have already chosen the values on which I will found my deliberation (ibid. p. 451).

Thus Sartre and Freud agree that viewing what is going on when one makes a decision is a superficial manifestation of a deeper intention. The difference is that for Freud, this deep intention is unconscious whilst for Sartre the basic intention is conscious even if it has never been expressed, even when the expression (which is reflective) appears to contradict the basic choice. Finally, I did what I wanted to do. It was a conscious choice, but which eluded the control of reflective will.

Sartre no more than Freud considers that a fundamental change is easy. It is difficult not because of the tenacity of the libidinal attachments or of the presence of unconscious conflicts. Rather, because every change of a detail in an individual's life is a challenge for the fundamental project: what appears to be the least significant change implies a disruption of being-in-the-world. To change the way in which I walk is to change my orientation towards life. We are radically free, writes Betty Cannon, we are not capriciously free (Canon, 1993, p. 61).

Now that each thinker's view has been understood apart, I propose to focus on their affinities as well as their differences.

IV. Sartre versus Freud

There are similarities between Sartre and Freud. Robert C. Solomon remarks that "the ongoing battle between Freud and Sartre and their followers often fails to take note of the similar complexity of these two great thinkers. Their opposing languages of 'mechanism' and 'bad faith,' and their supposedly antagonistic views on the existence of 'the Unconscious,' tend to distract from their mutual concern, undercutting the 'transparency' of Cartesian self-reflection (See Rorty, 1988)" (Solomon, 1999, p. 256, note 32).

Sartre himself points to some more specific similarities between his view and Freud's (1957, pp. 569-571). These include the idea that the personality is unified, that division can occur within this unity, and that this division implies the necessity of analysis, because once the problem is known a solution becomes possible. Both find a meaning in the symptoms of mental illness and both interpret the surface psychic manifestations (gestures, isolated acts, symptoms, tastes, all constitutive elements of concrete lived experience) in terms of a profound purpose. According to Sartre, "a gesture refers to a *Weltanschauung* and we *sense* it" (ibid. p. 457). But in Sartre's metapsychology the profound goal manifests itself in concrete choices, whereas for Freud one has to discover it *behind* those choices, in the instinctual life and the unconscious.

Neither Sartre nor Freud gives the subject of the analysis a privileged position regarding his subjective material, but for different reasons. For Freud, the analyst must fight the resistance of the patient in order to make conscious the unconscious material. For Sartre, an abyss separates spontaneous experience from reflective consciousness, but as the same person can know both these states, the final intuition of the subject of the analysis can be considered definitive. The therapist or counsellor can take her client as a partner in the common project of exploration and denomination of what Sartre calls the "fundamental project of being."

Both Freudian and Sartreian psychoanalysts agree that the individual is a non-fragmented whole. The "fundamental project" has the same importance for the latter than the "complex" has for the former. As the Freudian psychoanalyst looks in childhood for events which lead to this organized group of ideas and memories which constitutes the complex, the existentialist psychoanalyst wants to discover "the original choice" through which the client adopted his own vision of the world. The fundamental project and the complex both refer to the interpersonal world of childhood. And the two forms of psychoanalysis attempt to discover, according to Sartre's terms, "the crucial event of childhood and the psychic crystallization around this event" (ibid. p. 569). Nevertheless, the original other, as libidinal object in Freudian psychoanalysis, is totally different from the original Other as the first person who sees me and calls my name in existential psychoanalysis. The fundamental project is distinguished from the complex: the latter is unconscious and subject to the laws of nature, the former is conscious and subject to a permanent revision or even to a radical transformation. It is a *project*, a self-projection forward, from the past to the future.

The division within the unity is not the same for existential psychoanalysis and for Freud, for reflective consciousness and pre-reflective consciousness refer to the same conscious subject. Freud compares the psyche to a group of principalities at war—consciousness and the unconscious from the "topical" point of view; the ego, superego and id from the "structural" point of view. Finally, access to the knowledge which enables one to find a solution implies the submission of pre-reflective consciousness to reflective consciousness, according to Sartre, whereas it implies the transformation of the unconscious into conscious for Freud. Even if a therapeutic practice based on Sartre's metatheory will integrate some useful aspects of Freudian theory, it will adopt a resolutely contrary approach in the treatment of clients, whom it considers as conscious of the experiences which they will have to confront reflectively in order to revise their fundamental project of being.

Despite similarities, radical differences separate the two approaches, as Sartre notes in his criticism of the Freudian "empirical" psychoanalysis in *L'etre et le neant* (pp. 616-635). Sartre rejects Freud's determinism, his insistence on the unconscious locus of psychic life, his mechanical-biological explanations. He rejects the idea that nature and education, more than the original choice of a mode of being in the world, enable the explanation of human behavior. He rejects the resort to a psycho-biological residue as the libido in order to justify human motivations. Finally, he severely criticizes the notion of universal symbols (for example, snakes or water) and the nosology or classification of illnesses of Freudian psychoanalysis. As a perspective for psychoanalysis, Sartre proposes to reveal an individual's original choice of being in all its concrete richness, for this choice, though rooted in the concrete world, cannot be reduced to it. Due to the changing, even transformable, nature of this choice, existential psychoanalysis must be flexible in its interpretation of symbols and symptoms, not only for different individuals, but also for a particular individual at various stages of the therapy.

Though psychosexuality has a capital place in human development, it does not constitute for Sartre its motivating force. In place of pleasure as the organism's purpose, Sartre substitutes consciousness' tendency to establish itself as a value within concrete situations in the world. This is the "circuit of selfness" in which one uses a relation to objects and the other in order to create for oneself a solid sense of self. Existential psychoanalysis, nevertheless, aims at grasping the meaning of an individual's concrete choices as elements of the project of creation of value. In this system, general nosology is inefficient. According to Sartre, existential psychoanalysis should attempt to understand not the general structure of illusions or other symptoms, but rather the particular structure of each case, for example, why such an individual thinks he is Napoleon and not Christ or Einstein.

Lydia B. Amir 47

All the elements indicate a difference at root between Sartreian and Freudian metatheories. As Gerald N. Izenberg remarked (1976), all of Freud's and Sartre's divergences stem from their respective conceptions of meaning. For Freud, the meaning is evolutionist and neuro-physiologist. Meaning is reduced to the game of physical forces inside the human organism, combined with biological tendencies and laws. Behind the conscious life the unconscious phantasm is hiding, which is hiding the primary process, which finally is hiding the instinct considerd by Freud as "a border-concept between the animic and the somatic" (Freud, 1915, p. 167).

For Sartre, the pleasure principle and the death instinct are both replaced by the human desire to create values, which do not provide *a priori* pleasure or pain and which can be aggressive or pacific. To Freud's evolutionary neuro-physiological paradigm, Sartre substitutes an investigation of the intentional consciousness that creates meaning. Existential psychoanalysis, which considers that the laws of scientific materialism do not apply to the world of consciousness and which substitute motives for scientific causality, liberates itself completely from these ideas. It opposes to the Freudian conception of the past as a determinant force an understanding of the past and of the future as meaningful in terms of choices and values. In place of the concept of the drive as a biological instinct, Sartre prefers the concept of *desire*, later *need*, as lack(ing), which is found not in the biological withdrawal of the self but on the face of the world when it fits incarnated consciousness. Sartre replaces the mechanistic universe of the sciences of nature with the human universe of phenomenological investigation and ontological categories discovered within the concrete existence. Hence, when Freud and Sartre qualify the symptom as "meaningful," they do not mean the same thing.

The relationships that Sartreian consciousness has with its objects and the other are evidently not similar to relationships the Freudian psyche has. The psyche is opaque while consciousness is transparent. Freud imagines a third substance, a psychic glue which links the psyche with its objects: the libido or general sexual libido which emanates from a realm of instinctual life outside the reach of consciousness. In Freud's system, the other is not a subject but rather an object for the satisfaction of my needs. In the relationship between persons, as in everything else, the motivation comes from the obscure realm of the unconscious, from unconscious drives and desires, conflicts and complexes. At the end of the psychosexual development, the individual appears as an autonomous intra-psychic system. Without the intervention of psychoanalysis, the structural game between the ego, the superego and the id might stay essentially the same, like those infantile experiences which Freud calls "transferences."

When he describes the ontological structures of being, Sartre presents consciousness as open to its objects. Even if it can divide itself into reflective and pre-reflective modes, it remains in one piece, since it is the same consciousness which acts spontaneously and conceives reflectively its actions. Through an effort of attention, therefore, it is possible to decrypt one's project of being and change. Consciousness is consciousness *of* and *for* a particular future, which one attempts to bring into existence. Contrary to the Freudian psyche, Sartreian consciousness is not delimited and determined by the past. It therefore becomes capital for existential psychoanalysis to understand an individual's future projects, which is his or her meaning no less than its past, which is the background of that meaning.

Moreover, relationships with the other are not simply external and contingent. The other affects me in my being, and I have with him an internal and reciprocal relation of being to being. There can be at that point reason for conflict, especially if I try to use the other in my inauthentic desire of substantive liberty, but one can also witness the birth of a real intimacy and true reciprocity. (The early Sartre insists on the negative aspects of the ego, but Hazel Barnes remarks that there is a positive side to the Sartreian ego (Barnes, 1991), and in his biography of Flaubert (1971), Sartre recognizes the existence of positive possibilities for development of the ego.)

We can say that the main difference between Freud's psycho-biological metatheory and Sartre's ontological metatheory is the following: although both rely originally on phenomenological analysis and description, Sartre aims at discovering the ontological structures of human existence which manifest themselves in experience, whereas Freud attempts to discover the metabiological forces which lie behind human experience. As a theory which is "close to experience," Sartre's analysis fits better with various recent psychoanalytical approaches (Harry Guntrip, 1969; D.W. Winnicott 1965a, 1965b, 1971; W.R.D. Fairbain 1952; Michael Balint

1969; Harry Stack Sullivan 1940, 1953; Heinz Kohut 1977, 1984; see Cannon, 1993, chap. 4). But in contradistinction to many of these thinkers, Sartre proposes a metatheory, a philosophical investigation which goes past phenomenological analysis in order to elucidate the general structures of human reality. This enables him to understand psychological troubles as variations on the human problem, as manifestations of the various ways in which consciousness encounters the material world, the other and the self of reflective analysis, and in which it confronts or tries to avoid the anguish of responsible freedom.

Betty Cannon summarizes the differences that a Sartreian perspective could introduce in the practice of psychotherapy. Her work (1991) is almost unique within the literature on existential psychoanalysis. Existential psychoanalysis is an example of a metapsychology that recasts psychoanalytic theory in terms of essentially philosophical concepts, which are taken to be psychologically explanatory. Since its introduction to the English speaking world in the fifties by Rollo May, however, it has been dominated by a Heiddegerian perspective (Binswanger, 1963; Boss, 1963, esp. pt. II), a Husserlian perspective (the phenomenological psychologists of Duquesne University; Kockelman, 1967) or by an eclectic one (Van den Berg, 1955; Van Kaam, 1969; Bugental, 1965; Keen, 1970; Yalom, 1980), which use Husserl (1931), Heiddeger (1962), Jaspers, (1963, esp. pt. IV.) and Sartre (1957, pt. IV, chap. 2, and pp. 568-9).

A form of psychotherapy based uniquely on Sartre's ideas seems to be rare. It is true that Sartre writes: "this psychoanalysis has not yet found its Freud. At most we can find the foreshadowing of it in certain particularly successful biographies . . . But it matter little to us whether it now exists; the important thing is that it is possible" (1957, p. 575). Betty Cannon, however, contends that we waited too long for "a systematic application of Sartre's ideas to clinical theory and practice" (Canon, 1993, p. 14). Therefore, filling the gap in her book, she summarizes the differences that a Sartreian perspective could introduce in the practice of psychotherapy (Cannon, 1993, pp. 62-69).

Out of the seven she lists, one is especially relevant to the controversy over the unconscious. A therapist who adopts the Sartreian vision of consciousness instead of the Freudian psyche does not consider therapy a technique intended to make the unconscious conscious, but as a means of bringing a beneficial reflection on the pre-reflective experience of the patient, which until then would remain deformed or non-identified. Regarding the phenomena of self-deception, where Freud sees the indication of unconscious forces and processes, the existential therapist interprets them in the light of the gap between reflective and pre-reflective consciousnessess and in terms of the structures of bad faith.

The structures of bad faith—to lie to oneself by saying that one is free in a world without facts or by saying that one is a fact within a world without liberty—, can lead to a false conception of reality, which makes one resist consciousness in certain areas. From an existential point of view, this resistance is not tantamount to suppression or repression in the unconscious. It is possible that a person suffering from the first kind of bad faith would seem to have a suppressed knowledge of past wounds, whereas a person who suffers from the second kind of bad faith would seem to have suppressed her capacity to act in an autonomous and efficient manner. In fact, there is no suppression in the sense of "rejecting in the unconscious." It is rather a selective attention-inattention regarding the past or the future, founded on a particular fundamental choice of being. It is a reflective distortion, not an unconscious process.

The existential therapist does not look for an unconscious complex in order to explain the "pathology" of the client. She explores the ontological structures of this client's project of being, a project that she assumes is transparent and free. Its goal is not pleasure, (even if pleasure can be included as a subsidiary goal), but the creation of sense, of a "self" as value. Because the fundamental project is known consciously but not necessarily reflectively and even less precisely, the therapist refuses to consider the subject as privileged in his *knowledge* of the fundamental project at the beginning of the therapy and at the same time respects "the final intuition of the subject as decisive" (ibid., p. 574). Since reflective and reflected consciousness are the same consciousness, there is no reason to suppose that the client can understand the strategies of bad faith and reflective distortion which obscure the present reflective process in order to can see what is really going on. This is of course the view of therapists such as Betty Cannon. It is worth mentioning though that Sartre never said that self-knowledge was impossible without the help of another, as testified by his own existential psychotherapy, which is none other than his autobiographical novel *The Words*.

To the best of my knowledge, Shlomit C. Shuster is the philosophical counsellor who did the most extensive work on applying Sartre to philosophical counselling (1995; 1997; 1998a; 1998b; 1999; 2002 chap. 6). She considers, however, that Sartre's legacy lies elsewhere:

> At present, most applications of Sartre's philosophy to psychotherapy and counseling do not practice positive reciprocal relations and anti-psychiatric understandings as proposed in Sartre's work. However, Betty Cannon, an extraordinary Sartrean psychotherapist, considers that in Existentialist psychotherapy the therapist *may* abandon the neutral position of witness "when what the client needs is not neutrality but rather an experience of positive reciprocity" (1991, p.116). In the new profession of philosophical practice and counseling, the dialectical relation between the counselee and counselor is equivalent to the relation of positive reciprocity Sartre proposes as the ideal relation between people (Achenbach, 1984, 1985, 1992; Schuster, 1991, 1996). The future of Sartrean psychoanalysis depends not so much on people occupying themselves with intellectual existential analysis of human behavior in various practices, as it does on a mutual, reciprocal relation with the subjects involved. (Schuster, 1998a, p. 28)

In a former paper (1995), she explains that she had combined existential psychoanalysis with Sartre's existential philosophy and thus created what she calls "philosophical psychoanalysis" (Cf. Schuster, 1999, pp. 101- 107, especially p. 107, and 139-144, chap. 7; 2003, chap. 6; Raabe, 2001, p. 63).[14] Those counsellors who are interested in implementing Sartre's philosophy *a la lettre* should be aware of the following problem that may arise from his view of irrationality.

V. Sebastien Gardner's Criticism of Sartre's View

Sebastian Gardner's *Irrationality and the Philosophy of Psychoanalysis* is a defense of psychoanalysis against Sartre's criticisms, which "represents the most serious line of objection which it has to face" (Gardner, 1993, p. 227). It defends the view that "psychoanalytic theory provides the most penetrating and satisfying explanation of irrationality," with an "existential" point of departure," which is that "irrationality exists at the level of personal experience, where it is directly recognized" (p. 1). It is unnecessary as well as difficult to reconstruct here Gardner's arguments, though his major points are worth mentioning. Part one shows that "if the unconscious being is conceived as a Second Mind, it makes the Censor Criticism irrelevant to psychoanalytic theory" (Gardner, 1993, p. 87). Part two demonstrates that Sartre's construction of psychoanalysis as a response to self-deception is a mistake. Gardner quotes Jean Laplanche and Serge Leclaire:

> In Sartre, for instance, the critique of the psychoanalytic unconscious misconstrues the latter's radical heterogeneity by reducing unconscious contents to the misunderstood fringes and implications of present intention ... the questions thus posed (bad faith, conscious reticence, misunderstanding, pathology of the field of consciousness, etc.) ... we characterize as marginal in relation to a domain which is properly psychoanalytic (Laplanche and Leclaire, 1972, p. 129).

He adds that to say that the properly psychoanalytic domain possesses a "radical heterogeneity" is to reject Sartre's assumption that psychoanalytic theory is a theory of self-deception. Sartre's basic error is to have supposed, in taking Freudian explanation to rival the explanation of bad faith, that there is *but one* range of irrational phenomena to be accounted for; in fact, self-deception and psychoanalytic pathology are very different and can not both be spanned by one theory. This may be put by saying that the phenomenologist's layer of implicit meaning does not comprehend the unconscious proper. (On the relation of psychoanalysis to phenomenology, see Ricoeur, 1970, pp. 390-418.) To establish this, however, it must be shown that psychoanalytic explananda and explanations are at a significant remove from self-deception, for Gardner believes that Sartre is at least correct in thinking that the combination of ignorance and motivation uncovered in psychoanalytic interpretation has the outward appearance of self-deception. For among Freud's earliest psychoanalytic conceptualizations is the characterization of the hysteric as one who lies also to herself (Freud, 1895, p. 61). Moreover, many writers are quick to identify unconscious motivation and self-deception, if only implicitly. For example, Hartmann writes: "a great part of psychoanalysis can be described as a theory of self-deceptions" (1975, p. 64). Finally, Freud does not employ the concept of self-deception, although he confronts the concept of contradictory beliefs in some places (1909, p. 194 n1; 1916-17, p. 101; and 1895, p. 117 n.1).

Without assessing Gardner's opinion of Sartre's criticism, one illuminating point is worth elaborating on. Briefly stated, Sartre's view is to be rejected, according to Gardner, because it leads us to an "impossible" picture of the mind, of the sort which Sartre is committed to (Gardner, 1993, p. 2). He labels this the "metaphysical" strategy exemplified by Sartre's account of bad faith and finds it elsewhere in Continental philosophy (Gardner, 1993, p. 6). Generalizing from Sartre's views of irrationality to neighboring views and deeming them "metaphysical accounts of motivation," he thinks that there is undoubtedly something compelling about the underlying conception of irrationality to which they give expression. It is both "a *romantic* and a *tragic* perspective": it suggests that irrationality is so deeply bound up with what it is to be a person that irrationality is a necessary, legitimate way of pursuing one's destiny as a human being. Metaphysical accounts of motivation have other, more logical attractions. But, for obvious reasons, "unless one accepts in full the metaphysics behind such stories, not much can be taken from them" (Gardner, 1993, p. 39).

I would like to elaborate on this point, as I think that it should not be taken lightly. It is so often assumed that psychoanalysis demands a "metaphysical" price out of us, that it is often overlooked that the alternative (here, Sartre's philosophy) does too and sometimes without the same benefits.

Highly schematically, Gardner reconstructs Sartre's concept of bad faith as follows. We begin with the assumption that there are two modes of being: that of consciousness, for-itself, and of the physical world, in-itself. Both are possessed by persons. The distinction between for-itself and in-itself cuts across persons and supplies them with two sets of properties: persons as for-itself are transcendent (they are free, spontaneous, active, engaged with possibility, lack enduring properties) and as in-itself they have facticity (they are also objective, embodied, public, situated, open to characterization). The basic human motivational story, or "fundamental project," arises from the necessity of persons' reconciling these two radically different modes of being. This necessity comes about because consciousness, which is for-itself, experiences itself as "lack(ing)," as an "insufficiency" of being relative to in-itself and is compelled to try to rectify this deficiency. The fundamental human project, undertaken in response to the initial condition of ontological inequality, has as its goal overcoming the disparity of modes of being. Such a resolution is however a metaphysical impossibility, which means that the project is strictly futile and its manifestations necessarily irrational (See Baldwin, 1979-80). Sartre maintains nevertheless that to a limited extent the two modes of being of persons, transcendence and facticity, "are and ought to be capable of a valid coordination." Bad faith is distinguished by the fact that the individual in bad faith "does not wish either to coordinate them or to surmount them in a higher synthesis"; contradictorily, they "affirm facticity as being transcendence and transcendence as being facticity" (Sartre, 1958, p. 56).

Consider the waiter in the famous passage from Sartre who is "playing at *being* a waiter" and "plays with his condition in order to *realize* it." He seeks to "be immediately a cafe waiter in the sense that this inkwell *is* an inkwell," to realize "a being-in-itself of the cafe waiter" (Sartre, 1958, pp. 59-60). The properties of his behavior "jar" with those of consciousness; consciousness is ill-expressed in his behavior. The kernel of bad faith consists then in representing oneself in thing-like terms, i. e. representing the relation between oneself and one's states and actions as if it were the same sort of relation as holds between a physical object and its properties. Forms of behavior manifesting bad faith mimic thinghood because they misexpress one's nature as a conscious being. Bad faith is therefore a structure of motivated self-misrepresentation defined not by a configuration of propositional attitudes, as is strong self-deception as Gardner defines it,[15] but by a certain species of motive (the fundamental project) and means (the refusal to effect a coordination of modes of being; self-thingification). Its connection with self-deception is consequently contingent: bad faith, as in the case of the waiter, is fundamentally a form of self-misexpression.

Gardner's strategy is to evaluate Sartre's account in relation to ordinary or common-sense or folk-psychology, as this is also the parameter according to which he assesses psychoanalysis. He thinks that the differences between Sartre's account and ordinary psychology are deep and evident. First, Sartre's is a view of human irrationality motivated by *metaphysics* rather than psychology. Put another way: psychology is for Sartre the *vehicle* of metaphysics. Whereas the metaphysical characterizations of persons typically considered in analytical philosophy (such as those of Descartes and Locke) do no more than set the scene for psychology and leave questions of motivation open, Sartre's wholly determines motivation. It does this because specific motivational axioms follow directly from Sartre's metaphysics of persons. Sartre's vision can therefore soak up explanatorily any given instance of human behavior; particularly, of course, irrational phenomena, since these, involving as they do self-contradiction, stand as emblems of the contradiction which is constitutive of human existence (and thereby, for Sartre, serve to confirm his metaphysic of persons).[16]

Second, whereas in ordinary psychology the origin of rationality is located in the *conative* powers of the mind, for Sartre it is located in the mind's *representational* powers: specifically, in persons' representation of themselves. All that is needed for Sartre's account is bare self-consciousness, which implies that even if persons had neither infancy nor biological identity—that is, neither an opaque past nor needs—they would still be irrational.

Third, Sartre's explanation posits *irrational desire*, in the sense of desire whose *content* is irrational, in the form of desire for the metaphysically impossible transformation of the for-itself into in-itself. Ordinary psychology, by contrast, assumes for the greater part only desires whose content is roughly rational and explains irrationality by assigning *deviant causal histories* to such desires.

In the first two respects, psychoanalytic theory is aligned with ordinary psychology: its motivational assumptions do not derive from metaphysical commitments, and it explains irrationality by referring primarily to conation rather than cognition. However, psychoanalytic explanation shares the third feature of Sartreian explanation: at least in its full Kleinian form, psychoanalytic theory posits irrational desires under the name of fantasies.

Sartre's account of bad faith can be read as exemplifying a general method of metaphysical explanation of irrationality. On such accounts, the origin of irrationality is something like a *contradiction in reality*, in the following sense: irrationality is explained by the incapacity of persons' powers of representation to provide a consistent representation of reality, the inconsistent representation which produces irrational phenomena being germane to and systematically caused by the very attempt to represent. On such a view, inconsistent representation is not optional for the mind but forced upon it: persons are brought viciously into contradiction with themselves and made to be irrational through being made to represent reality. In Sartre's account, the relevant bit of representation-recalcitrant reality is one's own nature as a person.

Gardner finds other instances of the same strategy in Hegel (1977, sec. 78-84, 166-75) "from whom Sartre takes much of his conception of the fundamental project." In Nietzsche (1967, especially sec. 7): "at the time of *The Birth of Tragedy* the world's own irrationality feeds directly the irrational Dionysian 'art-states' of the human subject. Nietzsche's vision of the Greeks is substantially borne out by Dodds' account, in *The Greeks and the Irrational*, of the Homeric concept of fate, a direct injection, originating in supernatural agency, or irrationality into the mind of the individual." In Heidegger (1977, pp. 135-7) "who suggests that, because Being is 'concealed,' Dasein is 'especially subjected to the rule of mystery and the oppression of errancy'." In Merleau-Monty (1962, pp. 168-9, 377-83): "there is in human existence a principle of indeterminacy"; and, arguably, in Lacan[17] (Gradner, 1993, p. 39).

He thinks that speculatively, one might trace these metaphysics of irrationality back to Kant's bifurcation of human personality into phenomenal and noumenal aspects: "Kant was arguably the first to insist on, not human duality (a much older thought), but the impossibility of fully coherent self-representation" (Gardner, 1993, p. 253). And he concludes:

> Whatever one may think of such accounts, there is undoubtedly something compelling about the underlying conception of irrationality to which they give expression. It is both a *romantic* and a *tragic* perspective: it suggests that irrationality is so deeply bound up with what it is to be a person that irrationality is a necessary, legitimate way of pursuing one's destiny as a human being. Metaphysical accounts of motivation have other, more logical attractions: they solve the Special Problem of irrationality; [18] provide determinate explanations of all human desires; and with their addition, ordinary psychology is guaranteed to be Complete [to give full explanations] rather than limited. But, for obvious reasons, unless one accepts in full the metaphysics behind such stories, not much can be taken from them. (Gardner, 1993, p. 39)

Gardner's conclusion is that if we do not accept the psychoanalytic explanation of irrationality, then we are left with ordinary, or common-sense, or folk-psychology. This kind of psychology does not explain the three obvious cases of irrationality which commonsense acknowledges, that is, wishful thinking, self-deception and akrasia, or weakness of will. With regard to these, we have no difficulty in saying, in broad terms, what each of them consists in. Wishful thinking is a matter of believing something simply because you desire it to be so. Self-deception consists in getting yourself to believe one thing in order to avoid facing what you know to be the truth. Akrasia consists in failing to do what you know is the best to do. Gardner contends that ordinary psychology treats these cases as rational: "irrationality is off limits to ordinary psychology, or . . . ordinary psychology deals only with rationality" (Gardner, 1993, p. 16).

His central argument in favor of psychoanalysis is that "some irrational phenomena–the recognition of which is inevitable for participants in ordinary psychology–can not be explained by ordinary psychology, yet require explanation in terms congruent with the ordinary conception of persons; which is what psychoanalytic theory supplies" (p. 227). He thinks that on the one hand, psychoanalytic concepts are natural extensions of the ways of thinking of ordinary psychology. For example, the explanation of irrationality offered by ordinary psychology relies, fundamentally, on such basic notions as mental conflict and the power of desire to malform belief. Psychoanalytic theory exploits with much greater intensity the same resources. On the other hand, psychoanalytic theory is not just a terminological reformulation of ordinary psychology: it explains things that ordinary psychology can not explain and does so by employing a distinctive form of explanation which is foreign to ordinary psychology. Finally, he summarizes his position by saying that:

> Psychoanalytic theory should not be made to seem to appear out of nowhere; as if it had evolved autonomously in response to problems of psychopathology whose existence can only be witnessed in the seclusion of the clinical hour. Looked at in that hermetic way, psychoanalytic theory is bound to seem forever strange, arbitrary and unpersuasive. A fundamental and central contention of this book is that, on the contrary, psychoanalytic theory lies in a direct line of descent from

problems and strategies of explanation encountered and deployed in ordinary psychology—the form of explanation to which our everyday talk of people as believing, remembering, feeling and wanting commits us—and that it is with reference to these that its concepts should be understood and its claims to explanation measured. (Gardner, 1993, p. 15)

I think that Gardner's emphasis on the price we have to pay when using Sartre's view of irrationality is important. This claim might be generalized to many views of irrationality, and not only those listed above. The strength of the Stoics' view of irrationality, to take an example, stem directly from a metaphysics in which the rational equates the divine and the natural (Nussbaum, 1994). Any use of Stoics' tactics regarding the irrational loses most of its power when disentangled from their metaphysics. It seems that the Freudian view of irrationality, though it might offend some cherished opinions about our freedom, might not be the worst when it comes to adopting a metaphysic. The extent to which ethics, which are traditionally inserted within some metaphysics, can be useful apart from that metaphysics, is an important question especially for applied philosophers. I have dealt with it elsewhere, both generally and specifically, using Spinoza's ethics as an example (2003b). Though this general question is beyond the scope of this chapter, it is time to address the more modest one, regarding philosophical counsellors' possible attitudes toward the unconscious.

VI. Philosophical Counselling and the Unconscious

My opinion is that even if Sartre's views are to be rejected (Gardner, 1993) as well as other philosophic criticisms of psychoanalysis (Levy, 1996), and even if today's climate has never been so hospitable to Freud's theory of mind (Smith, 1999), philosophical counselling is still a valuable enterprise. Before probing the extreme possibility of Freud being right, let us consider the possibilities of the philosophical counselor regarding the unconscious.

1. As Peter Raabe rightly notices (2000), the line between Freudian or classical psychoanalysis and psychotherapy is becoming quite blurred. He quotes psychoanalysts Morton Aronson and Melvin Scharfman regarding

the fact that with the passing of Freud and the generation of his immediate successors there is no longer a uniformity of viewpoints on what constitutes psychoanalysis (Raabe, 2000, p. 81). Even Sebastian Gardner's defense of psychoanalysis, which was used here as a criticism of Sartre, is more a defense of its Kleinian development than its classical Freudian formulation. This situation defies a direct controversy between psychoanalysis and philosophical counseling, and certainly a controversy of the kind I have attempted to present here.

2. Many psychotherapies reject the unconscious or do not deal with it: Adlerian therapy, A. Ellis' Rational Emotive Behavior Therapy (1970), A. Beck's Cognitive Therapy (1979) and Existential and Humanistic therapies, to name a few.

a. These psychotherapies follow in this philosophy's traditional view of the matter. Looking back at the history of philosophy, one can see that most philosophies that proposed fundamental change while recognizing the irrational (Plato, Aristotle, the Stoics, the Epicureans, the Pyrrhonists, Spinoza) also gave explanations of how thought or rationality can affect feelings and desires, how reason can work with or against the emotions, bringing thus change in the way we feel. Most contemporary works on the emotions, moreover, hold some version of the Stoic view, viewing emotion as a belief or as involving belief (Nussbaum, 2001; Solomon, 1993; Ben-Ze'ev, 2000). Thus, many philosophical counsellors feel entitled to disregard the unconscious (Lahav, 1994, 1995, 1996; Blass, 1996; Rachel Blass is a trained psychoanalyst), while some maintain that it is important to gain freedom from it (Schuster, 1993).

b. Following A. Ellis' example, however, some philosophical counsellors choose not to dismiss the unconscious but to deal with it indirectly (Cohen, 1995). This option is well explained in Peter Raabe's excellent chapter on the difference between philosophical counselling and psychotherapy:

> But it might still be argued that despite all this task about our emotions being connected to our beliefs there are nevertheless deeply unconscious forces that must be dealt with. An examination of the emotions around an issue often reveals that they are in fact based on certain beliefs about this issue of which the client is not consciously

aware. The philosopher can be a very capable assistant to the person wishing to come to a conscious realization and articulation of such "unconscious" beliefs. I have put quotation marks around the word "unconscious" because I'm not convinced that it is accurate to characterize a belief as being unconscious simply because it has not been recognized by the believer as a belief he has. In other words, I think a person can live and act according to an unreflective belief—perhaps one that is unnoticed as unjustified, such as racism—that is not necessarily an unconscious belief. The point is that once the person has been helped to become aware of these beliefs—whether they are termed unconscious or unreflective—they can be scrutinized and evaluated. And once they have been evaluated as the cause of troublesome emotions they can be either altered or discarded. *In this way the philosophical counselor is in fact dealing with what a psychotherapist might call the unconscious* but in a different manner, and with more client involvement, than in *the approach advocated by classical psychoanalysis.* (Raabe, 2001, p. 175, italics added).

It seems to me, however, that according to the terminology used in this chapter, the right term should be the preconscious. For, according to Freudian theory, the "part" which can be accessible to argument would not be the unconscious but the preconscious. This applies also to Elliot Cohen's statement that he deals with the unconscious indirectly, that the "unconscious" is merely the unexamined or forgotten, or that the unconscious is investigated with more client involvement than the approach followed in psychoanalysis (Cohen, 1995; Raabe, 2001, p. 96). Note 6 below explains the difference between the unconscious and the preconscious, and if I am right in this understanding of psychoanalysis, then philosophical counselling is no substitute to it.

3. Some philosophical counsellors do deal with the unconscious in the Freudian sense, using the *I Ching,* for example (Fleming, 1996). A few Western philosophers (i.e. Schopenhauer, Nietzsche), moreover, who could be useful in philosophical counselling, embrace the unconscious yet urge us to change. According to Nietzsche, for example, change is possible, but it is mainly unconscious and does not need self-knowledge, just a strong will to

truth (or power).[19] According to Schopenhauer, one can know oneself only "retroactively," by looking back at one's actions towards the end of one's life. Change is possible but it is not voluntary. It comes from the "outside," very much like God's grace, though God does not exist in Schopenhauer's philosophy (Schopenhauer, 1958). These ways of accepting or even "working" with the unconscious within a philosophical context should be further probed and developed.

4. Finally, I would like to emphasize a last point regarding the relationship of thought and emotion, and its relationship to the viability of philosophical counselling. I agree with the fact that "it seems uncontroversial to conclude that if emotions are not simply irrational and causal but rather the different ways people conceive of themselves and their situations, then they can be changed by influence, argument and evidence." But I do not think it is necessary to conclude that "this is the view a philosophical counselor *must* take regarding the relationship between thinking and the emotions if they want to practice legitimate philosophical counseling and not some thinly veiled form of psychology" (Raabe, 2001, p. 176, italics added). I think that philosophical counsellors, depending on the goals of philosophical counselling, can hold many different views regarding thinking and the emotions. I would like to elaborate on this point.

The philosophical counsellor need not aim at providing complete self-knowledge, nor at realizing a fundamental change in the counsellee. As I explained elsewhere (Amir, 2003a), to my mind the important thing is that the philosophical counsellor clears up her mind about her own beliefs or suspension of belief on irrationality, the possibility of change and the role of self-knowledge in that process. It is no less important to share these views with the counsellee, so that the measure in which philosophical counselling can accommodate these goals could be clarified and explicitly stated. Even if the philosophical counsellor is pessimistic regarding the possibilities of fundamental change through discussion; even if she believes that change presupposes self-knowledge but that philosophical counselling cannot provide it; even if she thinks that no one knows how change occurs; even if she thinks, finally, that Freud's view of change is the right one—many avenues are still possible.

First, philosophical counselling can be a good detector of irrationality, even if it might not be able to state the cause of irrationality nor change the irrational into the rational. The way of detecting irrationality might be the same for the philosophical counsellor, the non-psychoanalytic therapist and the psychoanalyst, if the following quote depicts correctly the psychoanalyst's procedure:

> It is instructive at this point to note that *one* criterion by means one of which the psychoanalyst identifies behavior as irrational and uncon- sciously motivated is the *degree* of the agent's *inability either to bring rational criticism to bear on his own actions or to respond to rational criticism of them.* (MacIntyre, 1967, p. 252, italics added)

Or, as Joseph Agassi puts it: "as Freud was first to notice, self-deception usually rests on the stubborn *reluctance to consider alternatives* when these are *suggested by others*" (Agassi, 1997, p. 24, italics added).

Second, having detected an instance of irrationality, the philosophical counsellor might attempt to change it through a change of belief, that is, through evidence, argument and influence. If she fails, *one* possible conclusion is that this is a case that Freudians would diagnose as "repression":

> Certain features in contexts of failures of self-knowledge provide criteria to distinguish repression from other conditions. They revolve around the person's inability *to come to a realization,* i. e. to form a self-ascribing belief that is effective in correcting their behavior. (Gardner, 1993, p. 103).

Third, the counsellor might suggest at this point that psychoanalysis might be more helpful. She might even refer the client to a psychoanalyst, as there is no reason for non-cooperation between psychoanalysts and philoso- phers. The psychoanalyst can send the client back to her, after the repression "has been removed," allowing thus the continuation of philosophic discus- sion. Anticipating a possible misunderstanding, I would like to clarify that I do not *advise* to send a client to a psychoanalyst. My point is just that a philosophical counsellor can even be a believer in Freudian psychoanalysis, provided that she adapts the counselee's expectation to what she can offer.

Generalizing from ten years experience in practicing philosophical counselling, however, I would say that counsellees usually do not get in touch with the psychoanalysts or psychiatrists to whom they are referred, even if these kinds of therapies are better for them in the long run (that is, even if they can better meet their demands). Most of the time, I learned through experience, philosophical counsellors are the last resorts, as counsellees seem to be much more anti-psychologists or anti-psychoanalysts or anti-psychiatrists than most counsellors.

Fourth, in that case, or even one step before that (step two above)—provided that the counselor is reluctant to diagnose something as "repression" or that she does not believe in psychoanalysis—she can simply say that she does not know how to change the irrational behavior or feeling. Counsellee and counsellor can continue the sessions bearing both in mind that specific area of irrationality. Of course, if the counsellee came just to solve that problem, then the counselling sessions could be over. As there are degrees of irrationality (Agassi and Jarvie, 1987), the counselor might be helpful in many ways though conceivably completely helpless in one specific area, where irrationality is deep.

It seems, therefore, that the capacity of philosophical counselling to handle the possibility of the unconscious depends on its goals. One goal could be the enhancement of self-knowledge. I think that the philosophical counsellor who does not adhere to a *theory* of irrationality can point to the counsellee *when* he is being irrational, but not *why*. This statement does not even assume that anyone can actually answer the *why* question.[20] In the paper referred to above (Amir, 2003a), I have argued that just knowing that you are being irrational, though certainly an advance in self-knowledge, can make you feel worse, if it creates a feeling of frustrating impotence regarding change. This leads us to the second possible goal of philosophical counselling, namely, fundamental change.

The whole body of philosophical theories is meant to bring fundamental change through learning and practice. But it is directed to the truth-seeking and rationality-expanding person. Philosophy changes those who can be changed by thought, those who value thought so much that it changes their whole being. A philosopher *wants* to be less irrational. Most people, generally, do not want to pay the price, as being irrational is very convenient and being consistent is hard.

If you count on influence, argument and evidence to convince your client to change his irrational beliefs, you still assume a basic choice of rationality. To reiterate the example I used at the end of last section, if you use Stoic tactics you can bring change. But there is a whole metaphysics involved, one which explains why being rational is better than being irrational. Without this frame of mind, the counsellee does not have a strong impetus for leaving the irrational for the rational. How can you defend consistency and logical thought to someone who wants to stay irrational in some area of thought? Who, except the philosopher, has a passion for rationality? Since when has consistency been a goal for most human beings? As Gershon Weiler puts it: "Whoever is *knowingly* inconsistent is irrational but there is, of course, more to rationality than mere consistency" (Weiler, 1987, p. 303).

One might argue that the counsellee's suffering is his impetus for change. And if you can convince him that being rational would remove the painful emotion, rationality would not have to be wholly endorsed by the client but only used as a tool for feeling better. This strategy however assumes another form of rationality, the capacity to relate means to ends. Furthermore, it does not solve the problem of akrasia or weakness of will.

I do not think, therefore, that philosophical counsellors should guarantee fundamental change, although this is what philosophy is all about. Nobody *knows* how change occurs and there are many controversial views about the ways to prompt it (Kanfer and Goldstein, 1982). One thing we know is that when a person is ripe for change, anything works. Freud said that every neurotic (that is, us) wants change and does not want change at the same time. Even pinpointing that during philosophical counselling is illuminating, for it enhances self-knowledge and calls for reflection.

Mapping our irrational zones might seem a minimalist goal. It is still a valuable one, for knowing that I am being irrational is not just a prerequisite for enhancing my rationality, it already enhances my rationality. This does not betray philosophy's goals, though much more can be achieved depending on the counsellor's beliefs, the counsellee's capacity and the power of philosophy. Although we are, as Nietzsche memorably puts it, "in the phase of modesty of consciousness" (Nieztsche, 1968, section 676; Cf. 1977, sections 344-5), the remarkable ideals of philosophy still have a strong appeal. Brought to counsellees through the counsellor's knowledge and personality, they can create a thirst for change that would result in a conversion to philosophy, exchanging the narrow unconscious-conscious controversy for new horizons.

References

Achenbach, G.B. (1987). *Philosophische praxis*. Koln: Jurgen Dinter.

Achenbach, G.B., & Macho, T. (1985). *Das prinzip heilung*. Koln: Jurgen Dinter.

Achenbach, G.B.. (1992). Die "Grundregel" philosophischer Praxis. In *Psychotherapy und philosophie*. Paderborn: Junfermann Verlag.

Adler, A. (1927). *Practice and theory of individual psychology*. (P. Radin, Trans.). London and New York: Harcourt.

Agassi, J., & Jarvie, I. (Eds.) (1987). *Rationality: The critical view*. Dordrecht: Martinus Nijhoff.

Agassi, J. (1997). Self-Deception: A view from the rationalist perspective. In M.S. Myslobodsky (Ed.), *The mythomanias: The nature of deception and self-deception* (pp. 23-50). Mahwah, NJ: Lawrence Erlbaum.

Amir, L.B. (2003a). *The practice of philosophy – Philosophy and practice*. Unpublished manuscript, Tel Aviv University.

Amir, L.B. (2003b). *Virtue, happiness and management: A Spinozistic approach*. Unpublished manuscript, Tel Aviv University.

Amir, Lydia B. (2003c). *Autonomy, sovereignty and generosity: Nietzsche's ethics in management*. Unpublished manuscript, Tel Aviv University.

Baldwin, T. (1979-80). The original choice in Sartre and Kant. *Proceedings of the Aristotelian Society, 80*, 31-44.

Balint, M. (1972). *Amour primaire et technique psychoanalytique*. (J. Dupont, R. Gelly & S. Kadar, Trans.). Paris: Payot.

Barnes, H. (1991). The role of the ego in reciprocity. In R. Aronson & A. Van den Hoven (Eds.), *Sartre Alive*. Chicago: University of Chicago Press.

Beck, A., et al. (1979). *Cognitive therapy of depression*. New York: Guilford Press.

Binswanger, L. (1963). *Being in the world: Selected papers of Ludwig Binswanger*. (J. Needleman, Trans.). New York: Basic Books.

Blass, R.B. (1996). The "person" in philosophical counseling vs. psychotherapy and the possibility of interchange between the fields. *Journal of Applied Philosophy, 13*(3), 227-296.

Blondel, E. (1999). Nietzsche and Freud, or: How to be within philosophy while criticizing it from without. In J. Golomb, et al. (Eds.), *Nietzsche and depth psychology* (pp.

171-180). Albany: SUNY Press.

Ben-Ze'ev, A. (2000). *The subtlety of emotions.* Cambridge, MA: MIT Press.

Boss, M. (1963). *Psychoanalysis and Daseinanalysis.* (L. Lefebvre, Trans.). New York: Basic Books.

Bouveresse, J. (1995). *Wittgenstein reads Freud: The myth of the unconscious.* (C. Cosman, Trans.). Princeton, NJ: Princeton University Press.

Broad, C.D. (1925). *The mind and its place in nature.* London: Routledge & Kegan Paul.

Bugental, J.F. (1989). *The search for authenticity: An existential-analytic approach to psychotherapy.* New York: Irvington.

Cannon, B. (1991). *Sartre et la psychanalyse.* (L. Bury, Trans.). Paris: Presses Universitaires de France. From English: *Sartre and Psychoanalysis.* Kansas: The University of Kansas Press.

Carus, C. G. (1846). *Psyche.* Pforzheim.

Chapelle, D. (1999). Nietzsche and psychoanalysis: From eternal return to compulsive repetition and beyond. In J. Golomb, et al. (Eds.), *Nietzsche and depth psychology* (pp. 37-50). Albany: SUNY Press.

Cohen, E.D. (1995). Philosophical counseling: Some roles of critical thinking. In R. Lahav and M. Tillmans (Eds.), *Essays on philosophical counseling* (pp. 121-131). New York: University Press of America.

Davidson, D. (1980). *Essays on actions and events.* Oxford: Clarendon Press.

Davidson, D. (1984). *Inquiries into truth and interpretation.* Oxford: Clarendon Press.

Davidson, D. (1986). Deception and division. In J. Elster (Ed.), *The multiple self.* Cambridge: Cambridge University Press.

Descartes, R. (1637). *Discours sur la methode.* In A. & P. Tanney (Eds.), *Oeuvres de Descartes,*12 vols. Paris, 1897-1910.

Decker, H. (1977). *Freud in Germany: Revolution and reaction in science,* 1893-1907. New York: International Universities Press.

Dennett, D.C. (1991). *The intentional stance.* Cambridge, MA: Bradford/MIT.

Dennett, D.C. (1991). *Consciousness explained.* London: Allen Lane.

Dodds, E. (1951). *The Greeks and the irrational.* Berkeley.

Dretske, F. (1995). *Naturalizing the mind.* Cambridge, MA: MIT Press.

Ellenberger, H. F. (1970). *The discovery of the unconscious: The history and evolution of dynamic psychiatry.* New York: Basic Books.

Ellis, A. (1970). *Reason and emotion in psychotherapy.* New York: Lyle Stuart.

Fairbairn, W.R.D. (1984). *Psychoanalytic studies of the personality*. London: Routledge & Kegan Paul.

Feyeraband, P. (1963). Mental events and the brain. *Journal of Philosophy, 60*, 160-166.

Field, J.C. (1922). Is the concept of the unconscious of value in psychology? *Mind, 31*, 414-423.

Fleming, J. (1996). Philosophical counseling and the *I Ching*. *Journal of Chinese Philosophy, 23*(3), 301-317.

Freud, S. & Breuer, J. (1895). Studies on hysteria. In *The standard edition of the complete psychological works of Sigmund Freud*, 24 vols. (J. Strachey, Ed.), vol. 2. London: Hogarth Press, 1953-64.

Freud, S. (1900). The interpretation of dreams. In *The standard edition of the complete psychological works of Sigmund Freud*, 24 vols. (J. Strachey, Ed.), vol. 4 and 5. London: Hogarth Press, 1953-64.

Freud, S. (1901). Psychopathology of everyday life. In *The standard edition of the complete psychological works of Sigmund Freud*, 24 vols. (J. Strachey, Ed.), vol. 6. London: Hogarth Press, 1953-64.

Freud, S. (1909). Notes upon a case of obsessional neurosis. In *The standard edition of the complete psychological works of Sigmund Freud*, 24 vols. (J. Strachey, Ed.), vol. 6. London: Hogarth Press, 1953-64.

Freud, S. (1910). Five lectures on psychoanalysis. In *The standard edition of the complete psychological works of Sigmund Freud*, 24 vols. (J. Strachey, Ed.). London: Hogarth Press, 1953-64.

Freud, S. (1914a). On the history of the psychoanalytic movement. In *The standard edition of the complete psychological works of Sigmund Freud*, 24 vols. (J. Strachey, Ed.), vol. 14. London: Hogarth Press, 1953-64.

Freud, S. (1914b). Recollection, repeating and working-through. In *The standard edition of the complete psychological works of Sigmund Freud*, 24 vols. (J. Strachey, Ed.), vol. 12. London: Hogarth Press, 1953-64.

Freud, S. (1915). The unconscious. In *The standard edition of the complete psychological works of Sigmund Freud*, 24 vols. (J. Strachey, Ed.), vol. 14. London: Hogarth Press, 1953-64.

Freud, S. (1916-17). Introductory lectures on psychoanalysis. In *The standard edition of the complete psychological works of Sigmund Freud*, 24 vols. (J. Strachey, Ed.), vol. 1. London: Hogarth Press, 1953-64.

Freud, S. (1923). The ego and the id. In *The standard edition of the complete psycho-*

logical works of Sigmund Freud, 24 vols. (J. Strachey, Ed.), vol. 19. London: Hogarth Press, 1953-64.

Freud, S. (1925). An autobiographical study. In *The standard edition of the complete psychological works of Sigmund Freud*, 24 vols. (J. Strachey, Ed.), vol. 20. London: Hogarth Press, 1953-64.

Freud, S. (1926). Inhibitions, symptoms and anxiety. In *The standard edition of the complete psychological works of Sigmund Freud*, 24 vols. (J. Strachey, Ed.), vol. 20. London: Hogarth Press, 1953-64.

Freud, S. (1933). New introductory lectures on psychoanalysis. In *The standard edition of the complete psychological works of Sigmund Freud*, 24 vols. (J. Strachey, Ed.), vol. 22. London: Hogarth Press, 1953-64.

Freud, S. (1938). Analysis terminable and interminable. In *The standard edition of the complete psychological works of Sigmund Freud*, 24 vols. (J. Strachey, Ed.), vol. 23. London: Hogarth Press, 1953-64.

Freud, S. (1940). Splitting of the ego in the process of defense. In *The standard edition of the complete psychological works of Sigmund Freud*, 24 vols. (J. Strachey, Ed.), vol. 23. London: Hogarth Press, 1953-64.

Freud, S. (1970). *The letters of Sigmund Freud.* (E.L. Freud, Ed., & T. Stern and J. Stern, Trans.). London: Hogarth Press and the Institute of Psycho-Analysis.

Gardner, S. (1993). *Irrationality and the philosophy of psychoanalysis.* Cambridge: Cambridge University Press.

Golomb, J. (1989). *Nietzsche's enticing philosophy of power.* Ames: Iowa State University Press.

Golomb, J. (1999). Introductory essay: Nietzsche's new psychology. In J. Golomb, W. Santaniello, & R. Lehrer (Eds.), *Nietzsche and depth psychology* (pp. 1-22). Albany: SUNY Press.

Golomb, J., Santaniello, W., & Lehrer, R. (Eds.) (1999). *Nietzsche and depth psychology.* Albany: SUNY Press.

Graham, G. (Ed.) (1994). *Philosophical psychopathology.* Cambridge, MA: MIT Press.

Grunbaum, A. (1984). *The foundations of psychoanalysis: A philosophical critique.* Berkeley: University of California Press.

Guntrip, H. (1969). *Schizoid phenomena, object relations and the self.* New York: International Universities Press.

Hartmann, E. von (1869). *Philosophie der Unbewusstsein.* Berlin: Dunker.

Hartmann, H. (1975). *Ego psychology and the problem of adaptation.* New York.

Hegel, G. W. F. (1977). *Phenomenology of spirit*. (A. Miller, Trans.). Oxford.

Heidegger, Martin, *Being and Time*, trans. J. Macquarrie and E. S. Robinson (New York, 1962).

Heidegger, M. (1977). On the essence of truth. In *Basic writings*. (D. Krel, Ed.). New York.

Howard, A. (2000). *Philosophy for counselling and psychotherapy: Pythagoras to post-modernism*. London: Macmillan.

Husserl, E. (1931). *Ideas - General introduction to pure phenomenology*. (W. R. B. Gibson, Trans.). London.

Izenberg, G.N. (1976). *The existentialist critique of Freud*. Princeton, NJ: Princeton University Press.

James, W. (1950). *The principles of psychology*, 2 vols. Reprint. New York: Dover. (Originally published in 1890).

Jaspers, K. (1963). *General psychopathology*. (J. Hoenig & M. Hamilton, Trans.). Chicago.

Jung, C.G. (1968). *Analytical psychology: Its theory and practice*. New York: Random House.

Kanfer, F.H. & Goldstein, A.P. (Eds.) (1982). *Helping people change: A textbook of methods*. New York: Pergamon Press.

Kant, E. (1964). *Groundwork of the metaphysics of morals* (H.J. Paton, Trans.). New York: Harper & Row.

Keen, E. (1970). *Three faces of being: Toward an existential clinical psychology*. New York: Meredith Corp.

Klein, M. (1952). Notes on schizoid mechanisms. In M. Klein et al., *Developments in psycho-analysis*. London.

Kockelman, J. (1967). *Edmund Husserl's phenomenological psychology*. Pittsburgh: Duquesne University Press.

Kohut, H. (1977). *The restoration of the self*. New York: International Universities Press.

Lacan, J. (1975). *Le seminaire, I: Les ecrits techniques de Freud*. Paris: Seuil.

Lahav, R. (1994). Is philosophical counseling that different from psychotherapy? In *Zeitschrift fur Philosophische Praxis, 1*, 32-36.

Lahav, R. (1995). A conceptual framework for philosophical counseling. In R. Lahav & M. da Venza Tillmans (Eds.), *Essays on philosophical counseling* (pp. 25-47). Lanham, Md: University Press of America.

Lahav, R. & M. da Venza Tillmans (Eds.) (1995). *Essays on philosophical counseling*.

Lanham, Md: University Press of America.

Lahav, R. (1996). What is philosophical in philosophical counseling? *Journal of Applied Philosophy, 13*(3), 259-278.

Laing, R.D., & Cooper, D.G. (1971). *Raison et violence.* Paris: Payot.

Laplanche, J. & Leclaire, S. (1972). The unconscious: A psychoanalytic study. *Yale French Studies, 49.*

Lehrer, R. (1999). Freud and Nietzsche, 1892-1895. In J. Golomb et al. (Eds.), *Nietzsche and Depth Psychology* (pp. 181-204). Albany: SUNY Press.

Levine, I. (1923). *The unconscious: An introduction to Freudian psychology.* London: L. Parsons.

Levy, D. (1996). *Freud among the philosophers: The psychoanalytic unconscious and its philosophical critics.* New Haven & London: Yale University Press.

MacIntyre, A. (1958). *The unconscious: A conceptual study.* London: Routledge.

MacIntyre, A. (1967). Freud, Sigmund. In P. Edwards (Ed.), *The Encyclopedia of Philosophy*, vol. 3 (pp. 249-253). New York: Macmillan & the Free Press.

Marr, D. (1982). *Vision.* San Francisco: W. H. Freeman & Company.

May, R. (1950). *The meaning of anxiety.* New York: Ronald Press.

May, R. (1967). *Man's search for himself.* New York: Signet. Originally published in 1953).

May, R. (1983). *The discovery of being: Writings in existential psychology.* New York & London: W.W. Norton & Company.

May, S. (1999). *Nietzsche's ethics and his war on "morality."* Oxford: Clarendon Press.

Merleau-Monty, M. (1962). *Phenomenology of perception.* (C. Smith, Trans.). London.

Millikan, R.G. (1984). Language, thought and other biological categories. Cambridge, MA: Bradford/MIT.

Millikan, R. G.. (1993). *White Queen psychology and other essays for Alice.* Cambridge, MA: Bradford/MIT.

Moore, G. E. (1962). Wittgenstein's Lectures in 1930-33. In *Philosophical Papers.* New York: Collier Books, 1962. (Originally published in 1954).

Nagel, T. (1979). Brain bisection and the unity of consciousness. In *Moral Questions.* Cambridge: Cambridge University Press.

Nietzsche, F. (1967). *The birth of tragedy.* (W. Kaufmann, Trans.). New York: Vintage Books.

Nietzsche, F. (1974). *The gay science.* (W. Kaufmann, Trans.). New York: Vintage

Books.

Nietzsche, F. (1968). *The will to power*. (W. Kaufmann & R. J. Hollingdale, Trans.). New York: Vintage Books.

Nussbaum, M. C. (1994). *The therapy of desire*. Princeton, NJ: Princeton University Press.

Nussbaum, M. C. (2001). *Upheavals of thought: A theory of the emotions*. Cambridge: Cambridge University Press.

Olafson, F.A. (1967). Sartre, Jean-Paul. In P. Edwards (Ed.), *The Encyclopedia of Philosophy*, vol. 7 (pp. 287-293). New York: Macmillan.

Parkes, G. (1994). *Composing the soul: Reaches of Nietzsche's psychology*. Chicago: University of Chicago Press.

Place, U. T. (1959). Is consciousness a brain process? In C.V. Borst (Ed.), *The mind/brain identity theory*. Cambridge, MA: Bradford/MIT.

Popper, K. (1962). *Conjectures and refutations*. New York: Basic Books.

Putnam, H. (1960). Minds and machines. In S. Hook (Ed.), *Dimensions of mind*. New York: Collier.

Putnam, H. (1975). The meaning of 'meaning'." In K. Gunderson (Ed.), *Minnesota studies in the philosophy of ccience, vol. VII: Language, mind and knowledge*. Minneapolis: University of Minnesota Press.

Raabe, P.B. (2001). *Philosophical counseling: Theory and practice*. Westport, CT: Praeger.

Rank, O. (1936). *Truth and reality*. (J. Taft, Trans.). New York & London: W.W. Norton and Company.

Ricoeur, P. (1970). *Freud and philosophy: An essay in interpretation*. (D. Savage, trans.). New Haven, CT: Yale University Press.

Robinson, P. (1993). *Freud and his critics*. Berkeley: University of California Press.

Rorty, A. (1988). Deception, liars, and layers. In A. Rorty & B.B. McLaughlin (Eds.), *Perspectives on self-Deception*. Los Angeles: University of California Press.

Russell, B. (1921). *The analysis of mind*. London: Allen and Unwin.

Sartre, J.-P. (1936). *L'imagination*. Paris: Felix Alcan.

Sartre, J.-P. (1943). *L'etre et le neant. Essai d'ontologie phenomenologique*. Paris: Gallimard.

Sartre, J.-P. (1958). *Being and nothingness: An essay on phenomenological ontology*. (H. Barnes, Trans.). London: Philosophical Library.

Sartre, J.-P. (1964). *Les mots*. Paris: Gallimard.

Sartre, J.-P. (1965). *La transcendance de l'ego*. Paris: Vrin.

Sartre, J.-P. (1971). *L'idiot de la famille*. Paris: Gallimard.

Sartre, J.-P. (1972). *Situations IX*. Paris: Gallimard.

Sartre, J.-P. (1984). *Le scenario Freud*. Paris: Gallimard.

Schacht, R. (1983). *Nietzsche*. London: Routledge & Kegan Paul.

Schafer, R. (1976). *A new language for psychoanalysis*. New Haven.

Schilpp, P.A. (Ed.) (1981). *The philosophy of Jean-Paul Sartre*. La Salle, IL: Open Court.

Schopenhauer, A. (1958). *The world as will and representation*. (E. F. J. Payne, Trans.). New York: Dover.

Schuster, S.C. (1991). Philosophical counselling. *Journal of Applied Philosophy, 8,* 219-223.

Schuster, S.C. (1993). Philosophy as if it matters: The practice of philosophical counseling. *Critical Review, 6*(4), 587-599.

Schuster, S.C. (1995). The practice of Sartre's philosophy in philosophical counseling and in existential psychotherapy. *The Jerusalem Philosophical Quarterly, 44*(1), 99-114.

Schuster, S.C. (1996). Philosophical counseling and humanistic psychotherapy. *Journal of Psychology and Judaism, 20,* 247-259.

Schuster, S.C. (1997). Sartre's *Words* as a paradigm for self-description in philosophical counseling. In *Perspectives in Philosophical Practice, The Reader of the Second International Congress on Philosophical Practice* (pp. 20-34). Doorwerth: Vereniging Filosofische Praktijk.

Schuster, S.C. (1998a). Sartre's Freud and the future of Sartrean psychoanalysis. *The Israeli Journal of Psychiatry, 35*(1), 20-30.

Schuster, S.C. (1998b). Revisiting hope now with Benny Levy. *Sartre Studies International, 4*(1), 63-75.

Schuster, S.C. (1999). *Philosophical practice: An alternative to counseling and psychotherapy*. Westport, CT: Praeger Publishers.

Schuster, S.C. (2002). *The philosopher's autobiography, a qualitative study*. Westport, CT: Praeger Publishers.

Sruton, R. (1986). *Sexual desire: A philosophical investigation*. London.

Sellars, W. (1956). Empiricism and the philosophy of mind. In G. Gunderson (Ed.), *Minnesota studies in the philosophy of science*, vol. VII: *The foundations of science and the concepts of psychology and psychoanalysis*. Minneapolis: University of Minnesota Press.

Sellars, W. (1963). *Science, perception and reality*. New York: Humanities Press.

Smart, J.J.C. (1959). Sensations and brain processes. In C.C.V. Borst (Ed.), *The mind/brain identity theory*. Cambridge, MA: Bradford/MIT.

Smith, L.D. (1999). *Freud's philosophy of the unconscious*. Dordrecht, The Netherlands:

Kluwer.

Solomon, R.C. (1993). *The passions: Emotions and the meaning of life.* Indianapois: Hackett.

Solomon, R.C. (1999). *The joy of philosophy: Thinking thin* versus *the passionate life.* New York & Oxford: Oxford University Press.

Sullivan, H.S. (1953). *Conceptions of modern psychiatry.* New York: W.W. Norton & Company. (Originally published in 1940).

Sullivan, H.S. (1953). *The interpersonal theory of psychiatry.* New York: W.W. Norton & Company.

Van Kaam, A. (1969). *Existential foundations for psychology.* Garden City, NY: Doubleday.

Van den Berg, J. H. (1955). *The phenomenological approach to psychiatry.* Springfield, IL: Charles C. Thomas.

Weiler, G. (1987). Rationality and criticism. In J. Agassi & I. Jarvie (Eds.), *Rationality: The critical view* (pp. 297-308). Dordrecht: Martinus Nijhoff.

Whyte, L.L. (1960). *The unconscious before Freud.* New York: Julian Friedman.

Whyte, L.L. (1967). Unconscious. In P. Edwards (Ed.), *The encyclopedia of philosophy*, Volume 8 (pp. 185-189). New York: Macmillan & the Free Press.

Winnicott, D.W. (1965a). *The family and individual development.* London & New York: Tavistock Publications.

Winnicott, D.W. (1965b). Ego integration in child development. In *The Maturational Processes and the Facilitating Environment: Studies in the Theory of Emotional Development.*

Winnicott, D.W. (1971). *Playing and reality.* Harmondsworth.

Wisdom, J.O. (1963). Psycho-analytic technology. *The British Journal for the Philosophy of Science*, Vol. 7 (pp. 13-28). New York: 1963.

Wittgenstein, L. (1953). *Philosophical investigations.* (G. Anscombe, Trans.; G. Amscombe & R. Rhees, Eds.). Oxford: Blackwell.

Wittgenstein, L. (1958). *The blue and brown books.* Oxford: Blackwell.

Wittgenstein, L. (1966). *Lectures and conversations on aesthetics, psychology and religious belief.* (C. Barrett, Ed.). Berkeley: University of California Press.

Wittgenstein, L. (1979). *Wittgenstein's lectures, Cambridge, 1932-1935: From the notes of Alice Ambrose and Margaret MacDonald.* (A. Ambrose, Ed.) Chicago: University of Chicago Press.

Wittgenstein, L. (1980). *Culture and value.* (G. H. von Wright, Ed.; P. Winch, Trans.). Chicago: University of Chicago Press.

Yalom, I.D. (1980). *Existential psychotherapy.* New York: Basic Books, 1980.

Young C., & Brooke, A. (1994). Schopenhauer and Freud. *International Journal of Psycho-Analysis*, *75*(1), 101-118.

Notes

¹ Wittgenstein's thoughts on psychoanalysis are mainly found in five places in material so far published: "Wittgenstein's Lectures in 1930-33," as reported by Moore, G.E., supplemented by remarks recorded by Alice Ambrose and Margaret MacDonald in *Wittgenstein's Lectures*, pp. 39-40; *The Blue Book* (dictated 1933-34) "Lectures on Aesthetics" (1938) and "Conversations on Freud" (dating from the same period as Part I of *Philosophical Investigations*), both preserved in Rush Rhees's notes in *Lectures and Conversations*; and notes written by Wittgenstein collected under the title *Culture and Value* edited by G. H. von Wright and translated by P. Winch. For a comprehensive, critical overview of Wittgenstein's ideas on the subject of psychoanalysis, see Levy, 1996, chap. 1. For a defense of Wittgenstein's views, see Bouveresse, 1995.

² Donald Levy notes that "it is remarkable that this vast difference of viewpoint between Wittgenstein and the other philosophical critics of psychoanalysis, many of whom were influenced by him, has taken so long to be perceived, and not only in regard to psychoanalysis" (Levy, 1996, p. 4). For example, MacIntyre's *The Unconscious* follows in Wittgenstein's tradition, according to Smith (1999, p. 5). Yet, MacIntyre's argument is that the unconscious in psychoanalysis is unobservable in a way that separates it from legitimate unobservables in science; unlike them, he argues that the psychoanalytic concept of the unconscious is dispensable in principle (MacIntyre, 1958).

³ For philosophical critics of psychoanalysis in the analytical tradition, see Levy, 1996; for critics for both the analytical and the continental traditions, see Gardner, 1993; for a valuable response to Freud's (mainly) nonphilosophical critics see Robinson, 1993, which also contains a chapter on Grunbaum.

⁴ For Freud's main acknowledgement of the affinity of his thought with Schopenhauer's, see *New Lectures on Psychoanalysis*, Lecture 31. A number of writers have noted Freud's affinity with and references to Schopenhauer's work (Young & Brooke, 1994).

⁵ For the influence of Nietzsche on Freud, and in general, for similarities in their thought, see J. Golomb (1989) and J. Golomb et al. (eds.) (1999), especially J. Golomb, "Introductory Essay: Nietzsche's New Psychology," D. Chapelle, "Nietzsche and Psychoanalysis: From Eternal Return to Compulsive Repetition and Beyond," E. Blondel, "Nietzsche and Freud, or: How to Be within Philosophy While Criticizing It from Without," and R. Lehrer, "Freud and Nietzsche, 1892-1895."

⁶ Freud's theory of the unconscious underwent some changes, the various stages of

which, following J. O. Wisdom (1967), can be summarized as follows: The first phase involved the structure of preconscious motivation and preconscious distress, the combination of which constitutes a dynamism producing neurotic disorder. The second phase brought out an additional hypothesis of degree of repression. It would indeed characterize the first phase but would not be very obviously contained in it. The third phase brought out a distinction between the preconscious and the unconscious; the theory again remained the same, but it was stated in terms not of the preconscious but of the unconscious.

In order to differentiate between the unconscious and the preconscious, please consider the following examples: Freud attempts to smash accidentally an inkstand on his desk in order that his sister would give him a more desirable one. This is not a psychoanalytic irrational phenomenon (Similarly, see 1901, pp. 208-10). So it is accommodated as an instance of ordinary, self-deceptive irrationality within the operations of the preconscious (See 1900, p. 541; 1915, p. 173, 188-9; 1923b, pp. 20-21; and 1925, p. 32). The preconscious is the site of all the hidden intentions that Freud diagnoses in the *Psychopathology of Everyday Life* (e.g. 1901, pp. 175-6, 191, 211). It can easily become conscious as it is only momentarily unconscious. And we should add that Freud divides the *unconscious* in two: the profound unconscious, the source of the instinctual drives and of the phylogenetic memories, which can never become conscious; and the dynamic unconscious, where repressed desires and memories abide.

[7] He held that the superego—an unconscious judge and controller—rose from the internalization of the *real* experience of fear of the father. Yet the theory of the unconscious as opposed to the preconscious was a theory about fantasies that were never conscious in the first place, and it implied that a motive, the distress it causes, and the repressing factors have all been at all times unconscious. The discrepancy could prove fruitful, although it has never been exploited. J. O. Wisdom remarks that: "the two obvious ways of the contradiction would be either to hold the superego has unconscious roots and is not based primarily on the real experience of a real father or somehow work out a theory that an unconscious distress might be kept unconscious by an unconscious agency which had itself been at some time conscious" (Wisdom, 1967, p. 191). We will see below how this second option is relevant to Sartre's criticism of the censor.

[8] Melanie Klein, Freud's follower within the psychoanalytic movement, drawing on his mechanisms of isolation, undoing, splitting and projection, changed radically his theory. She showed that a structure of the unconscious alternative to the one Freud proposed is possible (1952). She is responsible for the last phase of the unconscious theory in which the idea of resistance, which has always been included in the theory, became the explicit theory of the superego. The basic idea is defense; it may be divided into (a) the classical idea of repression,

and (b) the latter idea of splitting, together with projective identification.

Dissidents of the movement developed different theories of the unconscious for the following reason. Freud's attitude towards the unconscious has been regarded as biological. But it was not so in a genuine sense, for all viable organisms display an organizing principle, not yet understood, which ensures that everything occurs in support of the continuation of life. This coordinating and formative principle underlies all organic properties, including the processes of the human unconscious, such as the imaginative and inventive faculties without which civilization could not have been developed. It has been widely recognized that this factor—although it has been emphasized in earlier views of the unconscious, for example, by Cudworth, Goehe, Fichte, Schelling, Coleridge, and Carus—is not adequately represented in the Freudian theory, perhaps because it was neglected by the physico-chemical approach to organisms dominant when Freud was shaping his ideas. "His theory of mind is overly analytic or atomistic, writes L. L. Whyte, "and must be complemented by a general and powerful principle of coordination" (Whyte, 1967, p. 187).

The lack of a general principle of coordination was recognized by three of Freud's colleagues—Alfred Adler, Carl Gustav Jung, and Otto Rank—who from different points of view, stressed the potential integration and self-organizing power of the unconscious or of the mind as a whole. The writings of these three display agreement that Freud, particularly in his early work, overemphasized the role of genital sexuality, unduly neglected the historical background of the individual unconscious, and failed to allow for the role of factors making for coordination both within each Freudian level of the mind and between the various levels.

Adler treated the person as a unity; he did not regard the unconscious-conscious division as basic and held that the inaccessible unconscious contains elements which have never been repressed, but which are simply not yet understood and are unconsciously assumed in the endeavor to adapt socially and to overcome supposed or real weaknesses.

The individual's aspiration or unconscious need to realize a potential unity was more deeply appreciated by Jung. He created the concept of the collective unconscious, which is not a "group mind" but the deepest level in the individual mind, consisting of potentialities for ways of thinking shared by all men because their genetic constitutions are closely similar and their family and social experiences share certain universal features. In a given society, the collective unconscious contains particular traditional symbols or archetypes which organize thought and action. The tension of superficially opposed aspects in the unconscious mind produces autonomous foci of energy, acting as complexes. The ultimate aim for Jung was not discovery of truth but acceptance of the role of deep psychology in the present historical situation.

Rank stressed the role of religious and aesthetic traditions in shaping the unconscious, and he saw in the life will a factor making for integration.

[10] "le language qu'il utilise engendre une *mythologie* de l'inconscient que je ne peux pas accepter. Je suis entierement d'accord sur les *faits* du deguisement et de la repression, en tant que faits. Mais les *mots* de "repression," "censure," "pulsion"—qui expriment a un moment une sorte de finalisme et, le moment suivant, une sorte de mecanisme - ,je les rejette."

[11] For an excellent account of Sartre's argument, see Gardner, 1993, pp. 43-52.

[13] "Chaque fois que les consciences observees se donnent pour irreflechies on leur superpose une structure reflexive dont on pretend etourdiment qu'elle reste inconsciente."

[14] In *The Philosopher's Autobiography: A Qualitative Study* (2003), Shlomit C. Schuster describes several instances of philosophical psychoanalysis. Her own psychoanalytic method for discussing the autobiographies of eminent philosophers originates in the psychoanalytic understandings of Jean-Paul Sartre, Gerd B. Achenbach, Marcia Cavell, and narrative and qualitative theories. Unlike Betty Cannon's interpretation and use of Sartre's Existential psychoanalytic method in psychotherapy practice, Schuster finds it unnecessary to preserve much of Freudian or neo-Freudian psychoanalytic methods, techniques, terminology, and labeling lingo. A similar approach, though not methodological bound as in the above-mentioned autobiographical study, Schuster practices in private philosophical counselling sessions. Sessions in which the use of Sartre's thought is evident she described in the chapter called "Yoni," one of the eight case studies found in *Philosophy Practice: An Alternative to Counseling and Psychotherapy* (1999).

See also Howard, 2000, pp. 341-355, for a possible use of Sartre within philosophical counselling. "There is a striking similarity between philosophical counseling and the general psychotherapeutic model known as existential therapy," writes Peter Raabe. As to the question of whether existential psychotherapy or philosophical counselling make better use of philosophy, Peter Raabe refers both to Tim Lebon, an existentialist therapist, who writes that existential psychotherapy "is perhaps the most advanced and well-worked out form of philosophical counseling," and to Ran Lahav, who suggests that only in philosophical counselling is the dialogue of a philosophical nature (Raabe, 2001, p. 85).

[15] Gardner differentiates between strong self-deception and week self-deception (Gardner, 1993, pp. 18-19). He thinks that the basic feature of all cases covered by the ordinary use of the term "self-deception" is motivated self-misrepresentation. More precisely, all self-deception involves what can be called a structure of motivated self-misrepresentation, which he defines as:

> A structure in which a psychological state S prevents the formation of another state S', where (I) S involves a misrepresentation of the subject, (ii) this feature is necessary for S to prevent the formation of S', and (iii) this structure answers to the subject's

motivation.

In this definition it is left open how such a structure may operate. A subject is self-deceived when he *believes one thing in order not to believe another*. So we seem to have:

Self-deception is a structure of motivated self-misrepresentation in which S and S' are *beliefs* and the process occurs through an intention of the subject's.

This identifies what he called *strong* self-deception. Weak self-deception, by contrast, is any structure of motivated self-misrepresentation that does not involve an intention.

[16] Gardner uses this as an argument against Sartre. In fact he directs towards Sartre the famous Popperian argument used against Freud (Popper, 1963) (which he addresses in pp. 236-238), without mentioning Popper. He thinks that metaphysical motivational stories such as Sartre's may consequently seem to have the advantage over empirically constructed stories, such as psychoanalytic theory's, that they never risk running out of explanation; whereas empirical theories may well have to adduce contingent constitutional factors at the end of the day. But the "explanatory totalitarianism of metaphysical stories" may equally be a reason for viewing them with suspicion (Gardner, 1993, note 45, p. 253).

[17] Gardner thinks that in these terms, Lacan's "decentred subject" is not a psychoanalytic concept: it is due to the concepts under which human beings fall qua language-users being *unaufgehoben*, and has more to do with Hegel's notion of alienation than psychological non-integration or conflict (Gardner, 1993, p. 278).

[18] According to Gardner, the real problem in understanding self-deception through ordinary psychology is what he deems "the Special Problem of irrationality," which makes sense only when we expect ordinary psychology to supply us with full explanations. According to Gardner, what is left over from ordinary psychology's explanation of self-deception is the fact of irrationality itself: the fact that the subject's mental life takes an irrational rather than a rational course, that self-deceptive intent is truth-violating. This he calls the Special Problem of irrationality (1993, p. 32).

[19] For Nietzsche's conception of change without self-knowledge, see May, 1999, especially pp. 20-23, 115-117; for a valuable discussion of the subconscious nature of drives in Nietzsche, see Parkes, 1994, especially pp. 293-9; for a good discussion of Nietzsche's determinism and how it sits with his individualism, see Schacht, 1983, especially pp. 304-12 and 335-8. For a discussion of the applicability of Nietzsche's conception of change, see Amir, 2003c.

[20] It is noteworthy that even Kant doubted whether we could disentangle the causes of our actions and thus whether we could know that we had done the right thing out of the right motive (i.e. the thought of one's duty to the moral law): "We can never, even by the most strenuous self-examination, get to the bottom of our secret impulsions [*Triebfedern*]" (Kant, 1964, chapter 2, p. 75).

Chapter 2

"Mankind Cannot Bear Too Much Reality": Wishful Thinking and the Unconscious

Andries Gouws

Freud and his legacy remain controversial. Though often pronounced dead, they refuse to die.[1]

This chapter is not meant as a wholesale defense of Freud. Its aim is limited: to show that *any* adequate theory of mind will have to posit something approximately like Freud's notion of the unconscious. It can also be read as a schematic statement of what I think must minimally be salvaged from Freud's notion of the unconscious.[2] Though Freud may need revision—*radical* revision, even—a wholesale rejection of his thought would cripple our ability to understand ourselves and each other. If philosophy is to educate humanity, it should first let itself be educated, among others, by Freud and his legacy.

* * * *

This chapter bases itself on the desire/belief schema for understanding and explaining human behavior (Dennett 1987; Davidson 1963)—a schema neither folk psychology nor scientific psychology can do without. I try, as point of departure, to systematize the distinction between two modes of dealing with desires: "the realistic mode" and (for lack of a better term) "wishful thinking." My ultimate aim is to show how wishful thinking gone rampant can lead to something like an unconscious. (I leave open the question how closely the unconscious resulting from this argument resembles the Freudian unconscious).

These two modes of dealing with desires form the two ends of a continuum, not a dichotomy:

1) *The realistic mode:* trying to satisfy needs and desires by thinking and acting in accordance with everything one has learned from one's dealings with reality (including the realities of one's own mind, especially one's desires). Freud would call this thinking and acting in accordance with the reality principle. This involves taking account of countless facts or circumstances that act as *constraints* on thought and action. This mode is obviously indispensable for *survival*, and indeed the satisfaction of biological *needs* is its paradigmatic example. Take the need for oxygen, for instance.[3] Our actions in securing oxygen have to comply with an extended field of knowledge and with the general requirements of logic. Ignore any of the relevant factual constraints and death can follow. Another odorless gas won't do. Don't make a fire in an enclosed space. Don't let children play with plastic bags. Trapped in a sunken ship, you can fantasize about fresh air and gain momentary comfort from it, but this in itself won't save your life. Verbal or symbolic equivalents won't do either. Most of the crucial facts on oxygen and our need for it can be established more or less reliably.

In terms of the desire/belief model: Here the satisfaction of our desires requires knowledge—true beliefs—about the world, and we try to extend and test our beliefs to ensure that they count as knowledge. We have as much of the required knowledge as is feasible. The functioning of the cognitive system generating these beliefs is ideally not subject to bias in the form of the distorting influence of desires. It is not a failure for the cognitive system to find that satisfying a desire is impossible or unfeasible.

2) *Wishful thinking*—the general tendency to see the world as in accord with our wishes, or as able to become so without our having to take account of the relevant and often onerous constraints. This mode thus *ignores, suppresses* or *distorts* facts that constrain the real satisfaction of desires or make such satisfaction impossible. Instead, it juggles around signs or representations in such a way that a mental *Ersatz* for a real satisfaction of the desire is obtained. (This typically does not bring the realistic satisfaction of the desire any closer). An essential feature of this mode is its general inadequacy for the satisfaction of biological needs such as those for food, shelter and protection against predators.

In terms of the desire/belief model: whereas in the realistic mode desires specify *what* sort of knowledge is required and then leave the cognitive system generating beliefs to function independently of desire, here desires influence cognition so that beliefs are selected, reformulated, distorted, suppressed etc. to accord with desires. Wishful thinking is only satisfied with beliefs that promise the satisfaction of desires; if the cognitive system produces beliefs according to which the satisfaction of the currently active desire is impossible, too costly or otherwise unfeasible, it is sent back to the drawing board.

Folk psychology acknowledges the ubiquity and importance of wishful thinking. Numerous sayings in different languages attest to this. For instance: "The wish is father to the thought." It is commonly acknowledged that when people cannot satisfy their desires by controlling reality, they engage in wishful thinking, especially in the case of powerful desires. (In many contexts the term "wish" already suggests a desire not connected to attempts to control reality).

These two modes of satisfying desires pose contrasting demands. The realistic mode has an intrinsic need to *know* and therefore to put beliefs and behavior to the test. The more realistic our thinking about the world is, the better our chances of avoiding dangers and securing the satisfaction of our biological needs (and the realistic satisfaction of our further desires). Wishful thinking, on the other hand, has no need to know and even resists acknowledging anything that threatens the possibility or feasibility of satisfying wishes in this mode; it is not interested in negative feedback. "*Reality is what hurts*" (Jameson).[4] The realistic mode tries to take account of innumerable constraints on thought and action while the other mode ignores such constraints wherever they would imperil the satisfaction of the desire in question. Therein lies their essential difference.

The term "constraint" is consciously vague and general. A great variety of phenomena fall under it. In most actions a great many desires and beliefs are involved that serve as constraints on what actions and thought processes will be (acceptable and) conducive to achieving our goals. I have a multiplicity of desires: I wish all sorts of positive things as well as to avoid pain, humiliation, stigmatization, embarrassment, damage, imprisonment, death, unhappiness, and illness for myself and my family[5], and in general with varying degrees of urgency for others as well, except those I do not wish well. Given any foregrounded desire—say the desire to go to an island in a light plane—I will generally try to satisfy it in such a way that the constraints posed by these other desires are not violated nor those posed by 'the facts.' I won't fly the plane myself if I am an inexperienced pilot—otherwise I could kill or maim myself, my family and innocent bystanders. I won't steal the money as this will incur the risk of imprisonment, humiliation, poverty, and so on, and also as I don't like the idea of the harm it does to other people. I won't fly there with just any air service. If I see PW Botha (an apartheid President of South Africa) on the way to the airfield, I won't drive him over or beat him up, even if I may have an impulse to do so, because I am not sure that that is what a decrepit old scoundrel like him deserves and as I am likely to be punished if I do so. I won't take a taxi for the 400 miles to where the plane leaves because that would be impractically expensive. I'll tell other people that I am going timeously. I'll get inoculations for myself and my family; I'll take along money. I'll discuss the trip beforehand with my family.

These examples are trite, but I give them to show the sort of thing I have in mind when I say that the realistic mode takes cognizance of constraints —constraints posed by my wishes and beliefs.

Wishful thinking can ignore these constraints. I can fantasize or dream that I take a taxi from my home to the distant airport; that I beat up PW Botha on the way; that I fly the plane myself; that I take the holiday while in fact already facing imprisonment for my debts, etc. Wishful thinking can ignore any constraints reality—of which my desires form an important part - puts in the way of the fulfillment of my wishes. To fulfill one wish (the wish for sexual adventure), one disregards others one usually sets more store by (the wish to be sexually faithful, not to hurt one's spouse or children, etc.), or disregards other facts.

So when I speak of constraints on action and thought I mean a variety of things like facts about the physical and natural world, social rules, facts about the likely consequences certain actions are likely to have (or the fact that we can't really foresee what the consequences are likely to be), one's desires, one's lack of knowledge etc.

A number of points concerning my notion of "constraints" deserve comment:

1. One can speak in terms of the constraints imposed by reality, and one can speak of the constraints imposed by our beliefs about reality. Whether I believe it or not, too much carbon monoxide can kill me. In trying to cope with reality, the aim is to develop responses and beliefs that take account of the constraints of reality. (Many of the responses and beliefs we do develop lie beneath the threshold of awareness).

2. Of course, even where my inclinations do not make me biased, I am

often wrong in my notion of what constraints reality subjects me to. Many constraints are unsharp:

a. Probabilities. I picture a notion of probabilities—the real probabilities are hard to ascertain, and, even if they weren't, my estimation of them usually won't have a mathematical form.

b. Social rules. How risqué can a joke be and still pass muster in a particular social setting? How can one create or rearticulate a role in which what is frowned upon in others becomes acceptable? A latter-day Oscar Wilde can perhaps say all sorts of things and get away with it, while you can't—you don't have the flair, timing and publicly established persona needed to do so. What sort of sexual behavior can the President of the US indulge in and still get away with it (be re-elected, not go down in the popularity polls, not be impeached, and so on). There is a reality out there to take account of, but it is hard do know, define or predict.

c. Our knowledge of many things is indeterminate. Try and say in explicit terms under what circumstances an object you push over the crest of a mountain will roll down the other side and under what circumstances it won't. Nevertheless most of us have a fair working knowledge—a tacit knowledge—of this sort of thing. The indeterminacy of the constraints does not make them constraints any the less—the object will either roll down the other side or it won't.

d. Many of our beliefs are overdeterminate or not determinate in quite the right way. "People cannot fly," thinks somebody in 1908, not having heard of the Wright Brothers. Yet for all practical purposes this belief will serve him well for the time being and in his own limited context at the other end of the world. "All mushrooms are poisonous"—quite a useful overgeneralization for somebody to whom non-poisonous mushrooms would never be a serious source of food.

3. These two poles are only ideal types. Most sustained trains of thought and action will display elements of both. Wishful thinking need only be 'unrealistic' on *some* points: we will generally acknowledge and try to take account of *some* disagreeable truths while whitewashing others.

4. Part of the reason why wishful thinking can actually be quite satisfying is that the distinction between reality and appearance (or representation or fantasy) often breaks down where social and mental life are concerned. (Wishes and fantasies are for instance themselves realities). Procedures for establishing the objective truth in this area are complex, unreliable or absent—interpretation is the main game in town. Even if we are open to

feedback, the feedback on many of our beliefs and actions will be inconclusive.

This leaves considerable scope for wishful thinking. Many social demands are met if they *seem* (to others) to be met; many social desires satisfied if they *seem* (to me) to be satisfied or are given a *symbolic* satisfaction.
In social reality wishful thinking is frequently self-fulfilling. (Think of the
delusions of grandeur with which people like Hitler started their political
career). The healing power of medicines for organic illness owes a lot to the
placebo effect.[6] The distinction between the two modes of satisfying desires
is thus not as simple as in the case of the need for oxygen.

5. Because our knowledge of constraints is so woefully inadequate, most
action is (or contains an element of) experimental action. Acknowledging
the need for experimental action and thought is acknowledging the constraint that there is a lot I do not know beforehand and can only discover
by trial and error. I don't know what the rules are governing this particular
social situation, so I try out various actions. How familiar can one be? How
much bad behavior will the other guys take from me? How explicitly and
aggressively can I try to safeguard my own needs or interests in a teamwork
situation? Often the results of such experimental behaviors will lie at the
level of behavior patterns that have been found to work, even if it is not
quite clear why they work and what would have happened had one gone
further along certain lines. Moreover, the behavior patterns thus generated
will usually to a large extent lie beneath the threshold of awareness. I don't
see myself as extremely cautious or wary, even where most informed and
impartial observers of my behavior would agree on such a description.

All these points are meant to emphasize that getting constraints right
is a tricky business; most of the time we get quite a lot wrong, even where
our beliefs and actions 'work' fairly well in practice.

The complexity and indeterminacy of many constraints, especially
social ones, can lead one to entertain the notion found in some versions of
postmodernism that reality simply *is* our construal of it. My whole approach
is premised on the notion that reality disagrees to a large extent with our
notions about it. This goes for *everybody*. "Reality" is thus not used as a term
for something about which a comprehensive account is possible: nobody can
give the rest of us a comprehensive account of what reality actually *is*.

I have now introduced and expanded on the notions of the wish-fulfilling and the realistic modes of dealing with desires and the way each is linked
to the notion of constraints. The important point that I want to make is that

the central distinction is not one between getting the constraints right and getting them wrong. In the realistic mode we also get them wrong a lot of the time. Rather, the central distinction is between wanting to find out about constraints and take account of them versus not wanting to—a distinction between wanting to know, even if what one finds out is disagreeable and not wanting to know except if it is agreeable.

****

The next step in our argument is building bridges from these notions to psychoanalytic notions. I will do so at three levels:

a. *The sort of phenomena psychoanalysis is typically interested in*, because they reveal aspects of our mental functioning that are usually ignored in general pictures of mental life (especially those that take man to be essentially a rational being). We focus on dreams, psychosis and the analytic situation. These phenomena are said to be manifestations of the unconscious. The unconscious has two aspects that are particularly important in the present context (these form the next two levels at which we build the bridge):

b. *The strange thought-processes that are typical for the unconscious.* Freud refers to this as the primary process while rational, realistic thought is said to be governed by the secondary process. What is characteristic of the primary process is its radical disregard for constraints. It can thus be seen as a radicalized form of wishful thinking.

c. *The notion that the unconscious in the psychoanalytic sense is* not only that which currently escapes consciousness but also *that which resists being made conscious.* We argue that wishful thinking requires an unconscious in this sense because its satisfactions are undermined by reflexive self-awareness that it is exactly that. All of us constantly engage in fantasies, and regularly, after a stretch in which we suspend disbelief, realize that they are but fantasies. Certain, mostly enduring, fantasies are however too important for us, there is too much at stake in them, for us to be prepared to relinquish them by admitting that they are but fantasies, wishful thinking. (Anybody trying to help us relinquish them, is likely to meet resistance). Wishful thinking thus requires something like the unconscious of which psychoanalysis speaks.

We said that wishful thinking was characterised by ignoring those constraints that stand in the way of the realistic fulfillment of our desires. Now my thesis is that, when many of the constraints sufficiently governing the realistic mode are bracketed *simultaneously*, wishful thinking starts displaying the features Freud ascribes to the unconscious or primary process.[7] The phenomena on which psychoanalysis puts great store all derive from situations where the constraints governing our dealings with reality are disabled (at least, to a considerable extent): dreams, the analytic situation and psychosis. Noy (1969) has convincingly argued that as feedback mechanisms are suppressed or disabled, behavior starts showing the features of the primary process.

1. *Dreams.* Freud himself relates dreaming to wishful thinking in the following quote: "When a dream deals with a problem of actual life, it solves it in the manner of an irrational wish and not in the manner of a reasonable reflection." (1925*i*—SE XIX: 127). Dreaming is insulated from the present demands of reality. Because there is no action in reality, disregarding reality in dreams does no harm. Is it at all strange if this maximum disengagement from the demands of external reality during sleep is used to ignore these demands wherever wish-fulfillment requires it?

2. *Speech in the analytic situation.* The analysand is denied the feedback and other cues we normally use to mind-read others so as to influence them (or adapt to them) in the realistic mode. Because they are frustrated, the analysand's desires become more urgent. Wishful thinking then has free rein, increases exponentially and tends towards the primary process. The analytic contract largely robs the analysand's words of the performative force and other consequences (e.g. negative sanctions) they would have had in normal interpersonal relations. Just as in the case of dreams, the bracketing of the reality principle is therefore largely harmless. (As with the suspension of disbelief while reading a novel, the reality principle itself comes to realize that its own bracketing in this context will not hinder our ability to deal with reality). The more the analysand realizes this, the more the constraints typical for the reality principle fall by the wayside in what is said in the analytic situation.

3. *Psychosis.* Freud (1924*b*; 1924*e*) and others interpret this as a condition in which reality-testing (acknowledging feedback and other constraints from reality) is radically impaired. The realistic fulfillment of desires is impeded, frustration mounts, wishful thinking holds sway, and the stage is set for a vicious circle.

All three of these phenomena which psychoanalysis takes to be paradigmatic for the unconscious can thus be seen as resulting from the easing of the constraints usually governing our dealings with reality in the rational, realistic mode.

****

The next step in our argument is to relate our notion of thought-processes obeying or disregarding the constraints involved in trying to take account of reality, to Freud's description of the nature of unconscious processes.

A constant in Freud's description of these processes is his notion of a primary vs. a secondary process. This is an abstract description of the mechanisms said to underlie two types of thinking. Tellingly, Freud himself uses synonyms of our "constrained/ "unconstrained" distinction: he speaks of *free* (unconstrained) and *bound* (constrained) energy.[8] The idea is that the mind initially follows the shortest route from picturing a wish to picturing its satisfaction; in the language used by Freud: energy flows unhindered from the representation of the wish to the representation of its satisfaction. In this, the extreme form of wishful thinking, there are no constraints on thought whatsoever: to picture the wish is immediately to picture its hallucinated satisfaction.[9] Where this happens with our primal needs, however, it soon becomes clear that the need in question has not been satisfied: the pangs of hunger persist or return. The subject then gradually learns what routes to actual satisfaction of the need are offered in reality (e.g. the mother may feed him if he cries). After such a learning process, the constraints imposed by reality are (to some extent) modeled by the constraints governing the processes of thought and action which have been learned to satisfy the need in question. In Freud's picture: the energy flowing from the wish to its satisfaction now makes all sorts of detours. The detours model the constraints operative in reality. (If you bite your mother's breast, you get a smack instead of milk).

I think all of what Freud says here in terms of energy being bound or flowing freely can be reformulated in more psychological, cognitive terms. The primary process then becomes a thought-process not obeying any constraints while the secondary process is one obeying countless constraints which represent an attempt to model the constraints in reality.

The primary process is wishful thinking squared. The more the constraints imposed by reality are ignored, the more mental life displays its features. The reality principle involves acknowledging a variety of heterogeneous constraints, which the primary process can disregard separately or simultaneously.

1. *Not looking at things in a larger context.* To acknowledge constraints across-the-board means to look at things in a larger context. To ignore all constraints, on the other hand, means matching a desire with its satisfaction without considering whether it is compatible with a larger field of facts and desires over a longer period. A maximum fragmentation—reducing the field of other facts and the time frame to a minimum and looking at desires individually rather than as a set—gives the greatest release from the constraints imposed by other desires, the facts and the time frame. Each desire then seeks satisfaction separately without considering the consequences for other desires. An example: in a dream or in reality, you set fire to your house so as to burn with it your wife's cherished collection of letters from her childhood sweethearts. In waking life few people would be prepared to pay such a high price, in terms of other desires, in order to satisfy this wish.

2. *Disregarding the constraints placed on the correct use of language.* Philosophers like Wittgenstein and Austin have impressed upon us that the words referring to things may be similar, associated or identical without the things themselves being thus related. We err wildly on this score even in our most rational, realistic moments.[10] In wishful thinking such confusions are actively courted, the ambiguities of language exploited to the hilt, and verbal solutions to problems equated to actual solutions. At the end of a psychoanalysis a man marries a woman whom he shares little with and who also shares little with the women who have attracted him in the past. However, her name and age (year of birth) are the same as his analyst's. Here the unconscious is taking identity of representation—name and age—as sufficient to treat what is represented as identical or interchangeable. (If we find it easier to believe that a man can marry a woman because she physically resembles somebody he was previously attached to—what better basis for partner choice is physical resemblance than this resemblance?)

What Freud describes as the unconscious is only partly characterised by outright errors; it also shows a radicalization of the figurative use of language. The "primary process," "condensation," "displacement," "symbolism," and other bizarre manifestations of "the language of the unconscious" as described by Freud can be seen as extensions of everyday 'indirect' or 'figurative' uses of language. (Allusions, metonymy, metaphor, anagrams, cryptograms, mnemonic devices, etc.). This is made easier by the very nature of language: the rules imposed by language are often unclear, i.a. because of the role played by exemplars rather than explicit rules. Semantic divergences from common usage generally show far less of a dichotomy between "correct" and "incorrect" uses than grammatical divergences do; what falls somewhere between standard and incorrect uses, we label as figures of speech, figurative uses of language. The loosening of constraints which we elsewhere described as characteristic of the primary process here allows uses of language which repeatedly and radically hyperbolize figurative uses of language.

Our view dispenses with any line pretending to divide the unconscious from the preconscious. (Freud flounders every time he presents them as a dichotomy rather than a continuum). In describing 'the unconscious' or 'the primary process' Freud describes a situation in which *every* constraint on thinking is optional. Where *some* constraints remain in place, he speaks of a *compromise* between the primary process and the secondary process. Our model describes this in a different way: in wishful thinking as many constraints are ignored as is needed to imagine a wish as fulfilled. There is thus a continuum between thought showing the features Freud ascribes to the unconscious or the primary process *in their pure form* and what he ascribes to the preconscious or secondary process *in their pure form*.

Above we stated that people engage in wishful thinking because the realistic mode cannot always deliver the satisfaction of desires. This insufficiently brings out the antagonism between the two modes. The realistic mode requires an ongoing monitoring of reality (including society, ourselves, and significant others). We can only understand particular experiences against the backdrop of a fairly comprehensive picture of the world.[11] The realistic mode is hardly effective if it is only switched on from time to time. Given any desire—say, the wish to become a professional boxer—adopting the realistic mode can reveal to us not only that the desire is unrealistic but also many other highly unpleasant facts—all the desires that we cannot fulfill and sufferings we cannot remedy. Importantly, it confronts us with many injuries to our self-love, our sense of our own excellence and exceptionality.

On the other hand, the wishful thinking mode works well only inasmuch as its mechanisms remain covert. This is hardly surprising. The more clearly I acknowledge that I magnify Jack's failings only so as not to feel inferior to him, the harder I find it to compare myself favorably to Jack because of these supposed failings.

The realistic mode thus comes at a stiff price: the loss of the illusions of wishful thinking. The wishful thinking mode does not come cheaply either: it chips away at the conditions to be met if we wish to satisfy desires realistically.[12] (Philosophers and lay people are more inclined to see that wishful thinking has a price than that the realistic mode does.) In most lives the costs and benefits of each mode shift from moment to moment, changing the attractiveness of each. In practice neither triumphs over the other, so that we occupy a—shifting—position somewhere between these two ideal-typical extremes, taking account of some constraints while ignoring others so that our more or less self-serving interpretations of things do more violence to some facts than others.

If this were all, neither mode would work well because of the interference of the other mode. The realistic mode would run aground because the unpleasant truths it needed were denied by the wishful thinking mode, while the wishful thinking mode would be undermined because the realistic mode exploded its illusions. To some extent this is of course exactly what happens. However, wishful thinking also follows strategies in which we can eat our cake *and* have it; strategies that allow us to *avoid* (for the moment) unwelcome truths instead of having to *posit untruths* in their place. (Explicit untruths will sooner clash with experience and be contradicted by people not sharing the illusion in question. Unwelcome truths that have been avoided can be acknowledged when they become unavoidable).

First, certain areas are designated as sanctuaries in which the reality principle may be bracketed without social sanctions or other negative consequences to the subject. *Culture* provides forms in which wishes can be fulfilled vicariously, ideally without significantly impeding my ability to deal with reality: jokes, myths, novels, films, TV. Dreaming and telling dreams perhaps serves a similar biological/cultural function.[13] The psychoanalytic situation, in which everything may be said with impunity, is an extremely important addition to this series of culturally constructed and sanctioned sanctuaries from the reality principle, that is: from the demand to take account of the constraints imposed by reality.

Such strategies tend to work by assigning wishful thinking and the reality principle to separate domains. Other strategies, however, aim to make these two modes coexist in the same space without hampering each other's operations unduly. In these strategies, forms of representation are chosen that help us to be as *unfully* aware of their content and its implications as possible, preferably without having to explicitly posit untruths or deny truths.

Before discussing these strategies, however, a subsidiary argument: what is problematic is not the notion that we can *lack* awareness of our 'mental contents.' It is rather the notion that there could ever be 'mental contents of which we are *fully* aware.' Such 'contents'—our representations of our beliefs and desires, for instance—generally make use of language and other (public) systems of signs, the meaning of which are by no means more obvious than that of public uses of signs. *The far-fetched hypothesis is not that of an unconscious but rather that of consciousness as traditionally conceived.* It is not clear what it would be for anything to be 'fully known.' If there were contents of consciousness 'inside' consciousness, these would themselves be known incompletely, perspectivally, etc. Consciousness itself can never be *fully* conscious. Knowledge or consciousness is a question of *interrelations*: for instance, knowing and understanding the *content* of a belief sentence is a matter of seeing what consequences it has when combined with other belief sentences. Even at best the process of thinking through consequences is far from exhaustive.

Above, we did not describe our two modes of operation in terms of a plenitude of consciousness or lack of it, but in terms of *wanting to know* and *not wanting to know*. In the realistic mode we want to know, regardless of whether this knowledge is pleasant or not, and in wishful thinking we don't, except if what is to be known agrees with our desires.[14]

Although we can never be 'fully aware' of anything, there are many ways to be as '*unfully* aware' of it as possible, if desired. Metaphors of visibility and invisibility, being out in the open or hidden, tend to govern our conceptions of consciousness and the unconscious. Such metaphors make us forget that things can be represented in such a way that their import is not acknowledged, even if the 'full light of consciousness' is cast upon them.

The difference between 'conscious' and 'unconscious' is therefore as much one of 'logic,' semiotics or semantics, as it is one of psychology (attention or lack of attention).[15] We never 'fully acknowledge' anything and the 'unconscious' is linked to things having a form allowing them to be as 'unfully' acknowledged as possible so that their (painful) consequences for our thought will be avoided wherever possible.

My argument assumes that the mind, whether conscious or unconscious, deals with words and other *signs*, not with supra-linguistic *propositions* or *ideas* not needing signs for their existence, which could then quite plausibly be conceived of as transparent, with their meaning or content taken as immediately given, or even these propositions or ideas themselves taken as being *none other* than their meaning or content itself. If an idea or proposition were to be seen by consciousness, it would therefore necessarily also be understood. If we then introduce a notion like 'the unconscious,' the natural tendency would be to conceive of it in terms of invisible or hidden propositions or ideas.

Our beliefs and desires aren't transparent to consciousness; there is no "belief or desire itself" which would be a mental content without being a representation or which would be a neutral representation. Inasmuch as beliefs or desires are represented at all, each of them can be represented in a variety of different ways, public or private. (It is an illusion to think that the representations we think with, or shaping our thought, are essentially private). What I believe happiness to be or what the happiness is that I desire can be represented in a painting, a story, a facial expression, a posture, a dance, a song, a story (fairy tale, myth, novel), a poem, a play, a theory, a definition, a daydream, a dream perhaps. Depending on which representations of it are available or preferred, the belief or desire will have different vicissitudes. Different representations have differing degrees of determinacy, different degrees and types of emotional appeal, and allow different sorts of reflection. They differ in their associations—think of "having sex," "fucking," "making love," "having intercourse," "consummating a relationship," "moving a penis to and fro in a vagina." The same act is denoted, but differently represented beliefs and desires about the act will tend to have different effects regarding exactly which further thoughts and actions they will contribute to. This multiplicity of representations is exploited both by the realistic mode[16] and by wishful thinking; in both cases those representations are selected that offer a route to the satisfaction of a desire.

Let us review some strategies for representing things in such a way that their import is less accessible to us:

1) A thought, memory or wish is *not verbalized* or only *verbalized in an inarticulate* or *euphemistic* way. (Peter calls the violent, sadistic films he loves "intense." A punitive mother calls herself "firm").

2. It is represented in a bodily or symbolic way. Our primary experience—or representation—of many moods and emotions is a bodily one —feeling pressed down (depression), having a spring in one's step, feeling nausea. When no beliefs, desires or other mental contents are represented in conjunction with this, the exclusively bodily representation can serve to ward off a realization of the further import of what is represented. Here is an example of a use of symbolism: N, a professional in her late twenties, recounts the following dream: "Tonight I had such a strange dream. I dreamt that I slid down a mountain side on a tree trunk with my father. We sat face to face and slid down a path that had been cleared among the pines. We kept on going faster and faster; my father pushed with his feet so that we would go even faster. Because he found it such fun, he said. And it was

fun, but I became frightened because it kept on going faster and faster. How on earth does one manage to dream such strange dreams? Do you know, I am convinced that dreams have a meaning." I find avoiding the standard Freudian sexual reading of a dream like this a bit implausible—not that we can tell apart from a context (for instance lots of free association over a long time) what the further import of this dream is: whether the dream is only and simply about the father, whether she is emotionally or sexually fixated on her father, whether the sex stands for an intimacy her father never gave her, for taking the place of her mother in her father's affections, for getting her father's attention by offering him the only thing (she thought) her father was interested in from women, etc.

3. It is *formulated in a technical or alien language*, so that its existential import is harder to grasp and easier to avoid. ("I have a problem with authority," instead of "I hate and fear my father").[17]

4. Truths about oneself are formulated in non-first person terms. "I" becomes "one," "you," "it," "she" or *they,*" as in Cavafy's (1975: 3) poem "Walls" (1896):

> With no consideration, no pity, no shame,
> they've built walls around me, thick and high.
> And now I sit here feeling hopeless.[18]

This is especially important where it involves seeing desires in others that one repudiates in oneself. A woman striving for a life of saintly self-sacrifice for her family finds herself endlessly obsessing about a neighbor who forsook her family to run off with a lover; she does not acknowledge that a desire to do something similar is not foreign to her and that her endlessly repeated condemnation of her neighbor is a way of exorcising this desire in herself.

5. We are of course also free to give *versions* of reality that satisfy (certain of) our desires without (so obviously) militating against the constraints constituting the reality principle. Depending on the wishes of the speaker, one and the same person can be described as brave or foolhardy, systematic or compulsive, realistic or unimaginative.

Needless to say there are also psychological strategies next to these semantic strategies: one 'doesn't think about it,' or 'forgets' it. This can be more relative or more absolute, depending on how easily somebody else's observations can make things accessible to the subject's 'consciousness.' One of the most common and effective ways of avoiding unwelcome thoughts, memories or desires is to physically avoid everything that we associate with them: people, cities, suburbs, buildings, rooms, music, hobbies or other activities, languages even.

It would be naïve to think that wish-fulfillment limits itself to a few predictable forms, such as those listed here: almost *any* mechanism used in the reality-seeking mode can also be used for wishful thinking. *Not* verbalizing is for instance typically used as an escape; however *verbalizing* can itself also offer an escape (e.g., from an indeterminate feeling of grief threatening to erupt into tears).

There are thus countless ways in which we can avoid a thought or its implications (and what is a thought minus its implications?) without explicitly having to deny it or assert its negation. We entertain a comforting world view. Inasmuch as we acknowledge painful truths, we render them harmless by *isolating* them so that they have no consequences for the rest of mental life. The more absolute this isolation, the more it is as if the thought had never been thought.[19]

Admitting the existence and pervasiveness of something like wishful thinking vastly increases our chances of self-reflexivity and understanding others, which require the concept of motivated error. This can be beneficial even if we can never ascertain that something constitutes 'wishful thinking' with the probability and precision typical for facts in, say, engineering or natural science.

****

I now discuss the most important building block in this reconstruction of the Freudian unconscious, which has not been foregrounded in my account up to this point: the fact that, according to Freud, the contents of the unconscious are firstly repressed wishes (desires), and only in the second place the unconscious memories, thoughts etc. associated with them. We mentioned above that the constraints ignored, denied or distorted by wishful thinking can be facts about the world as well as facts about our desires and showed how the existence or possibility of multiple representations of our beliefs and our desires facilitates this process. Our focus was on the case where the desire as such is not unconscious but only the mechanism by which it is satisfied—wishful thinking. When we have wishes which clash with our other powerful desires—especially our desire to meet the norms we think have to be met to be worthwhile, decent, admirable, moral, lovable, respectable (etc.)—these unacceptable wishes can be repressed (denied, disguised, misapprehended, etc.) because of wishful thinking. It should constantly be borne in mind that unconscious wishes in the strong, psychoanalytic sense are not simply wishes we aren't aware of but also wishes we don't want to be aware of so that attempts at making them conscious meet up with strong resistance.

The same process of wishful thinking can be applied to unconscious desires. However, where the underlying wish (desire) is already unconscious, a real satisfaction of this desire is possible that is entirely 'realistic' in the sense that it observes all the relevant constraints—even meticulously so. Because the desire is unconscious, the subject is not aware that the conscious actions leading to its fulfilments serve to fulfill the desire. In that sense its fulfillment is also unconscious. No further disguise beyond the unrecognizability of the desire itself is then strictly required.

If there is a hostile desire to put other people down a peg or two wherever possible, there are countless ways of doing so without recognizing this action as "putting others down a peg or two" or recognizing the existence of the desire to do just this. "I just spoke to Mary and she says that she finds you so terribly ugly"; "John tells me that he was very disappointed after your lunch together—when he helped appoint you he'd trusted you'd be intellectually more stimulating." Why is the person saying this? "Well, I just experienced this, so it's natural to tell you this." Or: "I'm just being truthful." Or: "You said the other day that you want our relation to be an honest one." The more available a legitimate motive is for the behavior in question, the easier it is for the repressed motive to ride shotgun on the behavior, undetected.

Note that the desire is here realised in a very real way. Hostile desires can similarly lead to accidents—coffee being spilled over somebody's drawing or over a resented child, breaking or losing a present from someone who has fallen out of your favor[20] (That it may be hard to determine in any particular case beyond reasonable doubt that an "accident" or losing something was actually thus motivated is another matter; the issue here is determining whether the existence of unconscious but active motives is plausible).

It bears emphasizing that the intended destructive outcomes of hostile wishes are easy to realize realistically in the real world. While the wish to be a great artist may be hard to realize—making attempts to realize it in the form of something like a fantasy more likely—the wish to hurt somebody or to hurt their feelings or to destroy something beautiful can easily be realized.

What makes even this 'realistic' satisfaction of unconscious desires again resemble wishful thinking is that we can eat our cake (satisfy our proscribed wish) and have it (see ourselves as not having or acting on the proscribed wish).

This extension of the desire/belief schema clashes with our normal way of breaking up the world into actions and events. We see action only where we see a desire (motive)—an accident is not an action. And which action we see depends on which desire we ascribe to it. We may reject psychoanalysis from our belief that these are two distinct categories, an irreducible either/or: active vs. passive; actions vs. events; things done vs. things undergone. Or psychoanalysis can convince us that mental phenomena can straddle these categories: there can be passivity in apparent activity and activity in apparent passivity. If we relativise such dichotomies, it may require a shift in our abstract conceptualization of things: the adoption of a notion of the mind as a self-organizing system in which everything (conscious or unconscious, apparently active or apparently passive) is geared to finding routes for the attainment of its goals (wishes, desires). A self-organizing system is not active in the way activity is normally conceived of, nor is it passive in the way passivity is normally conceived of. Such an approach has resonances not only with psychoanalysis, but also with Eastern philosophies like Zen, other forms of Buddhism, and Daoism (*wu-wei*: not-doing), which—not incidentally—also reject the notion of a self.

Application of the Foregoing to Philosophical Counselling

•   Raabe's (1991) depiction of psychoanalytic theory, psychoanalytic practice and the psychoanalytic notion of the unconscious in *Philosophical counseling: Theory and practice* (PCTP).

Peter Raabe, citing Ruschmann, points out that "psychoanalysis is often employed as an unfavorable example against which philosophical counselors demarcate their terrain" (PCTP: 81). This function as an Other is unlikely to be conducive to a fair appraisal of psychoanalysis by philosophical counselors. In fact I think few theoretical exercises could be as useful to philosophical counseling as defining their practices vis à vis those of psychoanalysis—but then not against a straw man but against this practice at its strongest. I trust that the current book is a step in that direction.

From the description PTCP gives of it, I don't recognize psycho-analysis as I know it from Freud's writings on psychoanalytic technique and on psychoanalysis in general or from my own experience in psychoanalysis. This is especially the case when it comes to references to the unconscious. The sources referred to in describing psychoanalysis aren't those to which I would direct somebody interested in finding out more about psychoanalysis; importantly, references to the writings of Freud and other prominent psychoanalysts such as Abraham, Firenczi, Anna Freud, Klein, Winnicott, and Lacan are sparse or absent. The best place to get a better view of how Freud conceived of psychoanalytic practice is his own writings on technique. Contemporary consensus on what psychoanalytic technique should be, would probably be even further removed from the picture sketched in PTCP. So let me start by indicating where my view of the unconscious and psychoanalysis differs from that given in PCTP.

- *The charge that psychoanalysis embodies the medical model.* (PCTP:82-108)

It is true that Freud is often not far enough from the medical model. He refers to the "doctor" and the "patient" (criticized PCTP:93), and he uses the language of pathology and cure extensively.[21] I would align myself with all those psychoanalysts who want to abolish these and other vestiges of the medical model in psychoanalysis. However, in countless writings, such as *The question of lay analysis* (Freud 1926e) and his writings on technique, his aim is to show how far the practice of psychoanalysis is from that of medicine and how little a medical training contributes to the making of a psychoanalyst, who is above all presented as involved in hermeneutic activity—reading the words of the client for their meaning. Psychoanalysis as he conceives of it is a *sui generis* practice. The rules for psychoanalytic technique do not, as in the medical model, distinguish between a phase of diagnosis and one of treatment. Free association does both. Though Freud was extremely interested in what it is that distinguishes the different forms of neurosis from each other and from psychosis, neither he nor any psychoanalyst I know would think that supplying the client with a label (88) is acceptable.

Due to various institutional and political factors, the practice of psychoanalysis in America was for many years limited to people with a medical training (against Freud's (1926e) plea for lay analysis); the resultant medicalization of American psychoanalysis is seen as an aberration by most European and many American psychoanalysts.

"One of the primary skills of the psychoanalyst is his ability to make a diagnosis based on symptomatology found in the latest diagnostic tools available—... currently ... DSM-IV" (87). Analysts in Europe—at the very least—tend to belong to a totally different world from the psychiatrist who proceeds in this way. No analyst I know would use psychiatric diagnostic manuals or standardized tests (87) in the course of accepting or treating clients; she would want to base her picture of the client entirely on what the latter says in the analytic situation. The psychoanalysts I know belong squarely to those who "'attempt to refrain from imposing on their clients any predetermined notions of what the problem may be'." (87)

Psychoanalysis does not as such address deviations from the normal (82). (Laplanche and Pontalis's (1988) authoritative 500 odd page dictionary of psychoanalysis does not even contain an entry for "normality"). Those American versions of psychoanalysis in which notions of normality and abnormality play a central role are viewed as a heresy by Lacanians and many other European and American psychoanalysts. In fact Freud is at pains to emphasize how widely people can differ and how wrong it would be to impose some straitjacket of normality on this variety: "Our aim will not be to rub off [*abzuschleifen* - grind off] every peculiarity of human character for the sake of a schematic 'normality,' nor yet to demand that the person who has been 'thoroughly analysed' shall feel no passions and develop no internal conflicts" (Freud 1937c: 250). The aim of psychoanalysis is thus absolutely not to modify "behavior ... to suit relevant norms" (PCTP: 82).

Referring to Dennett's notion of the three different stances from which a complex system can be viewed, Raabe says that psychoanalysis takes the design stance to clients, not the intentional stance. "In taking this approach [the design stance], the psychoanalyst is somewhat analogous to the surgeon whose expertise is concentrated on the removal of the tumor without the requirement of the conscious involvement of the patient. ... The psychoanalyst has no intention of helping the client to understand her utterances within the context of psychoanalytic theory." (94) It is true that the analyst won't couch what he says in the theoretical language of psychoanalysis, but in other respects this description is incorrect. The aim is a process in which the client, largely through following the train of her own free associations, but now and then helped by an intervention from the analyst, comes to see the meaning of these utterances—which consists largely in seeing how they are interconnected to each other and to material that has gone before. In fact I, together with many other philosophers (for instance Wollheim 1973; Davidson 1982), explicitly read psychoanalysis as a version of the intentional stance—understanding actions in terms of the person's desires and beliefs. However psychoanalysis combines this stance —as do Davidson (1963) and Dennett (1987; 1991), the philosopher who identified these stances in the first place—with the assumption that desires and beliefs, whether conscious or unconscious, are causal antecedents of thought and behavior. Not all causes are reasons, but reasons—beliefs and desires—are causes of actions. So when Freud speaks of the unconscious determinants of behavior or symptoms, he is not speaking of something that does not have the status of a desire or belief. The point is exactly that when unconscious desires and beliefs become conscious they become susceptible to evaluation and change.

In fact Raabe and the other sources he cites approvingly (mostly philosophical counselors or cognitive therapists) too often leave out the "desire" component of the desire/belief pair, thereby making it seem as if looking at the beliefs involved in emotions and behavior is already taking the intentional stance. Having left out desires, the unruly bit, emotions and behavior now seem much easier to bring under rational control through philosophical counseling. It is because desires can be stronger or weaker that Freud conceptualizes the mind as not only a field of meanings but also a field of forces. To Ricoeur (1972) it is an essential feature of Freudian theory that it is a "mixed discourse" which combines reasons (or meanings) and forces (or causes). I myself agree with Dennett and many other philosophers that this is not only a feature of Freud. The intentional stance has always been a causal stance. To be able to predict something, you must know what it is caused by; we posit beliefs and desires in others because only this causal schema will allow us to anticipate what they will or could do.[22]

I therefore do not buy the dichotomy running through much of PCTP: philosophical counselors deal with free agents whose actions aren't caused, but based on reasons; psychoanalysts see themselves as dealing with the passive, unfree victims of unconscious causes. The unconscious causes are themselves reasons, capable of being brought to consciousness and evaluated for their acceptability, and where we deal with conscious reasons. The fact that we are still in the field of causality means that the complete autonomy and freedom of the subject is also a myth. Where the subject's desires are sufficiently strong, and they can currently only be satisfied if they or the mechanism for their satisfaction remain unconscious, he will be unable to give them up freely. In Freud's terms: it is only if and as other desires or other possibilities for satisfying these desires become strong enough that the person will be capable of relinquishing them (though still only after a protracted battle).

•   *"[C]lassical Freudian theory ... posits the unconscious as having a psychic locality ... "* (96)

Freud was quite clear that this—only one of many metaphors he used for the unconscious—was no more than a way of speaking.

•   *That philosophical counseling is hermeneutical clearly distinguishes it from other forms of psychotherapy.*

Proponents of philosophical counseling "cite the importance of hermeneutics or interpretation of the client's personal narrative or 'text' as central to the philosophical counseling process" (101). But clearly psychoanalysis is all about interpretation. Freud's (1900a) *magnum opus* isn't called *The Interpretation of Dreams* without reason; and Ricoeur's (1972) big book on Freud is subtitled *An Essay on Interpretation*. So where does the distinction lie? The unconscious determinants (causes) of actions aren't meaningless physical facts but are as meaningful as conscious mental contents. The unconscious does in fact present itself to consciousness and insistently but only in disguised form. That is why psychoanalysis is a form of hermeneutics.

Having shown where I disagree with Raabe's depiction of psychoanalysis and the unconscious, I can now address the relevance of the unconscious to philosophical counseling. As I do not know the full range of positions seeing themselves as philosophical counselling, I address the philosophical counselor as if she embodies the view of philosophical counselling expressed in PCTP, completely.

I find myself in an uncomfortable position here: on the one hand I am convinced that philosophical counseling is and can be a useful, effective and efficient way to help clients with the difficulties encountered in their lives; on the other, my own experience as well as theoretical and practical leanings make me (largely out of sympathy with what distinguishes philosophical counselling from psychotherapeutic approaches) inspired by psychoanalysis. On some points, such as the efficacy of using bodily awareness as an entrance into working with emotions, desires and beliefs, I am even further away from philosophical counselling than psychoanalysis is.[23]

How would philosophical counselling and a psychoanalytic approach relate to each other? There is a large range of possibilities, and I must confess to being uncertain as to which of them apply:

• As to their *efficacy*, it could be that some variant of the one approach is simply better across the board than all variants of the other approach. This is unlikely in the light of research indicating that the personal qualities of a therapist (such as empathy, warmth and clarity) are far more important than the theory or technique she bases herself on.

• As to their *applicability*, each approach is probably typically better suited to a different kind of client or condition, with perhaps some area of overlap. Lacking therapeutic experience or theoretical knowledge in this area, I have little to say.

• As to their *compatibility*, it could be that the two approaches are radically incompatible so that an eclectic mixing and matching from the two approaches would be ill advised or alternatively that eclecticism is permissible and even advisable. I tend to think however that the approaches won't mix very well. Thus, if one starts introducing rational argument into a psychoanalytic therapy or does things like reminding the client that eating meat is incompatible with her ethical principles, it will be hard for her to stick to the fundamental rule of expressing everything that comes into her mind without any selection on the grounds of how reasonable, consistent, relevant, ethical, decent, embarrassing etc. it is. To introduce rational argument is to introduce norms into the analytic situation. Vice versa, if the philosophical counsellor starts working in such a way that material and processes typical for the *System Ucs* start being unleashed, a conscious, controlled therapeutic management of transference phenomena and a longer therapy with more frequent sessions may be required. However, I believe that it should be possible for the philosophical counsellor to use insights from the psychoanalytic domain without ceasing to be a philosophical counsellor; it may be that with time philosophical counselling can be honed in such a way that the training for philosophical counsellors teaches them how to deal with *System Ucs* contents or processes while avoiding dynamics incompatible with the philosophical counselling approach. As regards wishful thinking, its forms vary from those intuitively graspable to laymen with no knowledge of psychoanalysis at all, to those showing all the features of the unconscious. The less palatable the wishes or their method of satisfaction is to the "censor" (the person's internalized norms of decency, rationality, etc.), the greater will be the distortion. Where the material shows little distortion, i.e., where the *System Ucs* is less involved, philosophical counselling will be able to deal with the material without ado, typically in what Raabe describes as Phase 1. As the material starts showing more features of the unconscious, which means more distortion and that the frustrated wishes being expressed in this way are particularly powerful, dealing with it will in my opinion become less feasible within the parameters defining philosophical counselling. Nevertheless I do not wish to exclude the possibility that, with sufficient insight into the different nature and demands of rational conversation and working with the unconscious, individual therapists may find effective ways of moving between these modes and even be able to formalize their method and teach it to others. This may involve clearly labeling and otherwise demarcating these modes from each other—e.g. by having the client lie on a couch for free association, or the therapist being addressed as "Dr. Freud" for work in this mode. (I joke seriously here). Finding ways that enable one to move effectively between these different modes in one and the same helping relationship would be a major, extremely valuable innovation.

Having pronounced these caveats, let me express what I believe the Raabean philosophical counsellor could learn from my reconstruction of the unconscious. This reconstruction attempted to show how acknowledging the phenomenon of wishful thinking makes the existence of something like a dynamic unconscious plausible—a domain of motivated ignorance or motivated error when it comes to a person's self-knowledge, or more fluidly put, a person's ability to reflect on her desires and beliefs.

I would recommend that the philosophical counsellor finding my account plausible read Freud and other psychoanalysts to see what can be learned from them. Philosophers are by no means agnostic on the issues he speaks about; he challenges deeply held philosophical views on the nature of the mind and the best way to tackle difficulties of living. The philosophical counsellor would then have to see for herself whether any of these insights can be fitted into the commitments that made drew her to philosophical counselling in the first place. As in the next paragraph, I find that philosophical counsellors themselves will probably be better able to determine what in psychoanalysis is valuable to them, than people who already prefer psychoanalysis to philosophical counselling. Freud's example of self-reflection when it comes to theory and technique is something other approaches would do well to emulate and perhaps engage in debate. (This does not in the least require agreeing with Freud on any substantive issue).

Somebody finding my account plausible or psychoanalytic readings worthwhile could find a psychoanalyst she feels comfortable with or a therapist working on analytic lines to experience first hand what psychoanalysis is about. (Undergoing psychoanalysis is totally different from reading about it). What actually happens in psychoanalysis and what is valuable in it may legitimately be formulated in terms very different from those chosen by psychoanalysts themselves. The philosophical counsellor could then again investigate how much of what she finds valuable can be fitted into the commitments that made her choose for the philosophical counselling approach. (Or how those commitments need to be modified to accommodate valuable aspects of psychoanalytic practice).

Having understood Freud and experienced psychoanalysis first hand, I think the philosophical counsellor will be better able to articulate how and why philosophical counselling differs from psychoanalysis and how and why some aspects of psychoanalytic theory and practice should be rejected or possibly adopted.

I expect that the recommended reading as well as the experience of psychoanalysis will confirm my own interpretation of psychoanalysis which is quite at variance with the image sketched in PCTP. Rather than the analyst actively imposing, like an intellectual bully, his view on the passive client, disregarding what the client thinks, both client and analyst attend in a passive/active way to the client's free associations, each confident that her mind is a self-organizing system where the material will find its shape over time without needing an active controller to impose order on it, synthesize it, or develop and test hypotheses about it. Each goes into an active/passive, *wu-wei* (not doing) listening mode. (Freud says that the analyst opens her receiving unconscious to the giving unconscious of the client without the intervention of consciousness being needed). As in mourning, mental processes will take their course towards healing and integration; a conscious plan and goal-directed monitoring aren't needed. As in mourning, it would be unwise for the analyst to try to make the process more rational (by pointing out the irrationality of the phase of denial, or of anger at the person for dying) to make it lighter or to speed it up. All the client need do is stick to the rule of verbalizing aloud her associations as they occur and experience (and verbalize) the feelings that arise. As with mourning, it will be useless for the analyst to deal with anything out of context—denial in the anger phase, for instance, or anger after the anger phase has passed. The basic task of the analyst is to listen with as little of an agenda as possible.

I believe this description is close to the picture of the analytic process found in Freud's writings on technique. When I started meditating after completing my analysis, I was struck by how meditative the experience of psychoanalysis seemed, retrospectively. In both there is a softening of hardened habits and a letting go of restrictive definitions of the self in favor of an awareness of the ever changing flux of the experience of the here and now. If the analyst imparted labels or psychoanalytic theory to the client, the openness and freshness of this process would be destroyed.

I think philosophical counselling will to a large extent have to avoid working with the unconscious. (I again mean 'the unconscious' in the Freudian sense). It is generally not possible to lift unconscious contents out of their context and make them the object of rational scrutiny and ratiocination. What makes them unconscious is the purely associative way in which they relate to other material. The unconscious element which today has become conscious only leads to insight inasmuch as it is allowed to lead to the becoming conscious of other unconscious material with which it is bound up and so on. What makes it "unconscious" is to a large extent its (apparent) lack of connections to the consciously recognised aspects of the person's mental life; the processes of free association and working through allow these connections to become visible.

The philosophical counsellor may need to be conversant with the workings of the unconscious so as to be better able to devise a strategy that doesn't activate it, and so as to be able to handle it—even if only in the sense of putting the jack back in the box wherever possible—when it does arise. Short term counselling at the level of a fairly rational conversation between client and counsellor is probably not a setting in which a process in the client that is strongly dominated by the unconscious can be made productive—or even be prevented from doing harm. I have in mind phenomena such as powerful positive and negative transference, regression and acting out. In all these, powerful frustrated wishes are activated and seek satisfaction by wishfully experiencing the current situation, including the therapeutic relation, in terms of old traumas and aspirations. More generally, philosophical counselling may need to emulate the sophisticated reflection on technique found in Freud and other psychoanalysts, presumably as a way of not activating the unconscious and trying not to work at this level—but also as a way of dealing with these phenomena to the extent that they do arise in philosophical counselling.

From psychoanalysis philosophical counselling can also learn that a cooperative, satisfied, model client need not be all of this because of rational considerations; this behavior is very often a way of realizing the dream of being the ideal—and thus eminently loveable—son, daughter, spouse, friend or student. This demonstrates wishful thinking: because I would love to be the model client, I am the model client. Only with time do all the facts and feelings not accommodated by this ideal role accumulate and make the fantasy being lived out untenable. In psychoanalysis this bubble usually only bursts some way into the therapy, at a stage where short term therapy or counseling would already have ended. Philosophical counsellors and other practitioners of short term counseling or therapy may thus miss the instructive experience of the moment when, in psychoanalytic terminology, negative transference shows up what went before as having been to a great extent (positive) transference.

PCTP does not seem to take the phenomenon of resistance seriously. My paper points out two sources of resistance. I say that each of the two modes of dealing with desires—the wishful thinking mode and the realistic mode—comes at a price. The counselor trying to help a person get out of an impasse into which wishful thinking has taken him should expect resistance. This mode of tackling life has a payoff; the threatened loss of the satisfaction it gives, even if flawed, even if meager compared to the possibilities offered by being more realistic, will tend to generate resistance; the higher the stakes, the higher the resistance will tend to be. Put otherwise, the more realistic approach that the client is being encouraged to consider, comes at a price—quite apart from the fact that it may in any particular case fail to deliver the goods. A counsellor aware of the payoffs offered by wishful thinking and of the forces opposing its replacement by a different approach will perhaps tread more gingerly (and compassionately) than might otherwise have been the case.

References

Cavafy, C.P. (1975). *Collected poems.* (E. Keeley & P. Sherrard, Trans.). Princeton: Princeton University Press.

Davidson, D. (1963). Actions, reasons, and causes. *Journal of Philosophy, 60*(23), 685-700.

Davidson, D. (1982). Paradoxes of irrationality. In R. Wollheim & J. Hopkins (Eds.), *Philosophical essays on Freud.* Cambridge: Cambridge University Press.

Dennett, D. (1987). *The intentional stance.* Cambridge: MIT Press.

Dennett, D. (1991). *Consciousness explained.* Boston: Little, Brown.

Freud, S. (1900a). The interpretation of dreams. *Standard Edition, 4-5,* 1-621. London: Hogarth Press.

Freud, S. (1905d). Three essays on the theory of sexuality. In *Standard Edition, 7,* 123-243. London: Hogarth Press.

Freud, S. (1914g). Remembering, repeating and working-through. *Standard Edition, 12,* 145-156. London: Hogarth Press.

Freud, S. (1915c). Instincts and their vicissitudes. *Standard Edition, 14,* 109-140. London: Hogarth Press.

Freud, S. (1924b). Neurosis and psychosis. *Standard Edition, 19,* 149-153. London: Hogarth Press.

Freud, S. (1924e). The loss of reality in neurosis and psychosis. *Standard Edition, 19,* 183-187. London: Hogarth Press.

Freud, S. (1925i). Some additional notes on dream-interpretation as a whole. *Standard Edition, 19,* 123-138. London: Hogarth Press.

Freud, S. (1926e). The question of lay analysis. *Standard Edition, 20,* 177-258.

Freud, S. (1937c). Analysis terminable and interminable. *Standard Edition, 23,* 209-253.

Freud, S. (1950c). Project for a scientific psychology. *Standard Edition, 1,* 281-387.

Gouws, A., & Cilliers, P. (2001). Freud's "Project," distributed systems, and solipsism. *South African Journal of Philosophy, 20*(3), 1-21.

Jopling, D. (1996). "Take away the life-lie …": positive illusions and creative self-deception. *Philosophical Psychology, 9*(4), 525-544.

Laplanche, J. & Pontalis, J.-B. (1988). *The language of psychoanalysis.* London: Karnac Books.

Noy, J. (1969). A revision of the psycho-analytic theory of the primary process. *International Journal of Psychoanalysis, 50*(4).

Raabe, P.B. (2001). *Philosophical counseling: Theory and practice.* Westport, CT: Praeger.

Ricoeur, P. (1972). *Freud and philosophy. An essay on interpretation.* (D. Savage, Trans.). New Haven: Yale University Press.

Wittgenstein, L. (1961). *Tractatus Logico-Philosophicus.* London: Routledge & Kegan Paul.

Wollheim, R. (1973). *Freud.* London: Fontana.

Notes

[1] A previous, shorter version of this paper was published under the title "Wishful thinking and the unconscious" in *South African Journal of Philosophy* 22(4), 361-377, and another, still shorter version as part of the electronic proceedings of the Twentieth World Congress of Philosophy held in Boston in 1998 (Section: Philosophy of Mind).

[2] 'Schematic' because many of the features Freud ascribes to the unconscious are not accounted for. Other features are revised or reformulated.

[3] Note that "the desire to breathe" linked to this need does not have to manifest itself to consciousness; it normally only does so when breathing becomes or threatens to become difficult or impossible. The everyday desire/belief schema thus does not presuppose that we are necessarily aware of our desires or beliefs.

[4] Cf. this to Freud's idea that the external world is originally that which is *hated*:

At the very beginning, it seems, the external world, objects, and what is hated are identical. (1915c—SE XIV: 136).

Hate, as a relation to objects, is older than love. It derives from the narcissistic ego's primordial repudiation of the external world with its outpouring of stimuli (1905d—SE VII: 139).

[5] Freud is notorious for emphasizing that people often (also) desire things like these which we generally assume they (only) want to avoid.

[6] Even conventional medicine is deeply dependent on the placebo effect. John Forrester, in an unpublished paper given at the 1996 Louvain/Nijmegen conference on psychoanalysis, mentioned one study which ascribes as much as 70% of its effectiveness to the placebo effect.

[7] In this article I freely use terms from different periods and levels of Freud's theory: reality principle, unconscious, primary process, secondary process, etc. I am not convinced that Freud's metapsychological schematisations or systematisations were entirely coherent at any stage in his development, which somewhat mitigates the dangers of mixing and matching across different stages of his thought.

[8] Freud's energy talk used to irritate me until I studied his *Project* (Freud 1950c) and discovered there a highly sophisticated model of the neural processes underlying the mind —one which agrees in essentials with current models in distributed computing (Gouws & Cilliers 2001). The rest of this paragraph derives from this work.

[9] We can say that even where there is no hallucination, to represent a wish is to represent its satisfaction: the same phrase describes a wish and its satisfaction: "to play ball" or "to win the tennis match" or "to kiss Susan."

[10] Thus we may fail to see that the many different uses of the word "love" don't all refer to the same phenomenon: being attached to somebody, desiring somebody, being in love, wishing well (without necessarily desiring or feeling attached to); that "justice" works differently in retributive and distributive justice; that "rights" presupposing that the state provide or guarantee a certain minimum level of wealth (e.g. the right to employment or tertiary schooling) introduce a very new element relative to "rights" not presupposing anything of this sort.

In deductive arguments, often taken to be the locus par excellence of rationality, only the form (syntax) of propositions is important, not their content (semantics). They thus assume that the same word will stand for the same object. When this assumption does not work, we ascribe that to a fallacy, the fallacy of equivocation. ("Cats make good pets. Tigers are cats. Therefore tigers make good pets." If all examples of the fallacy were this easy to detect, it wouldn't have been necessary to identify and teach it). When the unconscious thus treats sameness of word as sameness of object, it is following an automatic procedure much like that found in logic. (In the *Tractatus* Wittgenstein, 1961, wanted to refine our logical notation so that our tendency to assume that sameness of word indicates sameness of object, and vice versa, would never lead to error: each simple object would have only one name and each name would stand for only one simple object. This shows how deep the intuition is that we should be able to treat things bearing the same name as the same).

[11] I mean this in a sense in which even utterly uneducated or unintelligent people have a complex picture of the world, which an AI expert system will find hard to equal, let alone outperform.

[12] Cavafy's (1975) poem "The Windows" (1897) eloquently brings out the way in which acknowledging reality can be psychologically threatening:

In these dark rooms where I live out empty days,
I wander round and round
trying to find the windows.
It will be a great relief when a window opens.
But the windows aren't there to be found -
or at least I can't find them. And perhaps
it's better if I don't find them.
Perhaps the light will provide another tyrrany.
Who knows what new things it will expose? (p. 25)

On the costs, for self and others, of the wish-fulfilling mode, see Jopling (1996, p. 534ff).

[13] I would however not want to insist that such a function would be *the* function of the phenomena in question.

[14] If we cut everything disagreeable out of what we know, we do not know very much—even about the agreeable parts of life.

[15] Lest the reader think that some essential Freudian distinctions are being disregarded here: the difference between what Freud calls "preconscious" and "unconscious" especially comes out when the subject resists having things translated into a balder, more accessible form.

[16] The same object can be represented as a "pencil," "cylindrical wooden object," "sharp object," "writing instrument," "consumer article," "backscratcher." Each designation will suggest different aspects, different uses and different things the object could replace or be replaced by; being able to see this variety is essential to problem solving.

[17] Philosophical thoughts invoked during philosophical counselling may carry with them this danger, even if the counsellor succeeds in formulating without using much technical jargon; "a problem with authority" would normally not strike me as overtly technical language. Can philosophical notions really be formulated in the "I won't eat that crap" or "I'm not going to let myself be screwed" blood and guts language that is sometimes required if we want to stay true to our experience of pressing real life difficulties?

[18] The poem closes with a statement that the whole process escaped consciousness:

When they were building the walls, how could I not have noticed!
But I never heard the builders, not a sound.
Imperceptibly, they've closed me off from the outside world.

[19] Cf. Freud's words in the following quote:

Forgetting impressions, scenes or experiences nearly always reduces itself to shutting them off. When the patient talks about these 'forgotten' things he seldom fails to add: 'As a matter of fact I've always known it; only I've never thought of it.' He often expresses disappointment at the fact that not enough things come into his head that he can call 'forgotten'—that he has never thought of since they happened (1914*g*—SE XII: 148).

This could be said whenever any of the mechanisms discussed above has occurred. (All of which can be regarded as ways of isolating material). Freud's quote again goes to show that his usual dichotomous way of talking about the distinction between conscious and unconscious is not always borne out by his own hermeneutic practice. Most of the 'unconscious' material that 'surfaces' during analysis is not totally strange to the analysand.

Laplanche and Pontalis (1988:232) summarize "isolation" as follows:

Mechanism of defense … which consists in isolating thoughts or behavior so that their links with other thoughts or with the remainder of the subject's life are broken. Among the procedures used for isolation are: pauses in the train of thought, formulas, rituals, and, in a general way, all those measures which facilitate the insertion of a hiatus into the temporal sequence of thought or actions.

[20] To the reader who is skeptical: would you be as skeptical if somebody who was resentful became *careless* or exercised less care than in the case of somebody he cherished unambivalently? Where do you draw the line between "not doing much to avoid harm" to "doing harm"?

[21] It must be remembered that he wrote in an era in which the idea of a legitimate non-medical profession of psychotherapists did not yet exist.

[22] If we accept that there are no regions of space or time where the laws of physics cease to operate, then we have to accept that the motions of our bodies (physical actions, words spoken or written) are caused by their physical antecedents and only by their physical antecedents. However, I also clearly believe that what people think and do (physical actions, spoken and written words) depends on their reasons – their desires and beliefs. Therefore desires and beliefs are causal antecedents of what people do. This doesn't mean that they are caused in a way which would exclude their being modifiable by argument or evidence or feedback the way we normally take desires and beliefs to be. If reasons are causal antecedents of events governed by physical laws, and all causal antecedents of physical outcomes must themselves be physical, reasons must have a physical embodiment. (Otherwise the physical antecedents of physical outcomes would be causally incomplete. Physics would discover that there are regions of space-time where normal physical laws break down). This is only one of many arguments why reasons should be taken as causes.

Chapter 3

Divided Loyalties:
Cultural "Weltanschauungen"
and the Psychology of
the Unconscious

Daniel Burston

Ever since Freud's (1910) polemic on *The History of the Psychoanalytic Movement*, the standard explanation for the split between the Vienna and Zurich Schools is that Jung broke with Freud over the sexual etiology of the neuroses and the centrality of the Oedipus complex. While true enough, as far as it goes, this explanation is like the tip of the proverbial iceberg, whose surface impressiveness detracts attention from the massive dimensions of what lies underneath. On closer inspection, it is more apt to say that in many respects Freud and Jung represent two diametrically opposed approaches to the study and interpretation of unconscious mental processes.

Freud leaned toward rationalism and Enlightenment thought, the aim of which was to dispel superstition, dogma and traditional constraints on unfettered inquiry, in the belief that freedom from illusion is the primary prerequisite for individual and collective emancipation. With this agenda in mind, Enlightenment thinkers attempted to debunk time-honored conventions and valorized dispassionate intellect at the expense of feeling, sentiment and "enthusiasm." And in keeping with this view, from the Freudian standpoint, the primary function of the symbol in dreams and mythology is to disguise the underlying meanings and intentions of the unconscious mind—in short, to misrepresent underlying actualities, to make them palatable (yet also indecipherable) to conscious ratiocination, and thereby subvert or circumvent the purposes of the conscious, rational ego, giving blind, unreasoning "instinct" an avenue of expression through the patient's dreams and symptoms.

In keeping with this rationalistic bias, Freud also tended to stress the irrational and perseverative features of unconscious mental processes, as evidenced, for example, in his theories of the repetition compulsion and the death instinct, which owe much to Schopenhauer, Nietzsche and von Hartmann, as Thomas Mann (1939) first pointed out. Because of his emphasis on the determinism of early childhood experience, the Freudian analyst typically approaches the symbolism of the unconscious with a desire to unmask it, or reduce its operations to the efflux of infantile and atavistic impulses. He (or she) hopes that by illuminating the patient's unconscious conflicts and the repetitive, self-lacerating or self-defeating patterns laid down in the depths of the patient's psyche, that reason will prevail and ultimately dissolve their harmful fixations and neurotic inhibitions (Riceour, 1970).

By contrast with Freud's approach, Jung's view of the unconscious mind derived from vitalism and the *Naturphilosophie* of Schelling and his followers, who construed the unconscious mind as one manifestation of an immanent (and generally unconscious) rationality that suffuses the entire cosmos; an intelligence imperceptible to and inexpressable in the limited language of an isolated, egoic consciousness (Ellenberger, 1970). Thus, in dramatic contrast to Freud, who regarded the unconscious mind as the backward, regressive part of the mind that resists adaptation to the demands of reality, Jung—like Schelling, Carus, Bergson and Samuel Butler, among others—regarded the unconscious mind as a reality oriented and progressive evolutionary force that propels the organism forward into genuinely new situations and conflicts and not mere repetitions of older ones (Burston, 1991).

As a result, according to Jung, the unconscious is guided by its own inarticulate reasonings, which often surpass those of consciousness in depth and acuity, and the function of the symbol is to express—rather than to repress—its underlying tendencies, in the hopes that the conscious ego, with its limited powers of observation, will take note of this communication from the depths of nature. Rather than seeking to unmask the unconscious, or rob it of its power to falsify or deform conscious awareness, Jung treated dreams and myths as the outward expressions of a supra-rational source of wisdom, and unlike Freud, for example, deemed the hegemony of reason as inimical to the life of the spirit (Hogenson, 1983). It is this global difference in outlook that sparked the initial debate between the Viennese and Zurich schools over Silberer's "anagogic method" of dream interpretation, which Freud belittled but Jung embraced and developed into his theory of the prospective function.

The upshot of all this, of course, is that in addition to their differences on the primacy of sexuality in the etiology of the neuroses, the centrality of the Oedipus, complex, etc., Freud and Jung were irreconcilably at odds on two basic points which are of at least equal importance, namely; the meaning and function of the symbol and the proper role of reason in our mental life. For Freud, reason alone enables us to gain mastery over our inner conflicts, and the atavistic and perseverative quality of the instincts which, left unchecked, would hasten our individual and collective ruin. For Jung, by contrast, reason is a limited and very imperfect instrument of adaptation that can scarcely fathom and seldom match the silent reasonings of the unconscious, and the function of the symbol is to communicate to consciousness what consciousness is not yet ready or able to comprehend as yet.

Personal Agendas and Intellectual Projects

Despite their divergent cultural and intellectual orientations, there are also important similarities between Freud and Jung that warrant attention and help explain their initial collaboration and the eventual rift between them. The first of these concerns does not have to do with the content of their ideas but with their ideas about themselves, their self-images, and the way these were shaped by their intellectual projects. Despite their indebtedness to philosophy and literature, Freud and Jung saw themselves, oddly enough, as empiricists of some sort. And at the same time, both Freud and Jung wanted to be culture heroes and preceptors to humanity and to be remembered as such many generations hence. Indeed, it would be fair to say that this ambition was probably their dominant passion, although they were not always aware of it as such, because their respective self-images as sober and impartial scientists frequently enabled them to hide this fact from themselves.

Other traits Freud and Jung shared were their great creativity and stubborn intellectual independence and their warmth and generosity of spirit, which alternated with tendencies to ruthless, calculating egoism and manipulativeness and a callous disregard to the real needs and interests of others. As a result of these vacillations, many of their followers who questioned their ideas or authority experienced the heat of their anger and intolerance and suffered greatly for it. So despite their intellectual differences, their styles of leadership were profoundly paternalistic. Clearly, if they had been less ambitious, less driven by their sense of mission, Freud and Jung might have been better and more balanced people. But they may also have been less creative and prolific and less memorable as a consequence.

As history attests, cultural heroes and preceptors to future generations are usually political or religious figures or exceptionally gifted and charismatic artists. The notion that a psychologist or psychiatrist could assume this exalted status—though plausible nowadays, thanks to their example—was an anomaly in their own day, a fact we are all apt to forget. Predictably, then, critics have often remarked on the religious and political coloration of their ideas and organizational structure. And it is no coincidence that Freud and Jung became rivals—not only because of their differences, as is usually alleged, but because of their similarities, which made them compete for the limelight and emphasize and often exaggerate their differences in the process.

In addition to all of this, Freud and Jung clashed for other reasons that defy easy categorization and could fall equally under the rubric of personal traits and/or cultural attitudes. To get our basic coordinates straight, let us start mapping them at the cultural/historical end of things. The Enlightenment tradition, in which Freud followed, by and large, prided itself on breaking with the superstition and dogma of past ages. It fostered great optimism about the possibilities of human progress, and tended to regard most of human history as a record of infamy, exploitation and prejudice, whose chief lessons are negative ones, that teach by example what we ought to avoid. Admittedly, their characteristic tendency to idealize future history for a fondly anticipated effloresence of rationality in a peaceful world of civic virtue and *esprit de corps* was blunted, in Freud's case, by the equally insistent pessimism bequeathed by Schopenhauer, Nietzsche and von Hartmann. However, Schopenahuer, Nietzsche and von Hartmann's withering skepticism about the idea of progress did nothing to dispel the dismal view of past history that the Enlightenment embraced. Indeed, their philosophies prompted them to view human history as a dramatic spectacle of misery and folly that will very likely unfold on a similar pattern in future, with only the players changing.

By contrast with Freud, whose Enlightenment leanings were leavened with Nietzchean pessimism, Jung embraced the cultural ideology of conservative Romanticism, epitomized in historian Jacob Burkhardt, which tended to idealize past history as a wellspring of sound precedent and pragamatic wisdom about how to live the good life. Conservative Romantics typically decried the Enlightenment's attempts to break with the past as intemperate desire to purge human society of its most balanced and humane features.

One practical consequence of their divergent cultural loyalties was that Freud and Jung tended to construe their own relationships to the past in very different ways. In true Enlightenment spirit, Freud wanted to break with the past, and accordingly, wrote as if he had personally discovered and charted the unconscious *de novo*, giving extremely scant acknowledgement to his 19th c. predecessors. Indeed, anyone well versed in 19th century thought can not help suspecting that a certain measure of *conscious* dishonesty and a need for self-aggrandizement accompanied Freud's tendency to unconscious plagiarism or cryptomnesia, which is now widely acknowledged, even by Freudians (e.g. Rudnytsky, 1987).

By contrast with Freud, Jung was generally quite pleased to acknowledge his predecessors, even while defending his own originality. Like most conservative Romantics, he had a sense of ancestral piety that was reflexive and tenacious. Though ancestral piety can degenerate into mere foolishness or idolatry, at times, it does have its uses. Because of it, Jung was able put Freud's contribution to the psychology of the unconscious in vivid historical context, and his essays and observations on this subject are still stimulating and insightful (e.g. Jung, 1914; Jung, 1933).

As previous authors have noted, of course, there is another world of difference between Freud and Jung; their attitude toward religion and psychotherapy. As a belated heir to the Enlightenment, Freud shared its hostility towards organized religion and to mysticism in all its forms. For Freud, religious belief was analagous or equivalent to a collective obsessional neurosis. Jung's attitude was quite different. Jung saw religious beliefs and experiences as paths to transcendence, wholeness and individuation—in short, as strivings toward health and integration. But though he welcomed dialogue with clerics and theologians of all creeds and confessions, Jung's temperamental leanings toward heresy and the esoteric rendered his attitude toward organized religion quite ambivalent, stressing the primacy of religious *experience* over mere religious belief. Consequently, unlike Freud, he welcomed mysticism as a legitimate path to transcendent knowledge, immersing himself in Gnosticism, alchemy, Kabbalah, Taoism and Tantric Yoga.

In keeping with their attitudes toward the sacred, Freud and Jung embraced two different epistemologies or theories of knowledge and two different approaches to therapeutic technique. Notwithstanding the emotional *catharsis* elicited by the lifting of amnesia, which presumably heralds the emergence of insight, Freud's method was distancing and analytical, and at the end of the day, valorized the fruits of careful observation and thinking purged of emotional influence and contagion. By his own account, anyway, Freud proceeded in a patient and methodical manner, collecting facts, noting anomalies, making inferences, checking hypotheses, and so on, without relinquishing his neutrality or engaging in significant self-disclosure. By contrast, Jung's approach to therapy valorized participation and empathic identification with the other in a direct human encounter; a kind of global, intuitive knowing that frequently bypasses discursive rationality and welcomes therapist self-disclosure, when warranted. Perhaps the simplest way to summarize these differences is to say that Freud's personality and cognitive style were predominantly Apollonian, while Jung's were predominantly Dionysian in character.

Individual and Collective Psychology: Religion, Politics and History

Finally, there is another realm of similarity and difference between Freud and Jung that is vitally important. While it is rooted in character and culture, and shaped by all the preceeding gradations of continuity and conflict, it may be more useful for us to approach it on a purely intellectual level. Despite important differences, Freud and Jung were both essentially Lamarckian in outlook. They believed firmly in the inheritance of acquired characteristics, and like American psychologist G.Stanley Hall, subscribed to the notion that "ontogeny recapitulates phylogeny." This guiding principle of their thought has been roundly discredited (e.g. Gould, 1977). And rightly so.

Nevertheless, this erroneous postulate provided the scaffolding for many theoretical innovations that seemed to impart a remarkable degree of intelligibility to many clinical phenomena, and more importantly, to social psychology and the fields of religion and politics. Having established their clinical positions, Freud and Jung moved swiftly to widen the scope of theory beyond the clinical setting to embrace the totality of human sciences. For if individual development recapitulates species history—for the sake of argument, anyway—one can only assume that a massive and complex interdisciplinary effort is required to assimilate and synthesize these various disciplines, which map different dimensions of these homologous processes. Physical and cultural anthropology, comparative religion and mythology, archeology, history, art, literature, neurology, genetics, linguistics—all are suddenly germaine and part of a bigger picture that beckons and calls for deeper exploration and ever more diligent theoretical integration.

Originally, Freud had hoped Jung would "conquer" religion and mythology for psychoanalysis. When Jung broke with Freud, Otto Rank, who was educated at Freud's expense, was asked to take Jung's place, as he did most dutifully for more than a decade before he in turn "defected." But while both Jung and Rank were excommunicated, they retained that astonishing breadth of perspective that Freud had encouraged in his more inquisitive and independent followers. For in essence and inspiration, depth psychology was never merely a clinical discipline, but a stubborn attempt to understand the individual and society in their historical, dynamic and dialectical interactions, free of the blinders of conventional prejudices. As a result, it is *inherently interdisciplinary* in scope and character, even if its original point of departure was the therapy of the neuroses. In attempting to discover homologies and connecting threads between psychopathological conditions, personality theory, social psychology, politics, religion, and so on, it implicitly opposed the prevailing division of labor between these disciplines, which persists (albeit in different forms) to this day.

In fairness, no doubt, academic specialization has created burgeoning bodies of literature and whole new scholarly industries. But in the process, it has contributed to the fragmentation of our image and understanding of ourselves and society, creating artifical boundaries and abstract entities were none previously existed; entities and boundaries whose ontological grounding, on deeper inspection, is dubious at best. Attempts to integrate these discourses effectively—or even to build bridges, to effect greater commerce between them—are often met with suspicion, resistance, derision, or worst of all, a frank and appalling indifference.

Unfortunately, attempts to narrow the scope of psychoanalysis and/or analytical psychology into one more clinical specialization—be it medical or psychological—collude with this general trend. With this regretable fact in mind, let us review Freud and Jung's efforts to make sense of the many striking isomorphisms between individual dreams and fantasies and the "collective representations" that comprise the standards and signposts of our collective ideologies. Since their theories about collective psychology lean on their views of clinical psychopathology, and vice versa, it might be wisest to preface our discussion of the linkages between these otherwise disparate discourses by a brief review of their clinical and biological rationale.

Drawing on 19th century neurology, on turn of the century embryology, and last but not least, on American psychologist G. Stanley Hall, Freud and Jung assumed that the ontogenetic sequence from conception to birth passes through a series of uniform phases, following a trajectory from the single celled organisms through plants, fish, reptiles, primitive mammals, and so on. Furthermore, they assumed that this miniaturized evolutionary process continues in the extra-uterine environment, though now the individual, who has attained a distinctively human form, recapitulates earlier phases of cultural or specifically human history, and not of other mammalian or pre-mammalian precursors to humanity (Gould, 1977).

Drawing on clinical data, Freud and Jung also assumed that psychological development, which ideally keeps pace with physical maturation, may undergo a more or less autonomous development under adverse environmental circumstances or the press of constitutional/genetic factors. When this occurs, the individual develops a neurosis, psychosis, phobia or perversion occassioned by an arrest in development (fixation) or a return to an earlier phase of psychological evolution (regression), which analysis attempts to ameliorate or dissolve, if possible.

Meanwhile, Freud and Jung assumed that a fixation on or regression to a particular point of the ontogenetic sequence results in manifest symptoms and unconscious phantasies whose content—while personal, on one level—hearkens back to an earlier phyletic or cultural/developmental stage, which continue to color, shape or frankly intrude upon or engulf our conscious, waking thought processes. In this way, the regressed individual, whose ego is weakened, is drawn back willy-nilly into the collective sphere (albeit without knowing it), and this would presumably explain the parallels between neurotic and especially psychotic phantasies and the mythological motifs or pre-literate societies and ancient civilizations, as well as many artistic motifs and preoccupations. Even the in absence of pronounced disturbance, Freud and Jung assumed that transient neurotic disturbances and crises of one sort or another are indelibly woven into the fabric of any "normal" human existence—Freud's "psychopathology of everyday life," Jung's "complexes." Though they evoke episodes or aspects of our personal past, of unresolved internal conflicts, these transient and relatively minor disturbances also echo aspects of our collective past, and the traumas and vicissitudes of prehistoric times, though more dimly and remotely, of course.

Furthermore, Freud and Jung both observed—paradoxically, perhaps—that in their emotional ties to their political, religious and military leadership, and with their tribe, nation, Church, etc., normal (i.e. symptom-free) people often give evidence of being at an infantile or childish level of development, which was explained in terms of collective narcissism, collective transference and/or the "incest complex." In short, the moment someone enters collective life—and in truth, once born, one never leaves it, save in psychosis or in death—he or she is swept up in mass psychological conta- gions and illusions of various kinds, which are often markedly discrepant with the level of development attained by normal people in their customary day-to-day conduct.

This kind of collective regression *within* the bounds of normality, freak- ish as it sounds, facilitates an ongoing "return of the repressed," whereby long forgotten episodes and processes from remote prehistory get enacted afresh. So despite progress in the mastery of nature, and changes in political and social organization wrought by technology and historical upheavals, the "timeless" character of the unconscious, first noted by Schopenhauer, dictates that the same collective dramas tend to be played over and over, with no real end in sight. Meanwhile, myth, ritual and religious ideas and artifacts (or their secular surrogates) provide the clue to the nuclear conflicts and dynamisms of collective life, and like the proverbial stars appearing in the astronomer's telescope, reflect events in a real but long since extinguished time, when these persistent patterns of unconscious functioning germinated, leaving traces that reverberate indefinitely into the future.

Of course, within the framework of consensus provided by their phy- logenetic perspective, Freud and Jung also *disagreed* on many things—in the end, quite vehemently. Freud, the Enlightenment thinker, wishing to break with the past, thought of our phylogenetic inheritance as a permanent threat to our rationality and as something to be analysed and overcome whenever possible. Jung, the Romantic, saw it as a potential threat to the ego's integrity and to collective well being, but also regarded it as a reposi- tory for the unconscious wisdom of the species, which we ignore at our peril and ought to respect and accept rather than analyse in the absurd hope of transcending our origins.

Another tactical difference within this strategic consensus were their notions of psychic energy, or libido, which occasioned some of the bitterest polemics, especially from Freud's quarter. Both Freud and Jung agreed that when the individual ceases to move "forward" developmentally, morbid- ity—in the form of fixation or regression—sets in. But Freud's notion of libido was specifically sexual in character, and tied to a host of mechanistic assumptions about the nature of the organism as a closed system that are now widely discredited (e.g. Bowlby, 1971). Jung's notion of psychic energy was more general, open ended and openly teleological in character (Jung, 1914). While subject to criticism, no doubt, it has the advantage of not blurring the boundaries between sexual needs and feelings and other human interests and concerns indiscriminately. It is one thing to maintain—as Jung doubtlessly would have—that sexuality suffeses every field of human activity; art, music, science, religion, psychotherapy, sport, etc. It is quite another to insist, as Freud did, on the *primacy* of sexual needs and interests over all others, or to see all other needs and interests as simply deflected or derivative forms of sexual desire—or failing that, of aggression.

Another aspect over the quarrel about psychic energy was that Freud and Jung had somewhat different attitudes toward regression. Both of them posited a primary regressive component to the psyche that runs counter to the normal "forward" flow of libido, even in the absence of external barriers and frustrations. Jung, to be fair, was first in the field, arguing that morbid fixation on the maternal imago—including overtly incestuous phanatasies—symbolizes a desire to return to intrauterine existence and give up one's individuated existence altogether, as a prelude to a longed for *metanoia* or spiritual rebirth. While indicative of a drift toward madness, regression may have a redemptive aspect and facilitate a genuine rebirth or renewal of the personality. These ideas were seized on later by Ferenczi, Balint, Winnicott and above all, perhaps, R.D.Laing (Burston, 1996).

Freud's approach was different. Regression was invariably a dirty word in his vocabulary and never an agent of integration or renewal. As Freud conceived it, regression can proceed in two dimensions: that of narcissism and that of Thanatos. The person who is narcissistically regressed has withdrawn all of his libidinal cathexes to external objects, all his connections to reality, and relates only to internal phantasy figures in an attempt to restore the conditions of intrauterine life (Freud, 1914). At this point in his theorizing, the connection between regression and the longing to restore intrauterine existence—which Jung drew attention to earlier (Jung, 1913)—is prominent, although the patent similarity was never acknowledged by Freud himself. This is a straightforwad example of the pupil teaching the master and the potentially embarrassing consequences of the same.

By contrast, the primary regressive urge Freud postulated in *Beyond the Pleasure Principle* (Freud,1920) was *not* linked with intrauterine phantasies, introversion etc, but with an ostensible urge in living things to revert to an inorganic state once their reproductive duties to the species are discharged, an idea derived from Schopenhauer and von Hartmann. As John Kerr and I have both noted elsewhere, the concept of the death instinct enabled Freud to maintain the primacy of the Oedipus complex in the collective unconscious and to the rob the maternal imago of the numinous power Jung, following J.J. Bachofen, had invested it with (Burston, 1991; Kerr, J., 1993).

In any case, as a result of the forgoing similarities and differences, Freud and Jung charted the contours of collective psyche in diverse ways with respect to 1) the unity or plurality of the "collective unconscious" and 2) the primacy of the paternal or maternal imagos in cultural, historical and individual development. Like Schopenhauer, both Freud and Jung regarded the unconscious mind as "timeless." The *a priori* Kantian categories, the laws of space, time, causality and logic that regulate the functioning of the reality-oriented ego (or persona) do not touch the deepest strata of the personality, which reach down imperceptibly into the well springs of instinct and collective life. So far, consensus prevails. It breaks down, however, when we try to account for the simultaneous unity and plurality—or unity in plurality—of unconscious mental life.

In 1912, as the mutual disenchantment between Freud and Jung deepened, Freud insisted with increasing vehemence that the startling multiplicity of mythological symbols represent so many derivative expressions of the self-same unitary or "core complex"—the Oedipus complex, as it is nowadays called (Kerr, 1993; Burston, 1994). Though he eventually made allowance for pre-Oedipal problems and processes in women, Freud always regarded culture and civilization as pre-eminently masculine achievements, in which women intervene merely as passive observers or objects of desire and never as the bearers of a numinous power or fascination akin to that of "the primal father" (Burston, 1989). As far as Freud was concerned, if the patient is male, ambivalence toward the father and fear of castration take precedence over all other developmental processes, unless the patient has developed a "reverse Oedipal complex."

Jung's collective unconscious was more pluralistic than Freud's. Instead of one archetypal drama being the nuclear or core complex, of which all others are derivative manifestations, Jung allowed for an indefinite number of collective representations, whose meaning or centrality varies with the needs, conditions and background of the subject. This flexibility regarding the plurality and co-existence of collective representations was quite commendable, up to a point, because it did not entail a reductionistic program of fitting the bewildering profusion of mythic ideas on the Procrustean bed of a single nuclear conflict. But it created a curious and possibly intractable philosophical problem. An indefinite and potentially infinite number of "archetypes" heightens the probability that some of the archetypes refered to are not *a priori* structures of unconscious life that are discovered through diligent search and comparison, but *post hoc* inventions created to suit the theorist's agenda and interests of the moment.

Fortunately, Jung did posit the existence of a nuclear drama which—though not subsuming others, necessarily—nevertheless assumed paramount importance because of its cross-cultural universality, namely the process of individuation from the mother (or maternal imago). In so doing, Jung was drawing on the (largely unacknowledged) ideas of J.J. Bachofen (1815-1881), a pupil of Savigny and the Historical School, and a prominent spokesman for conservative Romanticism, who lived in Basel, where Jung spent his childhood (Jung, 1963, p.111; Ellenberger,1970; Hogenson,1983; Burston, 1991). Bachofen, in turn, drew on the Historical School of Law, of which he was a well known representative and a broader philosophical tradition which included Herder, Lessing, Goethe, Hegel, Schelling, Carus, Schopenhauer and, somewhat later, his own protege, Friedrich Nietzsche

Unlike Descartes, Locke, Rousseau and Kant, who assumed that our everyday, egoic consciousness is a primary and self-evident datum of experience, Bachofen's German predecessors and contemporaries insisted that the conscious ego is a product of a developmental/evolutionary process in which the ego emerges gradually from a pre-dualistic unity with the surrounding cosmos—Romain Roland's "oceanic feeling." In this pre-differentiated matrix, cognitive schemata like self and other, subject and object, past and present, fantasy and reality do not yet exist. The path to a differentiated, adult experience is not smooth, however. In fact, it represents a precipitous "fall" from the enveloping protection afforded by the intra-uterine environment and union with the mother, which is nostalgically longed for ever after. The blissful sense of oneness with the cosmos the infant ostensibly experienced is not fully within the adult's grasp, however. Aesthetic, poetic or contemplative revery are the only means by which a sense of re-union with the cosmos are possible, and then only fleetingly (Abrams, 1971).

Freud's theory of narcissism and the gradual emergence of the ego from an undifferentiated matrix of instinct and fantasy (1914) bears a strong family resemblance to Jung's ideas (1913). Were it not for the bitter polemics that separated them, one would be inclined to see more similarities than differences in their approaches (Burston, 1991; Kerr,1993). Their doctrinal differences, which centered on anagogic ("non-reductive") dream interpretation, the primacy of the Oedipus complex and the libido concept, were sparked, perhaps, by clashing personal ambitions and/or by sexual secrets that each divined about the other circuitously—events which provoked much dissimulation and distrust, bringing out the very worst in both men (Kerr, 1993). But one can't help wondering whether these awkward antipathies over sexual secrets could have been overcome if the antagonism between them was not rooted, finally, in cultural and historical sensibilities that have yet to be adequately appreciated by all concerned.

Conclusion

However we may wish to construe the rupture between Freud and Jung, one thing is crystal clear. What prompted these disputes was *not* the clinical data per se. On the contrary, the way Freud and Jung interpreted their clinical data was determined by prior cultural allegiances and the fact that Freud was trying to transpose, collapse and in some sense contain the wealth of ideas and insights he gleaned from German Romanticism and Idealism into the framework of the mechanistic materialism spawned by the Enlightenment and mediated by way of Helmholtz, Brucke and Meynert—arguably an impossible project and one Jung finally could not endorse or embrace. Unlike Freud, he had no wish to wed the two divergent strands of the European *Zeitgeist* in what was ultimately a forced and unequal partnership. Nevertheless, like Freud, he saw himself as an "empiricist" initially, but soon abandoned that mistaken identity and became a phenomenologist of sorts (Brooke, 1991). His emphasis on the primacy of the maternal imago and the prospective character of unconscious mental processes reflects his indebtedness to conservative Romanticism—to Carus and Bachofen, in particular.

As the 20th century draws to a close, it becomes increasingly apparent that neither Freud nor Jung had a monopoly on truth and that both of their theories capture and express aspects of the unconscious mind that warrant careful scrutiny and respect (Burston, 1991). And by the same token, both approaches, taken to their logical extremes resemble nothing so much as a prototypical schizoid split. Because of his deep distrust of the unconscious (and of emotion in general), Freud's view of the unconscious was excessively *logocentric* or idolatrous in its one-sided overestimation of reason, as Jung among others alleged (e.g. Schachtel, 1959). Conversely, Jung's approach sometimes lapsed insensibly into mystical obscurantism and a virulent *irrationalism* that tended to debase or deny the efficacy and dignity of reason, as Freud and his champions have rightly objected (e.g. Fromm, 1947, introduction).

That said, it is also true that in many respects history has vindicated Jung—a fact seldom acknowledged in contemporary analytic historiography. Nowadays, we are witness to a startling profusion of psychoanalytic schools, ranging from object-relations theory, attachment theory, self-psychology, interpersonal psychoanalysis and Lacanian thought, as well as a comparable proliferation of post-Jungian approaches. Contrary to expectation, however, one development in the post-Freudian world that applies almost across the board is the gradual ascendency of the maternal imago to a position of equal or greater importance than the paternal imago in all but the Lacanian orientation, where the father's dominance is still absolute and uncontested. Rank, Klein, Fairbairn, Fromm and Bowlby, among others, have all acknowledged the primacy of mother-infant bond in developmental/clinical terms and have questioned the universality and/or irreducibility of Oedipal dynamics (Burston, 1989; Burston, 1991). Moreover, their ideas about psychic energy frequently stray in a Jungian direction. Yet Jung's followers, on the whole, are far more conversant in and receptive to recent innovations in psychoanalysis than the other way around. Let us hope that this sad state of affairs, which is rooted in a clash of nineteenth century sensibilities, ends sometime in the twenty-first.

Meanwhile, to some readers, dwelling on the pioneers' cultural-historical *Weltanschauugen* seems a little redundant by now. What's the point? Haven't we all moved on since then? And aren't our clinical concepts and practices mercifully free of much of the antiquated cultural baggage that both inspired and encumbered Freud and Jung?

Who are we kidding? Actually, it was Freud, a child of the Enlightenment, who tended to suppose one could develop a psychology of the unconscious on a purely scientific and empirical basis, free from extraneous considerations. Jung, by contrast, would probably have compared those who imagine they are free of cultural bias as heirs to Baron von Munchhausen. Jung always insisted that our cultural preconceptions shape our theories of human nature, and by implication, our clinical ideas and practices. If he was right, then our cultural preconceptions are no less powerful or influential for being unconscious. Indeed, the reverse is usually true.

The fact that the cultural preconceptions that shape our clinical theories and practices are less transparent to us that those of a previous generation is scarcely surprising. Hegel's observation that the Owl of Minerva only takes wing at dusk is quite apt here. However, the fact that this is a normal phenomena does not absolve clinicians of responsibility for trying to fathom the impact of their cultural embeddedness on their work and ideas. Meanwhile, if we fail to heed the past, we only impoverish our understanding of ourselves. The temptation to do so is doubly strong in an ostensibly "postmodern" world that is as anxious to sever its ties to modernity as the moderns were to repudiate their feudal forbears. Fortunately for all of us, the contemporary *Zeitgeist* also provides hermeneutics as an antidote. But that, as they say, is another story.

References

Abrams, M.H. (1971). *Natural supernaturalism: Tradition and revolution in Romantic literature*. New York, NY: W.W.Norton.

Bowlby, J. (1978). *Attachment & loss: vol. 1*. Harmondsworth: Penguin.

Brooke, R. (1991). *Jung and phenomenology*. London: Routledge.

Burston, D. (1989). Freud, the father and the philosophy of history. In L. Spurling (Ed.), *Sigmund Freud: Critical assessments*, (pp. 46-55). London: Routledge.

Burston, D. (1994). Freud, the serpent and the sexual enlightenment of children. *International Forum of Psychoanalysis*, *3*, 205-219.

Burston, D. (1991). *The legacy of Erich Fromm*. Cambridge, MA: Harvard University Press.

Burston, D. (1996). *The wing of madness: The life and work of R.D.Laing*. Cambridge, MA: Harvard University Press.

Carus, C.G. (1989). *Psyche: On the development of the soul*. Dallas: Spring Publications.

Ellenberger, H. (1970). *The discovery of the unconscious*. New York: Basic Books.

Freud, S. (1910). On the history of the psychoanalytic movement. M, Kahn (Ed.), *Collected Papers, Volume 1* (pp. 287-359). London: Hogarth Press.

Freud, S. (1914). On narcissism: An introduction. M, Kahn (Ed.), *Collected Papers, Volume 4* (pp. 30-59). London: Hogarth Press.

Freud, S. (1953/1920). *Beyond the pleasure principle*. In J. Strachey (Ed.), *Standard Edition*, Vol. 18. London: Hogarth Press.

Fromm, E. (1947). *Man for himself*. Greenwich, CT: Fawcett Premier Books.

Gould, S. J. (1977). *Ontogeny and phylogeny*. Cambridge: Harvard University Press.

Hogenson, G. (1984). *Jung's struggle with Freud*. Notre Dame, IN: Notre Dame University Press.

Jung, C.G., 1909, "The Significance of the Father in the Destiny of the Individual", in *The Psychoanalytic Years*, Princeton: Bollingen, 1974

Jung, C.G., 1913, *Symbols of Transformation*, trans. R.F.C.Hull, New York: Harcourt, Brace

& World.

Jung, C.G., 1914, *On the Nature of the Psyche*, trans. R.F.C. Hull, Princeton: Princeton University Press, 1960.

Jung, C.G., 1933, "Freud and Jung- Contrasts", in *Modern Man in Search of a Soul*, trans. W.S. Dillard and C.F. Baynes, New York: Harcourt, Brace & World.

Kerr, J., 1993, *A Most Dangerous Method, The Story of Jung, Freud and Sabina Spielrein*, New York: A. Knopf.

Mann, T., 1939, "Freud and the Future", in T. Mann, *Freud, Goethe and Wagner*, New York: Alfred Knopf.

Ricoeur, P., 1970, *Freud and Philosophy*, New Haven: Yale University Press

Rudnytsky, P., 1987, *Freud and Oedipus*, New York: Columbia University Press.

Schachtel, E., 1959, *Metamorphosis*, New York: Basic Books.

Chapter 4

Humean Character Revision: Reflections on Pride and Shame

Sylvia Burrow

Introduction

Psychological theories of motivation explain little, if anything, about the relationship between one's motives for acting and one's character. Philosophical counselling is a dialectical approach which provides a new way for people to learn philosophical tools enabling them to think and reason about the principles, values and commitments forming their characters. Philosophical counsellors typically refer to the Ancients to frame the discussion of one's beliefs, desires, and emotions. This approach is appropriate given the ancient view of philosophy as therapy, with its aim of weeding out internal inconsistencies between thoughts and emotions through philosophical dialogue. But consider character revision in light of Hume's account of motivation. Contrary to the Ancients, Hume famously held that reason alone can never motivate action but serves as a slave to the passions. So if philosophical counsellors consider that the emotions play the most prominent role in motivation as Hume thought, then bringing about character change is more a matter of reflecting on one's emotional responses rather than balancing one's reasons against one's emotions.

I plan to establish the possibility of deliberate character revision by upholding Hume's idea that the emotions are central to motivation. The most problematic psychological models of motivation suppose that external forces condition agents to act one way or another, usually through altering the unconscious desires from which action proceeds. I overturn these theories of unconscious motivation in favor of Hume's account of motivation, bringing to Hume's theory the idea that it is a mark of moral maturity that one reflect on one's own actions in light of their effects on others as part of character revision. If my account is limited to mature moral agents it will not undercut my theory, but it will show that not everyone may succeed in character revision. Everyone has the capacity to succeed, however. To a large degree, a person's capacity to successfully change her character lies in her ability to bear her own survey. Emotional responses like pride and humility, or shame, arise in response to reflection on one's own motives. I argue that pride and shame reveal whether or not one is maintaining integrity. Since we want to be able to bear our own survey, we are motivated to avoid doing that which brings about humility and to do that which brings about pride. Philosophical counsellors bringing persons to consider their emotional responses to their own motives encourage those individuals to take responsibility for their character traits. Counsellors endorsing a view of unconscious motivation, on the other hand, must suppose persons observe their own externally influenced motives just as anyone else would, which neither advances responsibility for one's own motives nor for one's very own character.

2. Observing One's Character

Psychological externalism dominates Anglo-American psychology.[1] Externalist psychological motivation claims that external forces outside of the agents' own cognitions motivate agents to act. Externalist psychologies can be alternately referred to as *socialization* theories, because they all share the characteristic that motives for acting, including moral motives, are the product of one's socialization. The roots of socialization theory lie in B. F. Skinner's radical behaviorism, which claims that behavior to act is defined in terms of observable responses rather than feelings, thoughts, or beliefs; persons act as they do because they are conditioned to do so. The socialization view entails that motives for action are unconscious or nonconscious, for actions are the result of social forces unwittingly influencing agents. Below, I outline the problems of accounting for both autonomy and self-respect that these sorts of psychological theories encounter. The alternative I develop in the remainder of this chapter is a philosophical account claiming both that we are social beings and that our individual thoughts, beliefs, and emotions consciously motivate. Hume's account of motivation grounds this sort of explanation, I argue, for it can describe how mature persons take responsibility for the development of their motives for action, and thus their own characters, in light of how their actions affect others. Externalist theories of moral motivation seem to deny responsibility for one's character development for they do not appear to offer *any* explanation of how persons can reflect upon and change their own character traits. Persons are cast as observers of their motives as much as anyone else is. Two externalist psychological accounts exemplify this view: operant conditioning and cognitive social conditioning.

Operant conditioning, or classical conditioning, is an early theory of observational learning first presented by Skinner. On this account, motivation changes on account of negative and positive reinforcement.[2] A certain stimulus produces a certain response, and when a particular stimulus-response pattern is reinforced, the individual is conditioned to respond.[3] If motivation is explained as Skinner thought, then persons' own thoughts and beliefs are in a "black box" and reasoning is irrelevant to one's actual motivations. Individuals are determined to behave in certain ways just as pigeons are trained to peck bars for food or rats to find their way to the end of a maze. Thus operant conditioning famously denies voluntary action. Moreover, it denies that reflection on one's own motives can change one's character or one's motivation. Enough has been written in opposition to Skinner to alleviate me of the task of disproving the plausibility of operant conditioning as an explanation of persons' motivation. R. M. Hare, for example, showed shortly after the view originated that operant conditioning proves inconclusive.[4]

In a move to offer an alternative to operant conditioning, but to preserve the idea that agents' motives result from social forces, Albert Bandura and Walter Mischel argue for a "cognitive social theory" of motivation. Cognitive social conditioning holds the following claims, each of which is aimed against operant conditioning:

a. one is not motivated in a mechanistic way, simply observed by noting a person's behavior

b. one does not have to experience reinforcement personally

c. conditioned behavior cannot be generalized from rats and pigeons to humans;

d. human behavior cannot be controlled by stimulus-response reinforcement.[5]

Bandura is the main proponent of social conditioning. Bandura's main claims are that memory plays an important role in determining the sorts of responses following certain stimuli, and that other people are the most important situational variable in a person's stimulus-response pattern.[6] Mischel advances a more complex theory of cognitive social learning variables, which include persons' expectancies, values, and plans.[7] Social conditioning does not prove any better than classical conditioning, at least not if the following is correct. Like classical conditioning, social conditioning denies that a person's own beliefs and emotions consciously *motivate* her actions, even if her values and plans are not *learned* through socialization: she is motivated because of social conditioning. This results in two problems.

First, social conditioning entails that an individual's moral motivation is nothing more than a product of society:

> all moral actions are molded by sanctions arising neither from an objective order of moral reasons nor from a subjective order of one's own desires and self-interpretations but rather solely from an environment populated by objectified 'socializers,' be they individual persons or institutions and other sorts of collectives.[8]

It might seem preposterous to think any person would hold this view about herself. But it is not so odd once one considers that psychology values that which can be measured and assessed through verification, predictability, quantifiability, objectivity, and reproducibility of experiments.[9] The method of study in psychology leads to conclusions supposing that the individual's own thoughts and emotions play a nonexistent role in determining action because they cannot be measured. Omitting an agent's own thoughts and emotions from moral action entails that moral action is not autonomous. Autonomous action is self-governed action, action arising from *within* oneself and not from without. Denying autonomy in a theory of motivation renders that theory implausible as an account of moral action, for moral action proceeds from autonomous emotions and beliefs.

Second, self-respect is impossible for those believing socialization theory is right, and if self-respect is impossible then that undercuts one's capacity for integrity. It devalues one's self-respect to think that one's moral principles, values or beliefs arise from external social forces.[10] As I hope to show later in this chapter, personal integrity consists of maintaining principles, beliefs, and values that are central to one's identity; those principles, beliefs, and values form an individual's central commitments.[11] If those commitments arise because of external social forces, then a person has no say in why she adheres to certain commitments over others. In that case, we should have no reason to think those commitments identify that person as the person she is. Consequently, there are no grounds upon which one's moral motivations can be said to reflect a person's identity and thus explain what it means to have personal integrity.

So both social conditioning and operant conditioning fail to provide the grounds upon which one can engage in voluntary character revision. People are attributed a passive role in the formation of their characters as that which is conditioned by others, and so it would appear impossible for those theories to explain how people could actively revise their characters. It is wholly unclear how externalist psychological theories could explain responsibility for one's character development since persons are cast as observers of their characters as much as anyone else is. The inability to take responsibility for and actively engage in character development is built into the above sorts of theories due to the definition of the person their models of motivation implicitly suppose. Motivation cannot be explained in psychology without at least a capacity for operant conditioning, according to psychology's definition of a psychological organism: "an organism is a psychological one just in case it is a motivated organism and it is a motivated organism capable of being operantly conditioned."[12] If this is right, then *any* psychological theory of motivation undercuts agents' capacities for autonomy and self respect, and so we would do best by turning to a philosophical account of motivation that does not rely on such a definition of a person.

An attractive alternative to externalist psychological theories of moral motivation will account for the ability of agents to reflect upon and endorse their own motives for moral action. I present Hume's theory of moral motivation as that attractive alternative, for it shows both that emotions are central to moral motivation and that moral development is a matter of deliberate character refinement. Hume's account of moral motivation, in its appeal to human nature, can show us how emotions and character development are related to moral motivation in a way that supports the aims of maintaining integrity and self-respect. This model of motivation explains the possibility of character revision in relation to one's capacity to be a moral person, which serves as a standard of excellence for motivation in general. If my account is correct, philosophical counsellors should take Hume's lead and engage their clients in discussion of their emotions as an essential part of broadening their understanding and development of themselves as moral agents.

3. Engaging with One's Character

Hume's moral theory is a good place to start to enrich one's understanding of moral motivation, for it is grounded in a conception of human nature. Philosophical counselling does not aim to cure people of illnesses or conditions, but to bring out a better understanding of oneself through dialogue. I can think of no better way of increasing that understanding than through exploring one's own understanding of human nature as a philosophical counsellor. This is not achieved simply through examining the relation between beliefs and actions, but through considering the role of emotions. To that end, Hume's account provides an excellent account of emotion in moral psychology. Hume's moral psychology explains the character revision that accompanies moral development through reflection on one's emotional responses. On Hume's account, emotions are both motivation to act and the basis of moral judgment. We judge a person's motive to act through judging a person's character, which is a judgment about the sort of emotions regularly bringing about action. If we have an impression of moral approbation that we regularly associate with the apprehension or idea of someone's action, then the action is virtuous, but if we regularly associate it with a feeling of disapprobation, then the action is vicious. Just or unjust actions are similarly judged by moral sentiment. Feeling approbation towards an action affecting the public interest indicates that it is just, and feeling disapprobation shows that it is unjust. How do we apprehend a person's emotional motive? Through sympathy and through a general understanding of human nature and observation of circumstance, we generate the emotion in ourselves that we infer the agent to have. I have developed the role of sympathy on Hume's account elsewhere.[13] Thus I will only provide a sketch of sympathy's relevance to moral motivation below.

Sympathy is essential to one's emotional judgments of approbation or disapprobation. Those who observe the effects of the virtues on others experience through sympathy the pleasure of those who benefit from those virtues. Virtuous action effects others in ways that gives rise to the moral sentiment of approbation that arises when we feel, through sympathy, the pleasure others receive from such actions; we respond with pleasure ourselves. This pleasure is moral approbation, and it arises even though we neither receive nor expect to receive any direct benefit from that quality of motive.[14] Pleasure in this case is not to be confused as the *aim* of moral action. Hume shares a similarity with Aristotle's view that pleasure completes the activity of moral action. For Hume, pleasure is not the end of moral action in the sense that we act to garner the approval of others, because the goal is already approved of.[15]

Sympathy is not itself a kind of emotion for Hume in the *Treatise*.[16] Rather, he explains that "sympathy ... is nothing but the conversion of an idea into an impression by the force of the imagination."[17] My *idea* of another's emotion is strengthened though my imagination until it is actually converted into a milder form of that emotion. In Hume's terminology, my idea "increases in vivacity" so as to become the passion itself. Sympathy is easiest with those to whom we are close: it reflects the *emotional* closeness present in the relationship. In having the role of changing our motivations, sympathy functions to change our immediate wants and desires. The change in motivation is one distinguishing mark between Humean moral theory and utilitarianism, for while utilitarians and Humeans are both concerned with what is useful or pleasing in society, it is not internal to utilitarian considerations that utilitarians will be motivated on those considerations. For example, the utilitarian may observe that giving up a right to private gun ownership would produce the most happiness in society if it prevents more deaths than owning guns will, but this need not *motivate* the utilitarian to act.

On Hume's theory, experiencing moral feelings of approbation or disapprobation towards our own proposed course of action *are* our moral motives for action.[18] Experiencing moral disapprobation in conjunction with the impression of pain motivates one not to do a particular act on the Humean account: motivation and judgment are internal to having a moral motive. This idea of moral judgment differentiates Hume from his contemporary Adam Smith, who only considers moral judgment to apply to other people. Per Smith's view, moral approbation or disapprobation *follows upon* comparing my emotional response to yours; so if we both have the same emotional responses to the same sort of situation, I morally approve of you, but if they disagree I disapprove of you.[19] This is not Hume's view of moral emotions. On Hume's view, to sympathetically engage with other persons, moral agents need to imagine what sorts of effects on others a person's character has, whether or not certain character traits are pleasing or useful to others or to oneself. Understanding what those effects are likely to be requires a general understanding of human nature. Since the point of sympathetically engaging with another is to understand the likely effects of a certain character trait, not its actual effects, we need to have a point of view from which to judge those effects as likely. That only comes from a general understanding of human nature.

Both for moral agents and moral judges, moral development depends upon sympathetic engagement with others. Sympathy matters to moral judgment in light of our relationships with others, for through sympathy we apprehend what others' emotions are or would likely be in response to another's action. We judge others from the point of view of the effects of the agent's character on those close to her, those in what Hume calls her "narrow circle." I consider it the mark of mature moral agents to be aware of the importance of their relationships with others and the importance of relationships to others in general. Similarly, a mature moral agent is concerned, in her motivation to act morally, to reflect the importance of her relationships in her motivation. Sympathy, as Hume explains it, is what I consider essential to that mature development of one's motives, in its role of changing immediate wants and desires: sympathy changes our initial emotional responses to reflect the evaluative role of reflecting on one's motives in light of the emotions those motives produce in others. Below I develop the idea that our concern with our own motives for action in light of others' responses is reflected in a desire to maintain integrity before others.

3. Integrity

Character revision through reflective endorsement of moral motives is central to having integrity. This endorsement may happen through the revision of reasons with the consequence of changes in beliefs, principles, or values. Or, one may revise one's emotional motives. In the latter case, other emotions need to counter the emotions we wish to revise. Below I will establish that the reflection of sympathy is central to having integrity. I appeal to three main classifications of integrity which, as Cheshire Calhoun points out, all share the idea that integrity is about standing for something.[20] In each case I show that generating moral motives through sympathy supports the reflection required for integrity.[21]

First, integrity can be understood as self-integration, characterized by a lack of ambivalence or inconsistency in desires. On this view integrity is about deciding what one stands for by deliberately rejecting some desires and wholeheartedly enforcing others. Inauthentic views make integrity impossible, for they have not been deliberately reflected upon nor accepted or rejected as 'outlaw' desires.[22] Weeding out emotional motives is thus central to integrity on this view. If we reject outlaw emotions because they are harmful or displeasing to either the self or others, this weeding out occurs as a natural progression of engaging in Humean sympathy. The effects of actions motivated by emotions have readily apparent events on the self. However, only through sympathy do we recognize those effects on others. If those sympathetic emotions outweigh our original emotions, then we will be motivated to act on emotions other than our outlaw original emotions. So engaging in sympathy is a deliberate way of weeding out those emotions if we actively take an interest in being sympathetic; character revision is thus a paradigmatic case of choosing to engage in sympathy. More on this below.

Second, having integrity—comparised of core projects and commitments without which one's life would be meaningless—can amount to being true to one's character. Were we come to possess those core views through socialization alone, we could not claim those views to be *our own*. Integrity demands reflection upon those views. Having integrity in this case cannot mean just upholding psychologically deep desires; we need to *endorse* the desires with which we identify.[23] To endorse those desires we need to reflect on what those desires are and uphold those that are important to our identity. If moral motives reflect character traits, then approving of one's moral motives entails approving of one's character traits. Since one's character traits are central to one's identity, approving of one's character traits is central to this picture of integrity. On Hume's view this may not involve a *conscious* deliberation over whether or not one wants to be an honest person or a temperate person, for example. But it involves no mysterious nonconscious processes either. Rather, I am either pleased or displeased by review of my own character. This is shown in my emotions of pride or humility.

Those traits that I am proud of are those that please me when I review them. Similarly, should I dislike the traits I have, I feel humility or shame. Emotional responses serve as judgments of one's character, thus reflection on one's moral motives consists of emotional responses. Feeling pride indicates that we want such motives to be part of who we are; feeling humility or shame indicates that we do not. So those emotional responses serve the same function and can give the same answers as reasoned deliberation over whether or not we want certain motives to form our identity. Sympathy is a necessary part of reflection on one's character, for character traits are pleasing or displeasing according to whether they are pleasing or useful to the self and others. So one must sympathetically understand how one's tendencies to act would affect others or the self as part of one's character assessment.

Third, having integrity can be said to consist of having basic values and principles which say that there are some things a person will not do. This view is rather narrow, for integrity also seems to be about not bowing in to others' demands, threats, reproaches; in short, integrity is also about not selling out to others' views. The justification for the view is that 'I couldn't go on as the same person,' but it ought to be extended to emphasize that 'I would be doing a wrong.'[24] This requirement ought to be common to any account of integrity.[25] If that is right, then we need to question ourselves as part of reflection, to recognize that we may need to revise our views in light of others' judgments; our own judgments are subject to the risk of reasonable criticism, reproach, and admonition by others.[26] This is what Hume's model of moral progress requires, as part of our evaluation of moral motives from a general point of view.[27] Emotional motives are subject just as much to assessment by others. But this does not entail that others' responses *create* our motives for action; they are simply what we consider if we are mature moral agents. If we act carelessly on our emotions without considering the emotional responses of others, then we are rightfully subject to criticism and reproach. Imaginatively producing their emotional responses in ourselves through sympathy moderates our own emotional motive for acting.

So in summary, lacking adequate reflection precludes having integrity on either of the above three views. Engaging in that reflection cannot ignore emotional motives if emotions are important to us as social selves, not *socialized* selves. Recognizing the emotional import of our relations to others requires actively engaging with their emotions. Sympathy calls on us to understand another's emotions through the work of the imagination; it takes us out of our own subjective, self-interested viewpoint, thereby correcting our own emotional motives in light of others' emotions. So on the view I am recommending, the reflection required for maintaining integrity involves us both in a broader understanding of society and of particular others.

My conclusion supports Calhoun's view that each of the above three conceptions of integrity must be broadened to show that integrity is a function of our relations to others, captured in the notion of 'standing for something.' Integrity concerns how we conduct ourselves in the face of others in two ways. First, what I stand for must be what I think all deliberators ought to do. I thus do not stand by something just as something I do for myself. Second, any shame I feel is not merely shame at my own lack of will or violation of a standard; rather, thinking one has no integrity signifies the revelation of one's inability of standing for something before others.[28]

We can understand Hume's claim that we feel shame upon reviewing our conduct in light of how it affects others as a failure to stand up for something particular, namely the sort of motives of which we would be proud. Consequently, shame is one indication of a lack of integrity. If Hume is right, we feel shame if we recognize we lack the motive in the first place, or we have the motive but fail to act on it. The latter does not occur if motives are emotions, for the emotions themselves motivate one to act. We may be thwarted in our actions, and that is why we may fail. But shame does not result simply from being thwarted in our actions. We can and do experience shame for lacking the sort of *character* of which we would feel proud. A recognition that we wish to improve our character and that we lack those motives that we consider virtuous of course indicates that we cannot say those motives are part of who we are. What to do?

4. Character Revision—Or Not

We can do one of three things. We can either aim to attain those motives we think are virtuous; take an uncaring stance to morality and do nothing; or hide our lack of moral virtue. Hume's answer to the first is that to attain virtuous character traits, one must act out of a motive of duty or obligation to perform those acts we would laud on account of their motives—but of course without having those motives. By invoking the *obligation* to act in similar circumstances as if we had the same sort of virtuous motive, we *develop* the moral motive through custom and habit; this is how we progress morally. Now this sketch of moral progress may or may not be empirically correct but at least anecdotal evidence suggests that, for example, a habit of acting kindly generally leads to kind motives. The more important point is that acting on a motive of duty indicates the desire to do that action before others that we would consider virtuous on account of its motives—we wish to stand up for that sort of motive as a virtuous one to have.[29]

Unfortunately, we don't always stand up for those motives we would think it virtuous to act from, because we can always just admit that we lack such motives and not try to develop them at all. The choice then is to either *hide* the lack of such motives or *not care* about one's moral worth in the eyes of others. The latter calls for a deadening of one's apprehension of others' judgments of oneself. This is achieved through *not* sympathetically perceiving others' reactions to one's character, which can be difficult to do. However, if one is surrounded by those who are dishonest thieves or cagey promise-breakers, it is all the easier not to worry how one looks in *their* eyes. That is, sympathy with those who are similar in their moral poverty will not produce any painful emotions.

If it were possible to have an entire society of individuals sharing the same happy propensities towards morally bad actions, then it might seem that such people would morally approve of each other. Since we morally approve of what generates a response of pleasure, a seemingly nasty society would be comprised of morally good people. But it is not Hume's claim that we could take pleasure in nasty acts, unless through some perversion of human nature. Hume's point is that we naturally take pleasure in what is pleasing or useful to others and displeasure in what is displeasing or not useful. And it is improbable that such knavery would be anything but harmful to those involved: breaking promises, for example, breaks down mutual cooperation in society, and it is harder to satisfy one's own interests alone than with the cooperation of others. And so it goes too with lying, stealing, or other activities breaking down the bonds of trust between individuals. In such a Hobbesian state of nature (which Hume denies would ever exist), no one would feel shame, for bonds within society mean nothing and so how one regards one's own character in light of one's relations to oneself or others would hardly matter.

So it seems best to hide one's lack of virtue rather than to belong to the sort of society in which we fear experiencing the reproach of another's gaze. This shows that we *do* care about morality, but do not want to be found out for our lack of moral worth by another. We would feel shame upon reflecting on others' reactions to our want of virtue, given the recognition that we are not standing up for what we see as the right thing to do, due to a deficiency of character. This shame indicates a lack of integrity in knowing what is good yet lacking the motive to do it. To hide the lack of a virtuous motive, I may do the sort of action that would follow from a virtuous motive. So a person devoid of gratitude may still be pleased to perform grateful actions and consider her duty fulfilled.[30]

Now on Hume's theory, if a moral action was artificially virtuous, as opposed to naturally virtuous, it would be done out of a motive of duty to do that which upholds mutual self-interest and cooperation in society. Motives of justice are such motives, and these arise purely through education and human convention. In this case I do not hide my lack of a virtuous motive. I really *do* have a virtuous motive, just not a naturally arising one. If I lack a natural virtue yet act *as if* I do, even out of a sense of duty, I may fool my companions and so avoid their reproach; but upon survey of myself I feel shame for lacking the natural motive to do what is right. It may be going too far to say, as Hume does, that such a person "may hate himself upon that account," but such a person will feel shame for not having the motive to do that which he thinks one ought to. This shame brings about a motivation to change one's naturally arising motives. Why is that?

We are not motivated to change our motives for action in light of others' responses to us so much as our own responses to ourselves. Displeasure upon one's survey of oneself triggers self-hatred in the serious cases and shame in more moderate ones. But we desire to be happy—or at least to relieve ourselves of anxiety. This is a common understanding of human nature that Hume upholds from the Ancients, Epicureans and Stoics. So we aim to rid ourselves of those motives that bring about shame and to bring about more approbation and pleasure. Pride is inherently pleasing, and it is also useful, asserts Hume: "'tis certain, that nothing is more useful to us in the conduct of life, than a due degree of pride, which makes us sensible of our own merit, and gives us a confidence and assurance in all our projects and enterprises."[31]

Self-satisfaction is of course quite agreeable to the person experiencing it, but Hume notes that we have to be careful not to let on quite how pleased we are: "We have, all of us, a wonderful partiality for ourselves, and were we always to give vent to our sentiments in this particular, we shou'd mutually cause the greatest indignation in each other...."[32] Should we lack many such favorable sentiments of ourselves, their very pleasure and usefulness brings us to further develop them. Should we both lack such favorable sentiments and the desire to further develop them, then I suggest that it will be necessary to cultivate one's sense of pride.

Thus, should philosophical counsellors want to help persons bring about a change in their motives, they should aim to develop those persons' capacity for self-reflection, which will bring with it the feelings of pride or shame. Should a person feel much shame or self-hatred upon his own survey of his motives, then the philosophical dialogue that will aid in his feeling pride will be a dialogue both drawing out his acknowledgement of the sorts of virtuous motives that *would* bring about pride upon his self-reflection and that focuses on the pleasure and usefulness of pride. The merits of feeling pride are twofold: it is both useful to ourselves and others, and it brings about pleasure upon our own survey and that of others.[33]

The wish to attain virtuous motives thus arises from the desire to feel pride rather than shame upon reflection of one's own character. To develop those virtuous motives, one acts *as if* one had those motives. So, one does the sorts of actions that would have resulted from emotions such as benevolence, courage, humbleness, etc. Custom and habit develops the attendant emotions through time. This explanation of moral development seems intuitively plausible. It also rings similar to Aristotle's account of how we become good practical reasoners: we have an idea of the virtuous person, and we aim to act like that person; over time, we generate the right sorts of emotions that attend actions done in the right way, at the right time, towards the right person, etc. The difference between Hume and Aristotle is that Hume gives a far richer account of the agent's moral psychology. And it is one that can help our own understanding of our emotional responses towards ourselves and others, as far as our own experience supports its views.

5. Conclusion

The experience of emotion is central to one's moral life, both in terms of one's moral judgments and one's moral motivation. Moral agents can get a better understanding of how emotions feature in that moral life through looking at the role of sympathy in Hume's moral psychology. Philosophical counsellors can accordingly encourage people to engage in self-reflection and reflection upon others' responses to themselves. Externalist psychologists suppose something like this: character revision involves pained introspection of how others have conditioned me to have the motives I do. I have argued that feeling pride upon reflecting on one's character encourages one to further develop those qualities that are pleasing or useful motives, and feeling shame calls for character revision. If the above account of Humean character reflection is correct, then reflection calls for me to generate a greater awareness of what sorts of motives give me shame and an understanding of what actions would follow were I to have virtuous qualities instead. I am successful at revising my character if I then aim to take on those actions that would exemplify the latter qualities, and custom and habit develops the attendant emotional motives in me that I originally saw lacking in myself. I am motivated to take on such actions through a desire for happiness and an aversion to pain and misery. I revel in feeling proud of my virtuous qualities and see the benefit in those around me from taking pride in my character. This view of character assessment and motivation relies on one's emotional responses to the self and others.

Socialization theorists deny the possibility of such moral reflection, because they cast agents' motives as conditioned by social forces. I offered two reasons for rejecting that view. First, an individual's motivation is just a product of society, so persons do not autonomously produce their actions, but simply observe their actions as anyone else would. If one's behavior does not arise from one's own beliefs, values, or emotions and is not meaningful to one's identity, there is little basis upon which to take responsibility for one's own character. And if one is not responsible for one's actions, then there is no need to reflect upon or alter one's motives for those actions. Second, socialization theory fails to account for agent self-respect and integrity, which further undermines the possibility of taking responsibility for one's own actions. Thus, unconscious or nonconscious psychological theories of motivation are poor theories to appeal to if the aim is to advance persons' responsibility for their motives and to encourage questioning and revision of those motives.

Philosophical counsellors can increase a person's awareness of the positive and negative aspects of her character as she judges it and no one else. This is not to say that one's judgements need be purely subjective. Through sympathetic reflection, one considers the emotional responses of others, especially those close to oneself, which is a mark of moral maturity. Of course, there will be people who do not wish to develop their characters through sympathetic reflection. If it is too hard for people to bear their own scrutiny or that of others, then they will find it best to surround themselves with others who share similar traits, thus avoiding censure. This in turn makes it easier to turn a blind eye to oneself. Turning a blind eye is impossible if one wishes to stand up for what one values, signifying integrity. As I argued above, having integrity is indicated by pride. So for people to be the sorts of mature moral agents who are responsible for their own character and who have integrity, character revision starts with the sorts of questions revealing whether or not they take pride in their characters.

Notes

[1] Thomas Wren, *Caring About Morality* (Cambridge, MA: MIT Press, 1991), 23. Wren notes that while psychology is beginning a trend towards cognitive approaches, the historical approach to psychological theories of motivation has its roots in socialization theory, which is the idea that persons are socialized to act as they do. Now, I do not mean to imply that externalist psychological theory is the only sort of psychological theory of motivation. Psychological theories of motivation roughly divide into two sorts: internal and external theories of motivation. (I follow Wren's terminology in this discussion of both internalist and externalist socialization theory.) Internalist motivation theories hold that agents' motivation is cognitive. Some personality theorists and cognitive developmentalist theorists like Lawrence Kohlberg and Jean Piaget exemplify internalist psychological motivation (See for example Jean Piaget, *The Moral Judgment of the Child* (New York: Free Press, 1965) and Lawrence Kohlberg, "Moral Stages and Moralization: the Cognitive-Developmental Approach," *Moral Development and Behavior* (New York: Holt, Rinehart and Winston, 1976). In fitting with the theme of this book, I only consider externalist psychological theories of motivation, for only these theories represent unconscious or nonconscious theories of motivation.

[2] A similar psychological theory is that of "vicarious arousal" in which observers are conditioned to experience emotional arousal from stimuli (usually painful) simply by observing others to be aroused (e.g. grimacing) by such stimuli (Thomas Wren, *Caring About Morality* (Cambridge, MA: MIT Press, 1991), 46). See for example Alvin Bandura *Principles of Behavior Modification* (New York: Holt, Rinehart and Winston, 1969) and S.M. Berger "Conditioning Through Vicarious Instigation" *Psychological Review,* 69 (1962): 450-466.

[3] See for example, Skinner, *Science and Human Behavior* (New York: Macmillan, 1953).

[4] H.J. Eysenck, "The Biology of Morality" *Moral Development and Behavior*. Austin, Texas: Holt, Rinehart and Winston, 1976), 117.

[5] "Cognitive Social Theories" *The Encyclopedia of Psychology* [online] ([retrieved September 7, 2002] available from: http://www.personalityresearch.org/cogsocial.html).

[6] ibid.

[7] ibid.

[8] Wren, "Caring About Morality," 26

[9] Wren, "Caring About Morality," 30

[10] Wren, "Caring About Morality," 33

[11] Bernard Williams, "Moral Luck" in *Moral Luck* (Cambridge: Cambridge University Press, 1981).

[12] Gareth Matthews, "The Idea of a Psychological Organism" *Behaviorism* 13, no.1 (1985: 37-51), 39. Matthews points out that this view ought to be upheld in psychology, as

both Philip Teitelbaum and V. G. Deither argue (but that it ought not imply that psychological organisms are incapable of purposive behavior). Matthews cites Teitelbaum, "The use of operant methods in the assessment and control of motivational states" *Operant Behavior* (W.K. Honig, ed. New York: Appleton-Century-Crofts, 1966) and Deither, "Microscopic Brains" *Science* (March 13, 1964: 1138-1145).

[13] "The Correction of Sentiment on Hume's Moral Theory" (presented at the American Philosophical Association, December 2001).

[14] David Fate Norton, "Hume, Human Nature, and the Foundations of Morality" *The Cambridge Companion to Hume* (New York: Cambridge University Press), 165

[15] Annette Baier "Moral Sentiments and the Difference They Make" *Proceedings of the Aristotelian Society Supplement* (1995, v. 60: 15- 30), 17

[16] Although I recognize that Hume's account of sympathy in the *Treatise of Human Nature* differs from his *Enquiry concerning the Principles of Morals*, space constraints limit my discussion of sympathy to the *Treatise*.

[17] David Hume, *A Treatise of Human Nature* (L. A. Selby-Bigge and Nidditch, eds. Oxford: Clarendon Press, 1978) hereafter cited as T; T: 427.

[18] Hume T: 401-404.

[19] Adam Smith, *The Theory of Moral Sentiments* (New York: Agustus M. Kelley, 1966).

[20] Cheshire Calhoun "Standing for Something" *The Journal of Philosophy* v.92, no.5 (1995).

[21] I am only considering integrity here in the context of one's moral character: integrity may be about preserving one's identity, upholding a set of principles consistently, or upholding principles consistently in front of others. In each case, what one considers essential to maintain to have integrity may be divided into either non-moral or moral principles and values. For instance, those who think integrity is consistency within one's principles must hold that if Hitler maintains his Aryan principles consistently, he has integrity. On this view, morality and consistency need not come together. They both come together on a view of integrity which holds that Hitler could not have integrity due to corrupt moral principles (Carolyn McCleod, "Integrity and Self Protection," unpublished). For the purposes of this discussion I only address what is morally important to maintaining one's integrity. This is not meant to exclude the possibility that integrity is also about maintaining what is non-morally important to us. It is to say that moral motivation incorporating Humean sympathy does not conflict with the demands of integrity, no matter what that conception of integrity.

[22] Calhoun, *"Standing for Something,"* 256. Calhoun points out that on this view, integrity is a matter of deciding what one stands for through rejecting and accepting certain desires on one's own settled reasons for taking the stand one does. This stems from Harry Frankfurt's account of voluntary action, in which only *persons* act from second order desires;

anything less makes one a *wanton* (Frankfurt, "Freedom of the Will and the Concept of a Person" in *Journal of Philosophy* v.68, no.1, January 1971). The process of acting on second order desires requires selecting and weeding out certain first order desires as motives. Gabriele Taylor follows up on this point, arguing that second order volitions are not one's own if adopted as a crowd follower or as someone shallowly sincere—the kind of person whose endorsements are not taken on for the long-term (Taylor, Pride, Shame, and Guilt; Oxford: Clarendon Press, 1985).

[23] Calhoun *Standing for Something*, 244

[24] Calhoun, *Standing for Something*, 246

[25] Lynne McFall "Integrity" *Ethics* (v.98, no.1, October 1987: 5-20).

[26] Calhoun, *Standing for Something*, p.251

[27]Annette Baier, *A Progress of Sentiments: Reflections on Hume's Treatise* (Cambridge, Massachusetts: Harvard University Press, 1991). She emphasizes that on Hume's view, I am aware of what sorts of effects your action would produce in others through my general knowledge of human nature, generated through conversations, observations, and other general experiences.

[28] Calhoun, *Standing for Something*, p.259

[29] Note that a motive of duty is required in addition to naturally virtuous motives. Two points follow from this. First, sympathy is required for the artificial duty of acting on a motive of duty just as it is for a natural virtue. Hume claims that a sense of duty cannot be wholly comprised of natural emotional responses, but that it is developed through education and habit because of the usefulness and pleasure of acting justly. Cultivating a sense of duty fills in the gap when either I am not disposed to act morally when I see I should, or if I have a morally virtuous motive but am not moved to act on it. So if I do not keep promises out of love and friendship, then I keep them because that facilitates our mutual advantage. In order to apprehend the pleasure and utility of keeping promises, I need to engage in sympathy with others affected by the promise- making. Second, sympathy is required for an obligation to act morally; it is not limited to moral motivation arising from emotion alone.

[30] Hume T: 479. Now Hume holds that we would still regard such actions done out of duty as morally meritorious: "But tho', on some occasion, a person may perform any action merely out of regard to its moral obligation, yet still this supposes in human nature some distinct principles, which are capable of producing the action, and whose moral beauty renders the action meritorious" [T: 479]. This is not convincing, for Hume never tells us what these 'distinct principles' are, and why it is we would find them morally beautiful. As it is, we could just as well consider such a person to lack integrity, in pretending to others that he is grateful when in fact, he only goes through the motions of a grateful person.

[31] Hume T: 596-7

[32] Hume T: 597

[33] Hume T: 607

Chapter 5

Sometimes a Cigar is Just a Cigar

Cameron Tsoi-A-Sue

Forms of therapy that center on Freudian psychodynamics are not therapeutic; the fundamental concept of the two-part human psyche, conscious and unconscious, is flawed, both practically and philosophically. The treatment models of psychodynamics are dehumanizing, create co-dependency, and encourage moral irresponsibility.

From the psychodynamic perspective, a human psyche, mind, thinking/feeling process, etcetera ... is a ball of forces, those of which we are aware, conscious, and those of which we are not aware, unconscious. The unconscious mind exerts influence over the conscious mind, creating profound internal conflict. Ergo, the unconscious becomes a boogie-man that preys upon and influences the conscious mind. The individual is then further distanced from moral or emotional responsibility for his or her actions. In psychodynamic practice, the separation of the human psyche into the conscious and the unconscious is destructive to ethical decision making. Philosophical counselling proposes a model of therapy and a view of humanity that ultimately places moral and emotional responsibility upon the individual, increasing personal autonomy.

The Freudian unconscious is defined as an area of mind containing repressed desires and taboo content. The three components of the unconscious are: id, ego, and super ego.

The id operates based on the pleasure/pain, attract/avoidance principle. One ought to act to increase pleasure, and avoid pain.

The ego is governed by the reality principle. The reality principle states that one ought to do what is best in terms of practical demands and the pressures of external reality.

The super ego acts by creating guilt when one surrenders to repressed desires or satisfies a craving for taboo content. For example, John (the universal client) wakes up. His alarm has gone off. John's unconscious desire is to go back to sleep (this is perhaps John's conscious desire as well). John's ego reminds him that he has to attend an early business meeting important to his career. John's super ego then causes him to feel guilty for his desire to remain in bed. What John does, says Freud, depends on which element of his psyche is in control at the moment of decision.

In psychodynamic therapy, the substance of the unconscious develops during the first six years of life. Therefore, there may be much in John's experience that he does not acknowledge or know.

The goal of psychodynamic therapy is to create awareness in John of unknown, deeply imbedded, unconscious conflict. Primarily, psychodynamic analysis uses two techniques—free association and dream analysis. Free association encourages the patient to talk aimlessly, wandering through his or her brain-stored visual images or personal archives. The therapist listens. He or she then interprets the possible conflicts between the patient's mind/body/feeling links based on the "free" associations John makes. It is presumed that John cannot interpret his own reality because he cannot be fully aware of it. The unconscious mind prevents John from attaining unified self-awareness, but the doctor knows and will guide John to where the doctor thinks John should go. Yet, if the doctor is wrong, only John suffers the life-based consequence. Or, the analysis shifts and continues ad astra.

Dream analysis is the analysis of dream content against the special knowledge the therapist is assumed to have, of both the symbolic meaning of dreams and John's psyche. For example, if John has a dream about eating an apple in a park, the therapist would examine the various components of the visual details of the dream, (the apple, the setting, the time, etc...) and make a judgement about John's unconscious motivations and unconscious conflicts. There are two major problems with these therapeutic interventions: 1.They are not therapeutic, and 2. behaviorally, they do not change destructive patterns.

Why? Because free association and dream analysis are carried out by a diversity of therapists. Therefore, the *Diagnostic and Statistical Manual of Mental Disorders* (*DSM IV*) notwithstanding, there is a diversity of analytical interpretations of content. Every therapist has his or her own unique cognitive process. Efforts to attain agreement among therapists that incorporate all of their various interpretations into a uniform diagnosis are implausible. Yet, a diversity of clients necessitates a diversity of therapists and therefore a diversity of interpretations. Human beings have both varied cultural biases and unique cognitive processes. Where one person might associate a fork with eating, another may associate a fork with a knife. John's associations do not necessarily mean that the therapist has discovered some unconscious motive or hidden desire. As Freud put it, "Sometimes a cigar is just a cigar." Conversely, John may have so many hidden desires in his unconscious, with so many associations, from so many different experiences, that no one interpretation can be universally correct. If no one interpretation is ever correct, how is John to achieve any internal harmony or feel certain of the psychological ground upon which he stands?

Frequently, psychology has been used to argue against philosophy. For example, John Stuart Mill's *On Liberty* states that human beings have a fundamentally positive community motive. That is, a group will generally act in its own best interests. In psychodynamic theory, there is no communal good will; groups do not always act in their own best interest. John's internal split is externalized, as is everyone else's in the group. Consequently, the group must be in conflict. For philosophical counselling to work, philosophy must be able to hold its own against psychodynamic theory or any other psychological theory or argument. Moreover, philosophical counselling must forge a link between the science of psychology and 2000 years of philosophical thought.

The primary purpose of psychodynamic therapy is the same as that of philosophical counselling, or of all therapies: to relieve human suffering. Yet psychodynamic therapies applied have led to a majority of psychiatrists embracing a chemical/biological view of mental/emotional imbalance. In other words, psychodynamic theories are quantitative failures. Why? Because the focus of psychodynamic therapy is the unconscious motive: John is seen, divided, separated, sectioned, and dissected, into a series of desires, impulses, and forces. Desires are divided into conscious and unconscious desires. Conscious impulses occupy conscious thought, belief, and action. Unconscious impulses influence behavior irrationally. Inexplicable behaviors are excused or defended with various rationalizations. It is as if John is a mechanism. When one piston of his psyche is repressed, another piston forces upwards into consciousness. John is a series of desires and responses, that, when in conflict, result in an exponentially larger number of impulsive behaviors. John is unaware of his unconscious chauffeur. He is driven, "around the bend," out of consciousness, and therefore out of control. For example, John wakes up; the conflicts begin between his id, ego, and super ego. John, unified, has no existence. He is simply riding with the more demanding portion of his mind. John, unified, is not the ruler, and John, divided, becomes his own victim.

If the goal of a psychologist is to relieve John's suffering, then John must be empowered to make decisions in keeping with his conscience. John must be able to make ethical decisions in order to be at peace. When the split between conscious and unconscious mind is presumed present, then John's ethical decision making process disintegrates. Within John, an 'us/them dichotomy' is created. But John is both 'us' and 'them'! The responsibility for behavior and motivation is placed upon John's unconscious mind, or parts thereof, and the forces competing for dominance within John. The therapist, who is also at the mercy of his own unconscious, attempts to decipher the 'real' dynamic of John's unconscious and correct John's conscious interpretations of his entire dynamic. John is at war with himself. The therapist can be presumed to have some conflicts, in spite of his enlightened state. The question arises, Who is driving whom, to what, where, and for what end?

Also how does John ever know that the actions he takes are exclusively his own and thus a cornerstone of his identity and that he is not overly influenced by his therapist? It seems as if, in the psychodynamic model, John must forever be in conflict and the therapist forever employed. John has limited responsibility for his emotions, actions, or decisions. The battle of id, ego, and super ego continues as one portion or another of the subconscious waxes and wanes in strength. John, as a whole, has had little to do with any final decision in his life. John is unaware of his entire internal dynamic. He cannot be held responsible for his ego's behavior alone. Responsibility necessitates awareness of the entire ball of forces that comprise John. One cannot ask John to make a decision to get out of bed if John does not participate in the decision making process, let alone be conscious that a decision has been made. In the psychodynamic perspective, John has few decisions to make until he is totally aware. So John cannot take part in his decision making process; John cannot make an ethical decision. Without an awareness of his unconscious, which is by definition impossible, John is morally paralyzed. How is this moral paralysis connected to John's emotional state, and where does philosophical counselling come in?

Ethics is a branch of philosophy. There are four considerations that must be regarded when an ethical decision is made. The skills required for ethical decision making are:

1. The ability to use logic to work through a dilemma,
2. An awareness of how decisions influence self,
3. An awareness of how decisions influence others, and
4. The ability to maintain a compassionate disposition.

Within the psychodynamic model, John cannot make ethical decisions. This does not mean that John does not use the skills of ethical decision making individually, or in different combinations, but for an ethical decision to take place each of the four skills must be operative. Philosophical counselling allows the teaching of the ethical decision making process to be a part of therapy. But how does the application of ethics connect to John's emotional state?

Making good ethical decisions through Philosophical Counselling involves integrating the elements of ethical decisions into everyday life. The existence or awareness of an unconscious is no longer necessary for a client to function in an emotionally healthy state. The responsibility for decisions rests with John, who, by the process of ethical decision making, necessarily becomes aware of the various emotional and external consequences and forces that will affect all concerned parties. John may not accept this responsibility, but it is his none the less.

If John is not a stimulus/response mechanism dominated by unconscious forces, then what is he? He is no longer a passive receiver of unknown information. He is no longer at war with himself. He is his own self-expert. He is active and participates in his interactions with both internal and external reality. He initiates and 'creates' his own reality on a daily basis. He consciously applies the principles of ethical decision making processes to the dilemmas of his life. The main concern of the counsellor is to help John clarify and express his concept of the problem. John need not have formal reasoning skills. Therefore, the counsellor may initially function as a learning resource, but eventually should attempt to transfer the reasoning skills to John. John may not apply reasoning to his emotions at first. Consequently, the counsellor must act as an emotional mirror, to help John understand the causes and results of his emotions. Another goal of the philosophical counsellor is to help John apply his own reasoning skills to his emotional dynamic. John can then becomes internally unified and independent. Philosophical counselling teaches these and other cognitive competencies.

Though the goals of psychodynamic counselling and philosophical counselling are the same, to alleviate human suffering, the methodologies are very different. Psychodynamic therapists interpret John's information, assuming that John himself does not know the true meaning of his own feelings or thoughts. The philosophical counsellor examines John's logical processes and functions as a passive facilitator of changes within John, such that he becomes a more cognitively effective and emotionally stable individual.

Philosophical counselling methodology distances the counsellor from the therapeutic process in a unique way. Because the philosophical counsellor functions as a facilitator of change, and not as a cause of change, the responsibility for growth and development is placed upon John. The responsibility of the counsellor, in this relationship, is to guide. Because the philosophical counsellor can claim a special knowledge in philosophy and does not claim special knowledge of John's secret thought process, a philosophical counsellor is an expert in ideas that can be applied to John's life, but he is not an expert in John's life itself. Only John is an expert in his own life. The Philosophical Counsellor does not teach his own philosophical bias or ethics, rather he teaches John to think for himself using sound reasoning and ethical processes. "Reason for a client, and solve his problem for a day. Teach a client to reason, and solve his problems for a lifetime."

For the philosophical counsellor, John is not a stimulus response engine. John is an aware consciousness who controls his interactions with his external reality. For John to control his interactions with his external reality, he must be aware of the reality and the mutual affects of his actions upon that reality.

However, controlling one's actions does not necessitate responsibility. When John is faced with a choice about anything, he must make a decision. For example, John wakes up and knows he must attend an important business meeting. John is still tired and wants to sleep, but he knows that his meeting may decide the future of his career. John has three options: to go back to sleep, to get up and attend the meeting, or to remain passive. No matter what John decides to do, he will alter his reality in some way. In this case John's work situation and the relationships associated with it are affected. John cannot avoid affecting a change in his environment, therefore John cannot avoid being responsible for his decisions. This does not mean that John always accepts his responsibility, but the responsibility is always there, and inevitably, John must live with the consequences of his actions. The model referred to in the above paragraph is called the Triacta Model of Cause and Effect in the Human Psyche. The psyche is composed of awareness, responsibility, and compassionate consideration of the effects of decisions made on the external reality.

When the philosophical counsellor, in his practice, adopts the Triacta Model three things must happen to/for John. The therapy must be John-centered. If John is presumed to be an aware being and the counsellor is to assist John, then the counsellor must assume that John has special knowledge of himself that the counsellor does not have. John is responsible for maintaining and increasing his autonomy. John must learn to be competent in his logical processes and learn to affect the changes in his life that he wishes.

When human beings are treated as engines, the process is essentially dehumanizing. In contemporary society, especially one in which computers are beginning to think and animals are learning to communicate using sign language, human beings stand out amongst other species less and less. With the unique ability to reason and project the possible consequences of reasoned actions into external reality, a new potential for humanity emerges. This person is an active and responsible participant in his society and can contribute to that society in a positive fashion. Adherence to psychodynamic therapies does not produce the kind of individual that the complexities of 'The global village' needs.

The mere study of philosophy alone, unapplied to daily life does not produce change. Psychodynamic theories and philosophy must integrate. Philosophical counselling can be the bridge between the new art/science of psychology and 3000 years of condensed philosophical brilliance and wisdom. Yet, when we accept and explore the responsibility that integrated knowledge offers, dehumanization and codependency diminish and fall away. New possibilities, dimensions and direction open for us all.

Chapter 6

Nietzsche and the Unconscious

David O'Donaghue

So in the soul of man there lies one insular Tahiti, full of peace and joy, but
encompassed by all the horrors of the half known life. God keep thee!
Push not off from that isle, thou canst never return!
—Herman Melville, *Moby Dick*

We are none of us that which we appear to be from the states for which alone
we have consciousness and words...we misread ourselves in this apparently
most clear script of our selves. And yet this opinion of ourselves...the so-called
"I," continues to collaborate on our character and fate.
—Friedrich Nietzsche, *Daybreak*

Sigmund Freud considered the ideas of the wandering, iterant, sometimes mad philosopher, Friedrich Nietzsche (1844-1900) as "too rich" for
him and declared that he had renounced the study of philosophy because
its abstractness was unpleasant to him.[1] Yet he wrote in *The History of Psychoanalysis*:

> In later years I have denied myself the very great pleasure of reading the
> works of Nietzsche, with the deliberate object of not being hampered
> in working out the impressions received in psychoanalysis by any sort
> of anticipatory ideas. I had therefore to be prepared—and I am so,
> gladly—to forgo all the claims to a priority in the instances in which
> laborious psychoanalytic investigation can merely confirm the truths
> which the philosopher recognized by intuition.[2]

We may smile at the term, "laborious psychoanalytic investigation," seeing
it as Freud's valiant but doomed attempt at creating a scientific credibility
for the insights gleaned from the methods of psychoanalysis. He needed
to distance himself from Nietzsche because he was aware of the striking

similarity of the description of human functioning by the intuitions of this philosopher and his own. As Harold Bloom has pointed out, there is likely to have been an "anxiety of influence" in Freud that required his overt disassociation with the titanic Nietzsche, in order for him to blaze his own theories of the unconscious. But, as Bloom goes on to say, the influence of the great predecessor brought both anxiety and security.[3] This chapter will describe how many of the dynamics of the unconscious were revealed in the writings of Nietzsche, making the late nineteenth century European intellectual soil ripe for the psychoanalytic harvest of Freud, Adler and Jung.

Nietzsche's philosophical position, developed in his productive years between 1871 and 1888, was built upon aphorisms. He chose not to write in the manner of the systematic philosophers (like Hegel) because he recognized the deception within metaphysical grand narratives in the face of the ever-changing non-hierarchical living world. For Nietzsche, aphorism allowed for fragments of insights to emerge without the accompanying demand of an overall logical structure. Despite various shifts of emphasis throughout his many texts, Nietzsche, by and large, maintained some consistent views of the nature of human functioning. Human beings, according to Nietzsche are born with a host of instincts and drives linking them more to the animal kingdom and nature than to human culture. These drives seek expression in an outward and immediate manner but are curtailed by the restraining forms of human culture into which one is born. "All instincts," Nietzsche wrote in *The Genealogy of Morals*, "which do not find a vent without *turn inwards*—this is what I mean by the growing 'internalization' of man: consequently we have the first growth in man of what subsequently was called soul."[4] The instincts of the free and wild human animal became turned backwards "against man himself." This was the origin of bad conscience, about which we will have more to say later. Nietzsche's words are too eloquent to paraphrase:

> It was man who, lacking external enemies and obstacles, and imprisoned as he was in the oppressive narrowness and monotony of custom, in his own impatience lacerated, persecuted, gnawed, frightened, and ill-treated himself; it was this animal in the hands of the tamer which beat itself against the bars of its cage, it was this being who, pinning and yearning for that desert home of which it had been deprived, was compelled to create out of its own self an adventure, a torture-chamber, a hazardous and perilous desert; it was this fool, this homesick and desperate prisoner, who invented the 'bad conscience.'[5]

This is the disease that Nietzsche felt has infected all of mankind, causing self-inflicted suffering and torture. However, it is a malady which Nietzsche thought could be cured. He saw the cure as one that could be undertaken by a very few who separate themselves from the herd and are able to tolerate an arduous and hazardous journey to self-overcoming. We will now look at the details of this diagnosis and its treatment.

Section I: The Drives

Nietzsche first mentioned the drives in "On Moods," by saying, "How often the will sleeps and only the drives and inclinations are awake!"[6] As a sort of twist on Plato's *Republic,* he pictured the psyche as a political realm where various factions vie for power. The statement he made about Wagner in *Richard Wagner in Bayreuth* can perhaps be applied to the genius in all of us:

> Each of his drives strove into the immeasurable, and each of his talents —from joy in its own existence—wanted to tear itself away from the others to attain its own satisfaction; the greater their abundance, the greater was the tumult and the greater their hostility when they cross one another.[7]

Talent, for Nietzsche, was vampirelike in that it sought to suck the energies from the other drives and endangered the individual with becoming possessed by only one tyrannical drive. This is very similar to Jung's notion of archetypal possession, when the ego becomes inflated with the power of the archetype and loses its own grounding. Nietzsche conceived of an entire host of drives, all struggling to dominate an individual. Each drive demands actions appropriate to its particular satisfaction. These drives include the scientific drive, the mythological drive, the political drive, the art drive, the drive for knowledge and even the seasonal spring drive. In his early writing Nietzsche disagreed with Schopenhauer that the drives could not be known directly but only through their representations. In the beginning he maintained that the entire *Triebleben*, drive-life, the play of affect, sensations and acts of will, could be known by us. But, by the time of *Daybreak* (1880) he saw that the drives largely function unconsciously. He writes in that work, "nothing can be more incomplete than one's image of the totality of drives that constitute one's being."[8]

One of the more interesting drives, the Dionysian, was articulated in Nietzsche's first work, *The Birth of Tragedy (1871)*. This drive seeks to nullify the *principium individuationis* by breaking down the personal boundaries between the self and the world and between individuals. The drive seeks a sort of particiaption mystique of merged identity with one's surroundings and the group. C.G. Jung would later explore this drive as part of the collective archetypal inheritance. Nietzsche's multiple and polyphonic drives resemble more the archetypal theories of Jung and James Hillman than the dual drive theory of Freud.

In *Composing the Soul*, an excellent book on Nietzsche's psychology, Gram Parkes describes how Nietzsche imagined the passions as animals within the soul, animate "beings" that must be feed, nurtured and eventually domesticated and trained.[9] Nietzsche fought the late nineteenth century Christian European tendency to distrust and squelch the instinctual life of human beings in the name of higher culture, seeing the need to coordinate and work with the drives. He did not wish to silence them nor to take away their power, but he did recognize that unbridled instincts do not serve the development of the individual. According to Parkes, he advocated a sort of training program for the wild beasts of the psyche so that they could be coordinated under a loyalty to a higher self.[10] He wrote in *The Wanderer and His Shadow*:

> All our drives must first become more anxious and mistrustful, then gradually acquire more reason and honesty, becoming more clear-sighted and thereby increasingly losing the grounds for mistrust of each other. In this way, greater, more fundamental joyfulness can arise.[11]

A very important aspect of Nietzsche is his emphasis on joy on attaining a coordination of the drives and in self-overcoming. He strongly rejected an attitude of Christian asceticism in handling the drives and, though he saw that self-overcoming is likely to involve suffering and hard work, it is not to be a mortification of the body or a mutilation of the instincts. He described this coordination more like a dance.

> There arises the danger of a feeble vacillation back and forth between different drives. A metaphor may help to suggest how this difficulty might be resolved: one must remember that the dance is not the same as a languid reeling back and forth between different drives. High

culture will resemble a daring dance: which is why one needs a great deal of suppleness and strength.[12]

The dance is an apt metaphor because it can allow for instinctual expression and joy within a form and a discipline. It can be further seen as an art form and can thus enrich and further higher culture.

Post-modernists often present Nietzsche as advocating a radical decentralizing of the self, reading him as challenging the notion of the necessity of unity in personal identity. In aphorism 105 of *Daybreak*, Nietzsche took up the question of the substantiality of the ego versus the *Schein-Ego*, the seeming-ego, created through an assortment of others' thoughts and opinions. Most people, he wrote,

> do nothing for their ego but only for the phantom of their ego that has been formed in the heads of those around them and communicated back to them—a result of which everybody lives in a midst of impersonal, semipersonal opinions and arbitrary and, as it were, poetical evaluations, each one always in the head of the other, and that head in turn in other heads: a wonderful world of phantasms, that yet manages to appear so sober![13]

We presume that our ego is in control of our lives and that we are rationally combating and controlling our drives in each moment. But Nietzsche challenges this by asserting that our so-called ego control is just the result of another drive.

> That one wants to combat the violence of a drive at all is not within our power, neither the choice of method nor whether that method will succeed. Rather, in this whole process our intellect is clearly just the blind tool of another drive that is a rival of the one that is torturing us by its violence: whether it be the drive for peace and quiet, of fear of disgrace and other evil consequences, or love. So while "we" think we are complaining about the violence of a drive, it is basically one drive that is complaining about another.[14]

It would be safe to say that Nietzsche believed we never can have the experience of being outside of our drives, that the drives are the very constitutive elements of what we experience as the "I." Most drive activity functions well below the threshold of consciousness, giving the illusion, for the most part, of a stable personal identity with consistent goals and values. During times of stress, however, when the ego-drive loses some of its control, we become aware of the diversity of our inner aspects in various symptoms and projections.

Nietzsche revealed a sort of presumption of consciousness when he writes "that all our so-called consciousness is a more or less fantastic commentary on an unknown, perhaps unknowable, but felt text."[15] Nietzsche was no doubt referring to Kant's declaration that the self, as numenal, cannot be known as it is in itself, but can only be known from the phenomena of its manifestations. These effects of the self are mistakenly assumed to be elements of its inherent nature, when they are more likely to be passing moods, thoughts, sensations and attitudes that do not adhere to anything substantial. "The ego is a plurality of person-like forces, of which now this one not that one stands in the foreground as the ego and regards the others as a subject regards an influential and determining external world."[16] Nietzsche conceived of the ego not as an island of rational reality testing that defends itself against the unconscious drives, but as itself constituted of the very drives that make up the unconscious. We are at one time identified and convinced by one drive and at another time by quite another drive. We subsume these drives under the general category of the "I" but they are, in fact, free of any ontological identity with whom we truly are. When one drive is in ascendance, the others are viewed as antagonistic and "not-me" and therefore are projected out on others or defended against. But in another moment that alienated drive might be the new identity of the "I" and the former identification is thrust out and seen as other. The effects of this model of the psyche can create an ontological insecurity, undermining any presumptions to grounding in a substantial self-identity. On the positive side, however, through resisting the tendency to look at the drives as being in opposition to the ego, one can liberate intense creative energy by exploring new aspects of drives as they expand and assist the ego in the art of living.

Nietzsche maintained that our conscious life is a product of deep-level fantasy determined by the current drive that is calling the shots. For example, when we are in the heroic drive, the world and ourselves become wrapped up in projects of challenges and battles. When the erotic drive dominates, the world and ourselves coordinate to build scenes of yearning and passionate release. Our drives act upon our perceptions of the world, causing us to selectively and artistically attend to those aspects in accord with the drive energy of that particular moment. Our beliefs and attitudes about ourselves and others become determined as drive-derivatives. This is the basis for Nietzsche's famous perspectivism—the replacement of an absolute standard for truth and values with a recognition of the inescapable subjective viewpoint of all value statements and metaphysical claims. Nietzsche declares that to experience is to fabricate.[17] But this fabrication is not ego-driven, but rather the result of the drives or instincts speaking through us. It is only in the false presumptions of the ego that "we" are the authors of these fabrications.

> We are buds on a single tree—what we do we know about what we can become of us from the interests of the tree!...Stop feeling oneself as the fantastic ego! Learn gradually to jettison the supposed individual! Discover the errors of the ego! Realize that egoism is an error...Get beyond "me" and "you"! Experience cosmically...What is needed is practice in seeing with other eyes: practice in seeing apart from human relations, and thus seeing objectively! To cure this enormous delusion of human beings.[18]

We are touching here on what I think will lead us directly into the nature of the *Ubermensch* and what Nietzsche meant by the need for mankind to surpass and overcome what it is to be human. With the concepts of the *Ubermensch* and the Eternal Return, Nietzsche distinguished himself from the camp of existential humanists in which we often find him, and finds more compatibility with the transpersonal psychologists. We will explore this distinction further in our conclusions.

So we can begin to understand the nature of Nietzsche's conceptualization of the unconscious as the repository for all human drives that may be aroused and awakened in the daily life of the individual. These drives are multiply determined by biological and archaic forces, so that the history of mankind can be read through their expression.[19] Some drives may never be expressed, since there may not be opportunities or triggers in the external life of the individual. Or the current identified ego (remember, also drive-based) may judge the nature of an unconscious pressing drive to be unacceptable to it and therefore will repress it. The energy from this drive, according to Nietzsche, will be turned against the individual, creating a vice-like torture of forced asceticism. All drives, in their claims to an absolute perspective, are errors. But, if no drive claims exclusive rights to an ego-identity then other drives can establish a sort of check and balance dynamic that prevents any tyranny among the drives and establishes a sort of inner harmony. As he wrote in his essay, *On Truth*: "The more individuals one has in oneself, the greater the prospect will be of one's discovering a truth—then the struggle is within him."[20] And later in the essay he described his advice to us as, "denying ourselves as individuals, looking into the world through as many eyes as possible, living in drives and activities in order to make ourselves eyes for that, giving oneself over to life from time to time so that one can later rest one's eyes on it, entertaining the drives as the foundation of all knowledge."[21] This sounds like a sort of abandonment to the instincts but actually the condition is one of discipline and order as we will see in section III. Parkes describes this condition as holding ourselves between and among the drives, while understanding ourselves as the play of drives themselves.[22]

For Nietzsche, rational thinking was a sort of law court where different drive claimants are brought before intentionality and testify to their relevancy in any particular situation of one's life. The verdict then allowed the winning drive claimant to interpret and color the situation to its own advantage. The fairer the hearing of the multiple claimants, the healthier the individual. In his stress upon the ultimate drive origin of human rationality, Nietzsche went so far as to undermine the presumption that the mind thinks its own thoughts:

> A thought comes when "it" wants and not when "I" will it...It thinks: but that this "it" is precisely the famous old "I" is, to put it mildly, merely an assumption, an assertion, and above all not any kind of "immediate certainty."[23]

Nietzsche indeed brought the death of man, not just the death of God.

Section II: The Sickness

Could consciousness itself be a symptom of this sickness which is man? Nietzsche seemed to think so. Consciousness for Nietzsche, as for Freud, is the region of the ego affected by the external world. Consciousness is always consciousness of a relation of an inferior to a superior. It is an ego in relation to a self. The lesser has the consciousness of a part of the superior which is not conscious. In Hegelian language the slave has consciousness while the master does not. Consciousness therefore is reactive to the influences of the superior force. This is very important for Nietzsche. Consciousness can only become aware of the effects of the superior force and can not itself be a creative force. Gilles Delueze examined Nietzsche's conception of reactivity in *Nietzsche and Philosophy*. He noted that the aim of Nietzsche's philosophical therapeutics is to find a way to shift the basically reactive condition of human consciousness to a more active and creative condition. Deleuze writes,

> The real problem is the discovery of active forces without which the reactions themselves would not be forces. What makes a body superior to all reactions, particularly that reaction of the ego that is called consciousness, is the activity of necessarily unconscious forces.[24]

Nietzsche said the only true science is that of activity and the science of activity is necessarily a science of the unconscious.

Nietzsche explained why consciousness can not be trusted as a means towards a *Wissenschaftslehre*, a science of knowledge, in the eleventh aphorism of *Joyful Wisdom*:

> Consciousness is the last and the latest development of the organic, and consequently also the most unfinished and least powerful of these developments. Innumerable mistakes originate out of consciousness... If the conserving bond of the instincts were not very much more powerful, it would not generally serve as a regulator: by perverse judging and dreaming with open eyes, by superficiality and credulity, in short, just by consciousness, mankind would necessarily have broken down... hitherto our errors alone have been embodied in us, and all our consciousness is relative to errors![25]

This "dreaming with open eyes" refers to Nietzsche's contention that we are constantly projecting our phantasies out onto the world even in full and clear consciousness. He recognized that these phantasies are fabrications and do not lead to foundational truths necessary for science. Also in this passage, Nietzsche recognized that our well-being is more dependent on the "conserving bond of the instincts" than on consciousness. Indeed, consciousness alone would lead humankind quickly into destruction. The birth of consciousness was brought about through the separation of human beings from the free expression of their instinctual lives. The intervening factor is culture. Because of culture, Nietzsche wrote in *The Antichrist*, "man is the most unsuccessful animal, the sickliest, the one most dangerously strayed from its instincts."[26] With the repression of the instincts mankind loses its vital and natural connection to life and replaces it with the poor and ineffective substitute of the various illusions of culture, "the greatest and most disasterous maladies, of which humanity has not to this day been cured."[27] In quite striking opposition to Hegel, Nietzsche did not see that the victory of Spirit through ever expanding cultural forms will herald a golden age for human beings. Rather,

> "Spirit" is to us precisely a symptom of a relative imperfection of the organism, as an attempting, fumbling, blundering, as a toiling in which an unnecessarily large amount of nervous energy is expended —we deny that anything can be made perfect so long as it is still made conscious.[28]

Obviously Nietzsche's therapeutics were not going to promote the conscious appropriation and processing of unconscious material as in Freud and Jung, His was a much more radical approach; that of respecting and feeding the unconscious instincts without translating them into conscious forms.

In the *Genealogy of Morals*, Nietzsche extended the active/reactive intrapsychic model of consciousness into the social world. He distinguished between the reactive, or slave morality, based on negation and *ressentiment* versus the master morality of the noble affirmation of power. Nietzsche traced the source of western morality to the attitudes of conquered people to their superiors. The will of the subjugated people becomes restrained by the conquerors. This will becomes reactive, in that it must react to the positive assertion of the superior group. *Ressentiment* is defined by Staten as,

> the reactive exercise of will, the will that would rather will nothingness than not will, the will of a subject who is powerless to do anything against that which makes him or her suffer and who therefore must "compensate" with an "imaginary vengence," a vengence in the depths of his inferiority, by redefining helpless passivity as a free exercise of the will.[29]

The conquerers in the assertion of their personal will are seen as evil while the victims, suppressing their will are viewed as good. This absolute reversal of the natural feeling of goodness in the expression of the will causes great harm to the psyche of the individual.

> All instincts that do not discharge themselves toward the outside turn inward—this is what I call the internalization of the human being: thus it was that the human being first developed what later came to be called the "soul." This entire inner world, originally as thin as if it were streched between two membranes, extended and expanded and acquired depth, breadth, and height as outward discharge was inhibited.[30]

Nietzsche attributed the entire internalization of consciousness to this primal repression of the instincts. He called this the intellectualization of the instincts and sees it as the basis for the forms of culture and religion. The "soul" is an artifact of this repression and internalization process. It appears from this that Nietzsche would abhor any psychology that attempted to fathom the inner core of a person. Soul is merely the result of repressed drives. This is why he could say of the Greeks:

> Oh, those Greeks! They knew how to live. What is required for that is to stop courageously at the surface, the fold, the skin, to adore appearance, to believe in forms, tones, words, in the whole Olympus of appearance. Those Greeks were superficial—out of profundity.[31]

It is an interesting twist that this "father of depth psychology" is here advocating our remaining at the surface amid the appearances and not digging for soul. There does seem to be a paradox here between the Nietzsche that claimed that we are hidden to ouselves and the Nietzsche that was content with appearances. Perhaps we can resolve this further along in our investigation.

Ressentiment, with its reversal of values and its thirst for revenge was characterized by Nietzsche in the figure of the Jewish Priest who makes a virture of a necessity. The impotence of the subjugated people is praised as the high value (humility and peacefulness) while the strong are condemned. According to Nietzsche, "Priests are the most evil enemies to have, because they are the most impotent. It is their impotence which makes their hate so violent and sinister, so cerebral and poisonous. The greatest haters in history —but also the most intellegent haters—have been priests."[32] A transition occurs as the human animal forces more and more of its instinctual energies underground, maintaining an outward aspect of cooperative geniality, while inwardly turning the more violent drives towards the oppressor, the individual himself. Nietzsche noted that the change in inner dynamics is reflected in the emergence of the Christian priest, who no longer calls out for vengeance against an external enemy, but places the source and responsibility for suffering within the individual himself. Now redemption can only come through suffering, so the priest inflicts the wound (of original sin) only to be in control of the only cure (renunciation of the ego and submission to the Church). This interiorization of guilt reduces the human animal to pure reactivity so that the active and creative life-forces wither away, or worse, continue to exert a destructive and torturous influence on the individual. Nietzsche considered this to be the condition of the overwhelming majority in Western Europe in the late nineteenth century.

Out of this condition developed the ascetic ideal. Nietzsche was both repulsed and drawn to the ascetic character. He found the renunciation of the instincts in the ascetic priest to be a perversion of the life force, but at the same time, he recognized that it was through a form of asceticism that the human animal can rise above the "human, all too human" and rise to the status of the *Ubermensch*. Staten articulates the distinction between the asceticism of the priest and that of a figure like Zarathustra when he writes, "Against a will turned toward the past, raging against its fixity, avenging itself by making others suffer, Nietzsche describes 'a will turned toward the future, a will that makes itself suffer in order constantly to remake itself.'"[33] The key here is that the will takes on suffering in order to transform itself. But why must the will suffer? Because it is full of errors and delusions.

We now return to Nietzsche's assessment that life is generally made up of the projections of our own fabrication. Life is utterly appearance, without any substance underneath. "We hide ourselves in life, in its appearance, its falsity, its superficiality, in its radiant deception."[34] Nietzsche used the metaphor, *vita femina*, 'life is a woman,' to describe both its allusiveness and its fertility. Blondel explains Nietzsche's choice of metaphor as follows:

This ontology speaks of being as a woman who has no being, as appearance and disguise, as the illusion and mystery of a woman who has no nature, who is pure spectacle—in a woman who, "when she gives herself, gives herself as spectacle...Appearance and appearing are the only reality of the vita femina...The notion of a truth beyond appearance, underneath or behind the veil, is rendered null and void. It is certainly true that life deceives us with her ambiguous apparitions; but she deceives us not because she conceals an essence or a reality beneath appearance, but because she has no essence and would only make us think that she does. Her 'essence' is to appear."[35]

We need to set aside Nietzsche's attitude toward women in examining the sense of this metaphor. He was trying to emphasize that life holds out a promise in its appearances, not a promise as to a goal but rather towards a possiblity. This brings out the second aspect of the metaphor. Though bad conscience is a sickness, it is like a morning sickness, in that it signals a pregnancy. Nietzsche said that it is the womb of all ideal and imaginative phenomena.[36] This pregnancy fortells of the creative opportunity when, liberating oneself from the conditioning of the bad conscience, one can move ahead into new ways of living. In realizing that all reality is a fabrication then one can do as Goethe advised and truly "create oneself."

Of course this move toward self-creation runs on the very precarious edge of the abyss of nihilism. In recognition that there are no grounds to values and metaphysical and religious claims, one risks falling into the deep depression of finding no value or purpose in life, so that everything is drained of meaning and significance. This was a real threat to Nietzsche in his life, as it was for Dostoevski and other existentialists. How do we live in a world that we see as built upon the values imposed by motives of power and control that have no true basis? Life shows itself to be an arena of manipulation and seduction, full of untruths and errors, some devised intentionally to control and suppress, others unconsciously accepted by the herd and affirmed as real. Nihilism is seen by many contemporary thinkers as the major malady of this last century.[37] Sass describes that nihilism can be experienced in two ways:

> as a vertiginous sense of power inherent in seeing reality as but a fig-
> ment of one's own, all powerful self; or as a despairing recognition
> of the ultimate meaninglessness and absurdity of the human world,
> a succumbing to what Nietzsche called "the great blood-sucker, the
> spider skepticism."[38]

Sass explains in *Madness and Modernism* that Nietzsche, early on in his first work, *The Birth of Tragedy*, recognized that the means by which we can accept and embrace this world devoid of its inherent values and mean-ing is through acknowledging the Dionysian drive within us. Dionysius is the Greek God of wine, inebriation, madness, and most importantly the dissolution of personal boundaries in the experience of the ever-flowing changable state of existence in which nothing remains the same and there is no firm ground that remains constant. This condition is described well by Hegel in the *Phenomenology of Spirit*: "The True is thus the Bacchanalian revel in which no member is not drunk; yet because each member collapses as soon as he drops out, the revel is just as much transparent and simple repose."[39] Through the god Dionysius the ancient Greeks recognized the ultimate importance of submitting to the multiplicity of manifestions of life through the drives and letting go of the need to control or contain them. But the Greeks also paired the god Dionysius with Apollo, the god of order and balance, and thus acknowledged that a balance of power must abide in the psyche between the powers of dissolution and abandon and the poweres of form and structure. Our next section will explore how Nietzsche conceived of this balance as a type of cure for the sickness of modern humanity.

Section III: The Cure

Nietzsche did see a way through the "death of God" and the transvaluation of all values. Once individuals are able to separate themselves from all prior metaphysics and moral ideas, they are capable of establishing a set of values and purposes that reflect their own unique being. But this process involves crossing the abyss of nihilism, in which everything is destroyed and there is no firm ground underneath one's feet. The experience of Nihilism can either be experienced with despair or with elation depending upon whether the individual can see it as an opportunity for personal creation. Since no "self" is inherently within the person to be discovered and then submitted to, the individual must build up a self *ex nihilo*. This section will explore how one is to do this in a Nietzschean fashion utilizing the various drive energies of the unconscious.

As shown earlier, Nietzsche maintained that there is a multitude of unconscious drives within us. These cannot be reduced to the sexual or aggressive and also do not necessarily work against the fashioning process of the self. In fact, Nietzsche maintained that it is important to harvest the passion and energies from the various drives in order to feel the vitality and creative forces in life. This is why he condemned the Christian religion for curtailing the life energies. However, a life that is tossed from drive to drive in a haphazard manner is not an elevated life, but one in which the person is at the mercy of their instincts. He or she is nothing more than an animal. And, though Nietzsche was quick to recognize that we are in most ways closely akin to the animal kingdom and therefore should not push away these animal instincts, he also envisions the human being as capable of surpassing the merely animal. This is not done, however, through, controlling the instincts through reason. Nietzsche criticized Socrates for over-intellectualizing life by believing the highest form of life was attained through thinking alone, that his diamon merely restricted him from acting rather than affirming authentic action itself. Nietzsche saw the necessity and advantage of the struggle between the instincts for domination in the individual. He wanted to keep the opponents strong and observes along with Heraclitus that "strife is the mother of all things." It is through this vigor, if the individual can tolerate it, that truly novel solutions arise. This can give birth to genius, as he showed through the examples of Goethe and Wagner.

The question, then, is how does one live with the multiplicity of drives, each seeking its own sole domination of the psyche? Walter Kaufman, in his classic work, *Nietzsche: Philosopher, Psychologist, Antichrist*, suggests how Nietzsche envisioned the governance but not suppression of the instinctual life. He notes that Nietzsche is one of the first thinkers to employ the word *sublimieren,* sublimation, in his work and that he anticipates Freud by over twenty years in the employment of this term to describe a means of utilizing instinctual energies without repressing them. In *The Will to Power*, Nietzsche used the term sublimation to describe how the sexual impulse could be channeled into creative spiritual activity instead of being fulfilled directly. He maintained that all self-mastery involved the transformation of the baser instincts into their more moderate and creative expressions in art, literature, governance, and other forms of civilization. In a very similiar fashion as Freud, Nietzsche believed that through sublimation the energy of the drive need not be repressed or lost but can find meanful and satisfying expression through productive means. This preservation of the drives is made clear in what Kaufman writes:

> Nietzsche believed that a man without impulses could not do the good or create the beautiful any more than a castrated man could beget children. A man with strong impulses might be evil because he had not yet learned to sublimate his impulses, but if he should ever acquire self-control, he might achieve greatness.

This is why Nietzzsche is often misinterpreted as praising the "blond beast" or the Borgia. Those who criticize do not understand it is not the cruelty that he praises but rather the preservation of instinctual energies that can be utilized for creative, live-affirming projects.

Humans cannot be very creative in chaos. If there is no guiding principle to organize the panoply of drives, then humankind is tossed from one fleeting instinct to another without ever being able to fully harness the instinctual forces for systematic ends. In Nietzsche's efforts to transvaluate all moral systems and in his attack on Christianity he deconstructed external systems of vices and virtues which have long organized human efforts at self improvement and abolishment of the baser drives. His challenge, then, was to find a means by which the multitude of drives could be preserved and yet governed. He found this through the will to power. Nietzsche maintained that all drives, even fully respecting their unique characteristics, are exemplars of one basic meta-drive, the will to power. The will to power is a universal principle that states that everything that is organized even for a moment wills to increase its power in confrontation with its surroundings. Pleasure and pain are epiphenomena in this striving for increased power. In the concept of the will to power, Nietzsche took Spinoza's understanding of *conatus,* as the effort by which everything endeavors to persevere in its own being, and extends it to include a dimension of striving beyond itself. Heidegger picks up on this striving beyond mere existence in his two volume study of Nietzsche when he wrote, "Only a more powerful heightening can counter the tendency to sink back; simply holding onto the position already attained will not do, because the inevitable consequence is ultimately exhaustion... To will is to want to become stronger."[40]

This will to power is the unifying principle to which Nietzsche appealed in his efforts at presenting a non-repressive structure under which the drives can be organized.

> Supposing, finally, that we were to succeed in explaining our entire drive-life as the development and ramification of one basic form of will—namely, of will to power...supposing one could find in this the solution to the problem of procreation and nourishment—it is one problem—one would then have the right to determine all effective force univocally as: will to power. The world seen from within, the world determined and defined in its "intelligible character"—would be precisely "will to power" and nothing besides.[41]

Nietzsche endorsed a type of monism in his more metaphysical moments, in seeing all things as expression of the will to power. He did not think that the reduction of all drives to this basic principle was in any way threatened their uniqueness but rather it preserved their essential dynamic. Some might argue that this flight into metaphysical reductionism is inconsistent with his overall trajectory, but let us for the moment entertain this notion and see if it solves the problem of the chaos of the conflicting drives. Indeed, Nietzsche saw that it is very healthy to have strong, conflicting drives battling for dominance within the psyche. Though this might produce suffering in the individual, it will make the person strong and creative and perhaps capable of producing original work.

Nietzsche maintained that the way to honor the uniqueness of each instinct without reducing it to another is to affirm the will to power of all instincts and allow them to develop momentary order out of the struggle. At any particular time one instinct might find expression while another is reacting to it. Nietzsche seemed to give no credit to a guiding "reality principle" as in Freud, where the instincts are modified through an understanding of the demands of external reality. In fact, Nietzsche disdained the socializing and refining forces of civilization and viewed them as manifestations of the errors of the dominant European Christian culture. This is one reason why his hero, Zarathustra, drew back away from society and sought his truth alone. Nietzsche endorsed no Freudian compromise formation with civilization. He described a compromise formutation, but it was between the personal instincts themselves. Strong instincts are like the best of oligarchical administrations, where the assertion of each individual instinct modifies and shapes the ultimate expression into a creative and novel response that will not overwhelm the person or lead to disaster.

The question is, with the diminishment of the ego and consciousness as the guiding and regulatory mechanism, can one trust that the struggle among the instincts alone will enable individuals to negotiate their lives in productive ways? Isn't giving over control to the instincts a form of regression and even psychosis? Haven't we won the conscious control of our lives over many years of evolution; how could it possibly be progressive to return to an unconscious state of merely living the instinctual? This is not how Nietsche imagined human development. He did not advocate a going back to the animal state but saw "man" as a bridge between the animal and the super-human, the *Ubermensch*. "Man is a rope, tied between beast and overman—a rope over an abyss."[42]

Who is the *Ubermensch*? Kaufmann writes that the *Ubermensch* is the symbol of "the repudiation of any conformity to a single norm: [the] antithesis to mediocrity and stagnation."[43] Man, according to Nietzsche, must be overcome. In our self-overcoming we approach the *Ubermensch*, but the *Ubermensch* is always on the horizon. He represents the anticipated yet seemingly impossible condition of overcoming what we are, the fabrication of our selves out of the deceptions of our culture. This is why we cannot trust our ego or our consciousness because these are merely the result of civilizing and erroneous forces. We must appeal to an unconscious part of ourselves that can organize the drives in a project of self-fashioning, an ever-changing process of the expression of the one will to power that unites them. As Sass writes,

> The Nietzschean hero would be a person who could hold all these rival perspectives in mind while still managing to act—a person who, while somehow remaining aware of the underlying flux in all its un-categorizable immediacy, as well as of the arbitrariness of all schemata or perspectives, could nevertheless, through force of will, draw from himself a firm horizon in which to live.[44]

As opposed to a will turned towards the past, raging against its fixity, resenting others and avenging itself by making others suffer, Nietzsche endorsed a will turned toward the future, a will that makes itself suffer in order constantly to remake itself. This task off self-transcendence means that the self must free itself from the remnants and lies of cultural conditioning and say "no" to the values and metaphysics that one has assumed unreflectively, in order to say "yes" to the self and the cosmos. The image of the *Ubermensch* is a symbol of the capacity possible within us to move from a reactive and resentful state of powerlessness to a condition of self-creation and affirmation of life. Life in its multi-faceted and ever-changing reality stripped of cultural and religious overlays. Nietzsche uses the image of Ariadne as the analog to this condition. She is able to release herself from the longing for the abandoning lover and arch-representative of the conventional "heroic" life, Theseus, in order to embrace Dionysus, the arch-representation of flux and change and organic growth. Socrates, in obeying the command of restraint of his quasi-divine daimon, epitomized for Nietzsche the prevailing use of reason and the life of the mind as a purely inhibitory agent. Dionysus, on the other hand, is characterized by fusion, spontaneity and the liberation of desire.

The fullest manifestation of the affirmation of life is in Nietzsche's admonishment toward *amor fati*, love of one's fate, "that one wants nothing to be different—not forward, not backward, not in all eternity."[45] This is the condition by which we can understand what Nietzsche means by his principle of the eternal return. I interpret this doctrine most usefully as a sort of moral imperative, such as, "I will seek to live my life and accept and embrace all that has happened to me and all that will happen to me, as if it were to reoccur, over and over, for ever." If I could do so, then I could truly say "yes" to my life and live solely from active and not reactive forces. As he writes in *The Gay Science*,

> My doctrine teaches: live in such a way that you must desire to live again, this is your duty—you will live again in any case! He for whom striving procures the highest feeling, let him strive; he for whom repose procures the highest feeling, let him rest; he for whom belonging, following, and obeying procures the highest feeling, let him obey. Provided that he becomes aware of what procures the highest feeling, and that he shrinks back from nothing. Eternity depends upon it![46]

The key here is the highest feeling of completely being the author of one's life. The recognition that all is necessary, not in a fatalistic way, but in total affirmation of past, present and future.

In *Human, All Too Human*, Nietzsche articulated the goal of this form of therapy: "You have it in your power to merge everything you have lived through—attempts, false starts, errors, delusions, passions, your love and your hope—into your goal, with nothing left over."[47] In this way individuals will not play victims and use their perceived powerlessness in the face of forces outside of themselves as excuses for resentment and inaction. Rather all of one's life will be embraced as necessary in fulfilling one's special destiny. Fate and destiny imply a lack of free will and indeed in a number of passages, Nietzsche seemed to echo the following deterministic position:

> To be sure, the acting man is caught in his illusion of volition; if the wheel of the world were to stand still for a moment and an omniscient, calculating mind were there to take advantage of the interruption, he would be able to tell into the farthest future of each being and describe every rut that wheel will fall upon. The acting man's delusion about himself, his assumption that free will exists, is part of the calculable mechanism.[48]

Nietzsche struggled with the same paradox as Spinoza in that both men denied freewill, yet described and defended an optimal way of being in the world. Both philosophers recognize that true freedom can be attained through acknowledging that one's life could be no different than it has been (freedom from guilt, resentment and regret) and that the future will be composed entirely of the elements of the past in a way that must unfold out of necessity (freedom from fear, rumination and anticipation). In truly adopting this attitude, individuals can transcend and overcome their worries and regrets and live in the indeterminate space of the present moment. This would be the final goal of Nietzschean therapy: not to promote and enhance determinate consciousness, but to allow for the guidance of the entirety of one's life—one's drives and failures and aspirations—which is much bigger than mere consciousness. This would create an opening for the possiblity of the *Ubermensch* to arise as a new creation, not based on the conditioning of the past. Zarathustra claimed that the *Ubermensch* was only a possibility on the distant horizon of human kind but I think Nietzsche might agree that we all have a bit of this *Ubermensch* within us and it is waiting in its cave to emerge when the time is ripe.

References

Ackerman, John. *Nietzsche: A Frenzied Look*. Amherst: University of Massachusetts Press, 1990.

Blondel, Eric. "Nietzsche: Life as Metaphor" in Allison, David B., ed. *The New Nietzsche*. Allison, New York: Dell, 1977.

Bloom, Harold. *The Anxiety of Influence*. London: Oxford University Press, 1973.

Deleuze, Gilles. *Nietzsche and Philosophy*. Tomlinson, Hugh, trans. New York: Columbia University Press, 1983.

Freud, Sigmund. *Interpretation of Dreams*. Strachey, James, trans. New York: Avon, 1965.

Hannah, Barbara. *Jung: His life and work*. New York: Putnam and Sons, 1976.

Hegel, G. W. F. *Phenomenology of Spirit*. Miller, A.V., trans. Oxford: Oxford University Press, 1977.

Heidegger, Martin. *Nietzsche*. Krell, David, trans. San Francisco: Harper, 1991.

Jones, Ernest. *The Life and Work of Sigmund Freud*. New York: Basic Books, 1953.

Jung, C. G. *Two Essays in Analytic Psychology*. Hull, R., trans. New York: Meridian, 1956.

_____ *Psychological Types*. Baynes, H.G., trans. Princeton: Princeton University Press, 1974.

Kaufmann, Walter. *Nietzsche: Philosopher, Psychologist, Antichrist*. New York: Vintage, 1968.

Klein, D.B. *The Unconscious: Invention or Discovery?* Santa Monica: Goodyear, 1977.

Klossowski, Pierre. *Nietzsche and the Vicious Circle*. Smith, Daniel, trans. Chicago: University of Chicago Press, 1997.

Levin, David Michael. "Psychopathology in the Epoch of Nihilism" in Levin, David Michael, ed. *Pathologies of the Modern Self*. New York: New York University Press, 1987.

Lowith, Karl. *From Hegel to Nietzsche*. Green, David, trans. New York: Anchor, 1967.

Nietzsche, Friedrich. *Beyond Good and Evil*. Hollingdale, R., trans. London: Penguin, 1976

_____ *The Birth of Tragedy*. Golffing, F., trans. New York: Anchor, 1956.

_____ *The Genealogy of Morals*. Golffing, F., trans. New York: Anchor, 1956.

_____ *Human, all too Human*. Faber, M. and Lehmann, S., trans. Lincoln: University of Nebraska Press, 1986.

_____ *Joyful Wisdom*. Common, T., trans. New York: Frederick Ungar, 1975.

_____ *Philosophy in the Tragic Age of the Greeks*. Cowan, M., trans. Chicago: Henry Regnery, 1962.

_____ *Thus Spoke Zarathustra*. Hollingdale, R., trans. London: Penguin, 1971.

_____ *Unfashionable Observations*. Gray, R., trans. Stanford, Stanford University Press, 1995.

Parkes, Graham. *Composing the Soul: Reaches of Nietzsche's Psychology*. Chicago: University of Chicago Press, 1994.

Roazen, Paul. *Freud and his Followers*. New York: New American Library, 1974.

Robinson, Daniel. *An intellectual History of Psychology*. Madison: University of Wisconsin Press, 1986.

Sass, Louis. *Madness and Modernism*. New York: Basic Books, 1992.

Simmel, Georg. *Schopenhauer and Nietzsche*. Loiskandl, H., trans. Urbana: University of Illinois Press, 1991.

Staten, Henry. *Nietzsche's Voice*. Ithaca: Cornell University Press, 1990.

Yalom, Irvin. *When Nietzsche Wept*. New York: Basic Books, 1992.

Notes

[1] Jones, E. p. 154.

[2] Freud, S. *The History of Psychoanalysis, p. 56.*

[3] Bloom, H. (1966) *The Anxiety of Influence, p. 89.*

[4] *Genealogy of Morals*, p. 176.

[5] Ibid.

[6] *On Moods*

[7] *Wagner in Bayreuth*, p. 3.

[8] *Daybreak,* p. 119

[9] Parkes, G. *Composing the Soul*, p. 283.

[10] Ibid. p. 278.

[11] *Wanderer and His Shadow*, p. 6.

[12] Human, All Too Human, p. 270.

[13] Daybreak, p. 105.

[14] Ibid.

[15] *Daybreak*, p. 119.

[16] *Kritische Studienausgabe*, p. 70.

[17] On Truth and Lie in the Extramoral sense, p. 82.

[18] Kritische Studienausgabe, p. 11.

[19] "I have discovered for myself that ancient humanity and animality, indeed the entire primal age and past of all sentient being continues in me...You still carry around valuations of things originating in the passions and loves of former centuries. In every feeling, in every sense impression there is a piece of [this] ancient love," The Joyful Science, p. 54.

[20] Ibid., p. 119.

[21] Ibid. p. 141.

[22] Parkes. op. cit. p. 305.

[23] Beyond Good and Evil, p. 17.

[24] Deleuze. *Nietzsche and Philosophy*, p. 40-41.

[25] *Joyful Wisdom*, p. 47.

[26] *The Antichrist*, p. 14.

[27] Ibid.

[28] Ibid.

[29] Staten, H. *Nietzsche's Voice*, p. 41.

[30] *Genealogy of Morals*, p. 16.

[31] *Nietzsche Contra Wagner*, Epilogue, p.2.

[32] *Genealogy of Morals*, p. 167

[33] Staten. op. cit. p. 50.

[34] *Ecce Homo*, 78.

[35] Blondel, E. *Nietzsche: Life as Metaphor*, p. 156-7.

[36] *Genealogy of Morals*, 19.

[37] see Sass (1982) and Levin (1987).

[38] Sass, p. 31.

[39] Hegel, *Phenomenology of Spirit*, . 27.

[40] Heidegger, *Nietzsche*, vol. I, p. 60.

[41] *Beyond Good and Evil*, p. 36.

[42] *Thus Spoke Zarathustra*, p.3.

[43] Kaufmann, p. 309.

[44] Sass, p. 153.

[45] *Ecce Homo*, sec. II:10.

[46] *The Gay Science,* sec. 126.

[47] *Human, All Too Human*, sec. 292.

[48] Ibid, sec. 106.

Chapter 7

Addressing the Crisis of Meaning: Towards a 'Psychotheological' Reading of the Unconscious

Fiona Jenkins

I love those who do not know how to live,
except by going under, for they are those who cross over…
—Nietzsche, Zarathustra's Prologue #4

Introduction

Philosophical counsellors have often staked their claim to a difference from conventional psychotherapy in terms of their capacity to address crises of meaning—disorders of mind or spirit irreducible to pathological factors and requiring a specifically philosophical form of engagement. Provisionally accepting this self-definition, we might ask, what could be the importance of taking account of the unconscious when addressing a crisis of *meaning*?

Since the notion of the unconscious is often understood to refer to a site in the person of merely pathological pressures, many philosophical counsellors consider the unconscious to lie outside the provenance of their expertise (if they believe in its existence at all). If, however, the unconscious is somehow bound up with what we refer to as the sense of there being or not being 'meaning' (hence if 'meaningfulness' is not limited to what can be grasped consciously and by cognitive means) then the unconscious would be something that must be addressed just in so far as the question—or crisis—of meaning is being addressed. In addressing such a crisis of meaning, indeed, it seems that something which is and must remain *enigmatic* is being evoked. If it therefore appears unlikely that an answer to the sense of life's meaninglessness can come through any simple formula or practice, then we are lead to consider ways of approaching this problem that are neither prescriptive nor strictly a matter for a cognitive therapy. Our question about the importance of the unconscious might then become: How can philosophy engage the sense of enigma that attaches to the problem of what the sources of a sense of meaning (or of 'proper' meaninglessness) might be? And what would lead us to think that the question of meaning touches on something that eludes the conscious self and its capacity to reason or otherwise take full responsibility for itself?

What Is The Meaning Of A Crisis Of Meaning?

The 'crisis of meaning' is often linked in a rather casual but nonetheless significant way with the crisis Nietzsche spoke of when, in the persona of a madman, he announced the death of God. The era of nihilism ushered in by this event is one which for Nietzsche has an enigmatic aspect, bound up with a fundamental equivocality. Nihilism takes an 'active' and a 'reactive' form. In the former case it is the sign of an "increased power" of the spirit, whereas in the latter it signals a decline and a recession of these powers.[1] But of what power does Nietzsche speak? Active nihilism is perhaps the ability to confront the meaningless vista of existence after the death of God has deprived us of an ultimate horizon and to do so without despair. Passive nihilism, meanwhile, gives into what remains an unconscious desire to re-institute an ultimate source of authority. He writes in a note dated 1887:

> The nihilistic question 'for what?' is rooted in the old habit of suppos-ing that the goal must be put up, given, demanded *from outside*—by some *superhuman authority*. Having unlearned faith in that, one still follows the old habit and seeks *another* authority that can *speak un-conditionally* and *command* goals and tasks. The authority of *conscience* now steps up front (the more emancipated one is from theology, the more imperativistic morality becomes) to compensate for the loss of a *personal* authority. Or the authority of *reason*. Or the *social instinct* (the herd). Or *history* with an immanent spirit and goal within, so one can entrust oneself to it. One wants to get around the will, the willing of a goal, the risk of positing a goal *for oneself*; one wants to rid oneself of the responsibility (one would accept fatalism). Finally, *happiness*—and with a touch of Tartuffe, the *happiness of the greatest number*.[2]

There is much for a philosophical counsellor to consider in this passage as an exemplary analysis of what a person who faces this type of crisis of meaning might seek. At the very least, there is a trenchant warning to the counsellor about offering a set of responses to a crisis of meaning that would ultimately fail to address the bottomless character of this problem, evading the abyss into which it seems impossible for us to gaze. It is clear that Nietzsche sees a number of complex substitutions occurring once the sense given to life by the faith in a God whose purposes the world was once thought to contain has been undone. Since the theological ground of the plenitude of meaning 'disappeared,' we seem unable to confront what appears as a 'senseless' world and we therefore seek partial solutions for our sense of lack in a variety of moralistic gestures. But what does Nietzsche intend by stressing the importance of a set of evasions that are equivalent to a refusal to either will or to risk 'positing a goal *for oneself*'? Here, one might imagine, would lie the general form of a diagnosis and thus answer to the problem of meaning that escapes mere 'substitution.' On a familiar view of such an answer, the meaning that was once held to derive from the sovereignty of God must now be acknowledged to derive only from the sovereign self. The interesting and problematic point to consider, however, in offering some such 'answer' to nihilism, is the character of the substitutions Nietzsche lists. Although all involve turning oneself over to the authority of something other than oneself, this 'turning over' can nonetheless have a profoundly *internal* character. 'Conscience,' for instance, despite its being in some deep sense a matter of one's own capacity to decide moral matters, remains a 'substitution' for the 'personal authority' of God. 'Reason,' too, which one might think of as integral to any autonomous ability to posit goals—and certainly would be within a Kantian framework for considering such questions—remains no less a substitution for God's role in providing purposes than the turn to social *mores* or a faith in the necessity of the historical process.

How, then, do we move beyond the domain of substitutions in reconfiguring our orientation towards problems of meaning? By speaking of an *unconscious* habit of seeking purposes beyond oneself, one might indicate only that this habit is unknown or unacknowledged, so that by bringing it to consciousness it would in a sense become cured. As soon as we 'know' that we continually desire to re-institute an authority that would bear the ultimate force of God's commands we can begin to learn to 'do without' such reference points. This would be the existential hero's form of asceticism, requiring of him that he reconstitute himself as 'center' of the meaning of events by becoming self-conscious of and resistant to the 'habit' which drove him to renege on his own responsibility. It is an easy reading to make, moreover, of what Nietzsche is saying here. But is it the only sense we can give to what is unconscious in the 'habit' at the root of passive nihilism, always looking for a source of meaning outside the self? Is the unconscious habit only to be understood as that pathology of self to which self-knowledge responds with an enabling clarity? Instead I would suggest that we pay attention to how the unconscious habit of which Nietzsche speaks pertains particularly to problems of authorization.

The 'old habit' bound up with a desired sense of meaning is further bound up with the sites of institutionalization of authority. The goal 'given' by a superhuman authority can be more or less adequately provided by the substitutive forms of conscience, or reason, or 'the herd.' The question here is whether we respond fully to the issues Nietzsche raises around authority by imagining the problem is simply how to become an individual, to honour one's own authentic ground of being, to learn to think and act through positing a goal *for oneself*, thus shifting the bases for authority from the outside to within. Or whether there is something too straightforwardly oppositional about this 'for another' or 'for oneself' schema which fails to do justice to the problem of what it is to be oneself in view of an *authority* integral to meaning though non-identical with it, which never entirely respects the difference between self and other; an authority which must always construct oneself-as-another and the other-as-self.

This latter way of looking at things might allow us to deconstruct the over-simplistic sense that meaning *either* comes from 'elsewhere' (from some transcendent ground of being) *or* from 'inside,' from some capacity for generating one's own sense of purpose. In place of this opposition, stressed by a certain existentialist way of thinking, the problematic of nihilism might be articulated less around the question of the *source* of authority (inside or outside) than around its *force*—its ability to command. In other words, the problem of meaning and the issue of positing a 'goal' for oneself cannot be fully grasped through a simple division of what is internal and thus assumed to be fully 'mine' and what is external and can thus be understood as imposed upon me. Further, we should note that the ability of authority to command always bridges a relation between self and other, precisely because to accept the force of *authority* is never simply to be *forced*. Authority proper, that is, symbolic authority, is at its most radical level, always powerless. As Slavoj Žižek puts it, "it is a certain 'call' which cannot effectively force us into anything, and yet, by a kind of inner compulsion, we feel obliged to follow it unconditionally." Indeed, by virtue of this unconditionality, "authority is inherently paradoxical", since "we obey a person in whom authority is vested irrespective of the content of his statements (authority ceases to be what it is the moment we make it dependent on the quality of its content) yet this person retains authority only insofar as he is reduced to a neutral carrier, bearer of some transcendent message…".[3] There is something about authority that forbids it from ever being fully rationalized, for whereas reasons persuade, authority *commands*. Equally, there is something about authority that refers it beyond what an individual can be imagined to contain by himself.

Now we may begin to forge some links between the question of authority—that is, the character of *recognition* of authority and its *power* to compel—and the question of the unconscious and its status. The unconscious, in the sense I want to begin to delineate here, would not be posited primarily as operating on the terrain of what is 'unknown' in the self qua '*hidden*' force, but more specifically would be invoked as operative at that problematic nexus of authoristy and selfhood, where in order for there to be authority at all—even the authority of 'positing one's own goals' —some *split* in the self, some division of what commands from what obeys must be assumed. Similarly, the goal that is posited 'for oneself' can never be sustained simply through one's own effort of willing, since it must contain that element of externality that enables it to either command the will or allows the will to *desire* it. The 'unconscious,' we might postulate, is bound up with this 'split' aspect of authority and with the feeling of compulsion which we seek to problematically 'assume' as our own in securing for ourselves a sense of meaning *commensurate* with the force of authority. If this can be made to seem plausible, as I shall try to show it might be in the sections that follow below, then the problem posed by nihilism might now be said to lie precisely in the nature of the attempt to 'cover over' this split and through one 'substitution' or another to disavow the rupture it affords to any project of identifying the sovereign self with the 'source' of meaning.

Taking up this line of thought would lead us to think of the 'power' Nietzsche links to active nihilism less on the model of self-determination (that is, of *autonomy* in the Kantian schema, which opposes the *heteronomy* of pathological influence) and more on the model of what he calls in his narrative of Zarathustra an 'undergoing,' a process I shall suggest we must ultimately conjoin to Nietzsche's interest in an *aesthetics* of existence. Nietzsche often suggested that life would be unbearable without art. The role he saw art playing for us, however, was never that of simply securing for us an illusion of harmony and meaning. Rather, Nietzsche conceives of art precisely in terms of a 'split' between what he refers to as the Apollonian and the Dionysian impulses. Whereas the Apollonian art-impulse allows us to sustain a sense of beauty and measure in the universe, the Dionysian allows us to experience the ultimate groundlessness of that vision of order.[4] In the 'paradoxical' combination of these two impulses in Greek tragedy, Nietzsche saw a model for the complex response to the 'death of God' that is demanded of us today.

An aesthetics of existence is that which sustains us in our desire for life but without allowing us to believe in any fundamental meaning that would *ground* (or ultimately explain) our lives. A similar role is played in Nietzsche's late thought by the figure of eternal return—which offers an image of life desired endlessly but without this desire ever finding a ground outside the passage of time itself.[5] The problematic 'gap' that opens up at the point of authority's excess of force over meaning coupled with an insistent reference beyond itself, is met in the thought of eternal return, *not* with the attempt to *close the gap over* but with an *affirmation of desire for life in excess of ultimate meaning*. The importance of the unconscious emerges here in an ambiguous way as the abyss of consciousness—that out of which it rises and into which it sinks. Consciousness is defined by Nietzsche as 'superficial' not by contrast with something 'deep' but rather as the *closed* system of intelligibility contrasts with the *abyssal* activity of unconscious life.[6] Consciousness forms 'closed' circuits of interpretation in a sense that allows us to equate what is compelling with what is meaningful, thereby evading the paradoxical character of authority's form, which eschews rationalization whilst always also referring beyond itself. In a sense, then, the problem with the structure of faith that began with God's authority and is now repeated in the many substitutive forms Nietzsche details in his treatment of nihilism, is not that it fails to originate in the *self* but rather that sense of the meaning provided by this structure fails to *exceed* the closure enforced by the requirement of intelligibility.

In other words, far from demanding a retreat from an externally derived to an internally derived sense of the sources of one's goals and purposes, Nietzsche's analysis of nihilism would point us to consider a problematic refusal of exteriority (resulting in formalism) which runs through all these 'closed' references to authority that substitutes for God. One could even say that the crisis of meaning arises out of the *rationalization* of authority in a sense that would include as problematic the attempt to make *oneself* the foundation of all authority. Eternal return, on the other hand, is above all else, *not* a closed circuit of repetition, but offers the attempt to think *out* of a crisis of meaning *into* an ability to desire a life that is and remains enigmatic; a life that is never *reducible* to my goals and will.

Let me now explicate further the considerations which lead me to these last, perhaps rather odd and surprising formulations.

The Unconscious Of A 'Psychotheology'

In what follows, I deploy Eric Santner's idiosyncratic 'theological' reading of the nature and task of psychoanalysis in order to further explicate the role one might accord here to an 'unconscious.'[7] Santner's study bears the title, "On the *Psychotheology* of Everyday Life" to mark its difference from the psycho-pathology of which Freud himself spoke. It is a philosophical re-reading of Freud's notion of the unconscious very much driven by the Nietzschean problematic of nihilism, transcribed by Santner as the problem of "law in force without significance," that is, precisely the formalism we identified above. It is in this specific sense of an element in the thinking of a 'psycho-theology' that I shall suggest the unconscious has a bearing on the question of what it is that philosophical counsellors might need to bring into consideration when they address crises of meaning. On my argument this will include the unconscious, but not in the way that the unconscious is commonly understood, that is, as the site of unknown and unknowable drives, traces of a past which it would be the task of therapy to mould, domesticate, make livable, or eradicate by bringing them to consciousness. Rather, I shall suggest, we might give an account of the unconscious which locates it on the terrain of Nietzsche's problematic of nihilism, one where the full and honest consciousness of the self-responsible self is less the issue than is the ability to be open to the enigma of that 'liminal' domain of the 'authorization,' in excess of all content and pointing towards some transcendent authority which we attempt to invest with a foundational role in order to avoid the anxiety provoked by the ungrounded and the abyssal. On a Nietzschean account of the necessity of 'undergoing' this experience, the problem would be how to translate the transcendent reference implied by authority into a relation to exteriority; for to 'undergo' the transformation promised by the thought of eternal return is to experience desire as that which places one in the midst of life without narrowing this desire to the desire for a ground of *meaning* felt by one who would be, in lieu of God, a sovereign subject.

Eric Santner alerts us to the case of Judge Daniel Paul Schreber who suffered a 'breakdown' at the moment of his investiture as a high ranking authority in the judiciary, a crisis he himself interpreted as a crisis of meaning. Santner interprets the judge's 'breakdown' in relation to problems of authority and authorization, and these in turn to crises in the relation between validity and meaning. Schreber's 'breakdown' occurs as he gazes into the abyss of authority into which he is now required to step. Why, then, is it necessary to invoke the unconscious at this point?

The unconscious is interpreted by Santner (following a Lacanian reading of Freud) as

> [the] psychophysical inscription of the procedures—and impasses—of symbolic investiture and legitimation, procedures that are bound up with the notion of sovereignty. The unconscious, in other words, forms the locus of psychic activity whereby a human being becomes a 'subject' by metabolizing its existential dependency on institutions that are in turn sustained by acts of foundation, preservation and augmentation. And by 'institution' I mean all sites that endow us with social recognition and intelligibility…[8]

What is the unconscious on this interpretation? To put it in broad brush-strokes, it is the 'liminal' domain of responsibility and authorization, a constitutive condition of subjectivity that is disavowed by the fully 'conscious' and responsible self. Such a self is one that seeks to 'close the gap' between command and obedience or between the 'external' and the 'internal' force of authority, through a process of rationalization integral to the notion of autonomy (that is, being oneself the source of the law one obeys). To relate this consideration back to our earlier reading of Nietzsche, we might approach the significance of the problem of meaning according to two alternatives, only the second of which invokes the unconscious:

1. There is no meaning 'out there', I have to make it myself. (Existentialist hero)

Versus

2. The experience of meaninglessness demands interrogation of how I take myself for a subject of meaning; placing emphasis on the inter-dependency of 'I' and 'thou' will lead to the question, How can I hold myself open to 'liminal' moments of authorization, to enigma, and the abyssal?

Let me expand a little upon this second trajectory of thought.

The unconscious is an 'inner strangeness' which, according to the Lacanian theorist Jean Laplanche is constituted by "the traumatic encounter with the dense, enigmatic presence of the Other's desire."[9] In other words it is a function of (constitutive) relationship—relationship upon which the subject's very existence depends; a relationship that forms subjectivity, authorizing and legitimating that subject who will call him or herself 'I.' The capacity to say 'I' is thus formed through the address or request for response that issues from another. When the 'I' fully assumes the status of 'subject' (and thus of what is imagined to be a self-identical authority) it takes itself to be responsible *for itself* in a sense that disavows this relation to the other, covering over the 'strangeness' that persists at the heart of self. But when subjectivity suffers a crisis, the problematic character of consti-tutive dependency again comes to the fore. Santner's description of the 'subject of psychoanalysis' therefore invokes a subject suffering 'symptoms' of meaninglessness which demand interpretation in terms that relate what they are symptomatic *of* to all the ways in which we find ourselves 'inscribed' in symbolic orders or 'out of joint' with them, and variously attempting or failing to 'cover over' the gap that opens up at these points.

These modes of our inscription are said to be 'unconscious' insofar as they always remain outside the grasp of full cognitive apprehension. The question is, however, what sense we should give to this being 'out of grasp'? Again, it is helpful here to be guided by an open (enigmatic) versus closed (intelligible) articulation of the difference between unconscious and con-scious life, rather than by the metaphor of surface versus depth. As an infant no less than as an adult one is, as Heidegger put it, 'thrown' into relations that are and remain irreducibly enigmatic. By 'enigma' here is intended the thought that one may be aware that something is meaningful without knowing *how* it is meaningful or *what* it signifies. Such is the situation of the pre-linguistic infant and, indeed, it is a condition of the possibility of learning language at all that this enigmatic sense of unfathomed meaning be present. The infant must be aware that there is a force to language prior to grasping the meaning of particular sounds. But such, too, is the situation of the individual in the nihilistic age who confronts enigma in the 'trace' left by the death of God.

The formalism that haunts the attempt to find substitutes for the replete moral universe in the authority of conscience, reason, and so on, must be referred to the attempt to raise the experience of authority to consciousness and thus to bring it into the order of intelligibility. In a crisis of meaning, conversely, the subject is returned to an enigmatic sense of imperative *force without significance* that can only further hollow out the life that bears it insofar as the degree of mastery the pre-cognitive infant does attain remains, in this case, ever out of reach. Even this comparison, however, may mislead us into thinking that it is in principle possible to 'master' meaning. For the instance of language and its status is an important site of irreducible enigma, the mastery of which we tend to exaggerate, imagining that an exhaustive determination of meaning is possible. This, in a sense, is the central preoccupation of Wittgenstein's *Philosophical Investigations*, which never ceases to remind us of the enigmatic yet deeply compelling life of words. Here the lesson we must learn from Wittgenstein is that we fail to exhaustively determine the meaning of a word *not* because we ourselves lack a full comprehension which we may expect will come later, but because the meaning of a word is always 'structurally' incomplete, always open to the dimension where 'words fail.'[10] In this sense, too, then, there is in language a 'structural' unconscious, an opening onto enigma which unfolds in the gap between the *force* of the sense of the meaningful and the ultimately unapproachable question of *what* it means.

Philosophy And The Cry Of Abandonment

At least two questions might arise for a philosophical approach to counselling out of what has been said already.

1. How can philosophy engage—in distinctively 'philosophical' ways— with a crisis of meaning that has the kind of form described here, in which emphasis has shifted from what I earlier described as the heroic-existential problem of 'laying meaning into' an inherently meaningless world (that is, a problem of *creating* meaning through a kind of extreme self-reliance) towards a concern with 'enigma'? If enigma cannot by its very definition be cognitively grasped, then what are we to do with it at all? And how can this 'excess' that seems to drive the nihilistic world to demand meaning and seek

substitutes for what it senses is lacking be either appreciated or become the means of some more fruitful transformation?

2. How can counselling practice which cultivates, amongst other things, a certain 'openness' towards a client take on an interpretation of itself which is sensitive to the difficulties introduced by supposing one's interlocutor to be a subject-with-an-unconscious, rather, that is, than being simply an individual with more or less confused ideas that might, with the help of philosophy, come to be clarified, thereby allowing rational self-determination to become the basis for a life?

On the first point Santner's account takes what he calls a 'theological' direction—but this is not a direction that for him would *exclude* philosophy. It is interesting to note that whereas Freud saw in the case of Judge Schreber a subject whose paranoid delusions were fantasmatic elaborations of a homosexual panic, Schreber himself, aware that his crisis was a crisis of meaning, expressed the view that "theologians and philosophers were better prepared to profit from his memoirs than the sort of neurologically and forensically trained psychiatrists who treated him."[11] Why and in what sense are philosophers to 'profit' from this case and perhaps have something to say in response to it?

Schreber's 'delusional' experience turned upon his sense that the world had been destroyed as a result of a profound imbalance between God and nature, and he referred to his feeling of undergoing this experience as a 'soul murder.' The hypothesis that what Schreber found himself subject to here marked a crisis in subjectivity itself, an inability to 'assume' or 'metabolize' the symbolic investiture held out to him, as he was inducted into the office of *Senatspräsident*, allows us to consider how this confrontation with abyssal 'enigma' marks every performative moment of language. Authority is always in some sense 'magical,' as is the performative which 'brings into being what it names' whilst also, implicitly, citing the previous and future instances of such an exercise of power. Again, one might say its force always exceeds its capacity to 'do' what it claims. There is then, on the one hand, a *surplus* here, a surplus of force over significance, whilst on the other, a *lack*, the lack of any ultimate foundation to sustain authority. Successful investiture with the mantle of authority requires what we saw Nietzsche describing in the passage above as a variety of substitutions, all of which are more or less effective in stabilizing this point of instability. Reason, conscience, or the herd all allow us to identify ourselves with the origin of authority, in a *closed* relationship that forswears exteriority. In other words, they allow us to reduce the anxiety of the enigmatic gap between commanding and obeying, speech and understanding, force and meaning.

If philosophy has anything to do or say here it is first of all called upon to bear witness to the sheer anguish of an experience like Schreber's. But is it not also called upon to do justice to the possibility that *this* is the difficult terrain on which we need to walk if we are to avoid *either* that conservative acceptance of substitutions for God's authority which hold us securely in our place in the symbolic universe *or* the assumption that the self-founded being of the existential hero would present an apt alternative? The collapse of what Santner refers to as "the practical unity of life" leaves Schreber with the sense of profound *abandonment*.[12] Can philosophy hope to offer a *cure* here—or only some means of recognition, some affinity with the crisis by which Schreber found himself wracked, some acknowledgement that the undergoing of this disaster bore conditions wider than the misadventure of a single man? How can philosophy hear and respond to the cry that resonates in Schreber's anguish: *Why hast thou forsaken me?*

Here, in the experience of abandonment which so often corresponds to the sense of meaninglessness, the existential hero would, perhaps, enjoin us to renounce our reliance upon this mysterious other and the implicit desire for redemption; to renounce the desire for a plenitude of meaning that must come from *without* in favour of resolute self-determination. Another response, however, more attuned to what is at stake here for the enigmatic borders of *all* authorization might seek, along with conventional psychoanalytic practice, a 'working through' of that abandonment implicit in *all* self-other relations. Abandonment in this sense does not signify some substantive lack of individual love, some personal trauma of the neglected self, nor the 'actual event' of the death of God; rather it corresponds to the necessarily enigmatic question of the other's 'meaning' for which an analogue was previously found in the infant's pre-linguistic experience. Lacanian psychoanalysis puts this problem in terms of the nagging question of one's place in the Other's desire, that 'what do they want of me?' which intersects the experience of becoming a fully fledged interlocutory partner *via* a never-transcended unconscious trace of ungraspability.

It is possible to again find a Wittgensteinian parallel to this thought where in *The Philosophical Investigations* we see the plain language-games of ordinary interaction—"pass me a brick, mate!"[13]—slowly excavated to reveal an insistent core of enigma which is miscast by philosophy as the enigma of that which is *hidden* and must be brought to light. One could argue that an engagement with the problem of the unconscious is figured in Wittgenstein's commentary upon the philosopher's desire to find a "final analysis of our forms of language, and so a single completely resolved form of every expression," and this, "as if there were something hidden in them that had to be brought to light."[14] The mistake in reading Wittgenstein would be to imagine that with a turn to the everyday he exposes and denounces the illusion of 'depth' in favour of consciousness of the full adequacy of meaning to *use*, or that he 'shows the fly the way out of the fly-bottle' to re-enter a surface world where nothing in or about expression is enigmatic any more. For what such readings miss is the importance to the Wittgensteinian 'therapy' of holding open rather than closing off to a sense of difficulty. Philosophy may indeed be "a battle against the bewitchment of our intelligence by means of language."[15] The seduction it battles, however, is one that is irreducible in that aspect of 'being in force without significance' that was earlier attested to as integral to authority and as the most elementary component of the experience of alterity as 'ungraspable.' The problem therefore becomes, as Stanley Cavell has eloquently argued in his readings of Wittgenstein, one of ardent negotiation with the skeptical impulse, now cast as the desire to reduce enigma *either* to the frightening possibility of unfathomable depth or to the equally frightening gesture of postulating that there is *nothing* there at all, that all is surface appearance.[16]

Contrast this skeptical impulse, then, in its desire for resolution, with a passage from Wittgenstein engaging with the enigmatic quality of the cry:

> But here is the problem: a cry, which cannot be called a description, which is more primitive than any description, for all that it serves as a description of the inner life. A cry is not a description. But there are transitions. And the words 'I am afraid' may approximate more or less than a cry. They may come quite close to this and also be *far* removed from it. We surely do not always say someone is complaining because he says he is in pain... But if 'I am afraid' is not always a cry of complaint and yet sometimes is, then why should it *always* be a description of a state of mind?[17]

What is a cry of abandonment? How should we 'read' it or respond to it? In the cry—'*Why has thou forsaken me?*'—our existentialist hero hears speak an inner state of mind whose sense of enigma can be overcome. A cry which is cast as a description of an inner state of grief and loss is one, it is imagined, that might be dispelled through the realization that what it longs for simply lacks all existence. The surface form of language that cries for God is here contrasted with a deeper psychic truth. The one who cries is driven by the unconscious 'habit' of reneging on responsibility for positing his or her *own* goal, and philosophy will serve to insist upon the *falseness* of the object taken by this habit. Acknowledgement of the *fact* that *there is no one there* at all becomes a means to the assumption of full self-responsibility. But notice Wittgenstein's riposte to this type of reduction when it serves to reduce the enigma of the cry. For him, the cry 'I am afraid' may *not even be* the description of a state of mind. Nor is it *simply* an expression, like an involuntary groan might be, for it is certainly articulated; 'I am afraid', may, Wittgenstein says, simply 'approximate' a cry, may 'come quite close to this and also be *far* removed from it.' Why, then, does Wittgenstein speak of the expression 'I am afraid' in this *enigmatic* way? Does he perhaps seek to capture something of the liminal inarticulable life of words which in their force of expression exceed what can be contained within the interiority of a 'description of a state of mind'?

If the unconscious traverses the domain of linguistic intelligibility, as I have suggested we might read its effect, we must displace our understanding of its domain from what is 'hidden' in the forces that act upon the mind, towards a sense of its play in the excess of force over anything we can pin down as the contentful meaning language bears. As is the case with language in general for the pre-linguistic child, here the utterance 'I am afraid' grips us with a force in excess of its translatability into 'the description of a state of mind.' But what is the character of this excess? Wittgenstein at one point suggests that if we want to know what 'I am frightened' really means we must ask after its *context*[18] (as if 'context' as a 'surface' concept might appropriately displace the problematic 'depth' concept of intention). Yet this remark occurs only half way through the line of meditations that reach their culmination in the note previously cited, and I take this to indicate at least some hesitation over the thesis so often attributed to Wittgenstein that the context of an utterance would serve to *determine* a meaning. The thought he dwells with towards the end of his ruminations would rather be that meaning is never fully determinable, that we are always driven towards its enigmatic quality. This reflection would follow in turn from the thought that even an apparently self-descriptive utterance like 'I am afraid' does not refer us only to a 'state of mind' but at once to what that mind encounters as *other* to itself. The cry of abandonment refers us to how 'being afraid' *inhabits* a body, and to those relationships between self and others that are mediated by the possibilities and the impasses of language. According to Cavell, to deny the unconscious life of the self is to deny embodiment, to deny the ways in which we find ourselves 'thrown.'[19] Again, how can philosophy and the marriage of philosophy with a counselling process be true to such reflections?

Knowledge And Acknowledgement

On Cavell's reading of Wittgenstein, the all important difference between skepticism and philosophy as re-interpreted above, can be rendered as the difference between 'knowledge' of another mind and 'acknowledgement'; the difference between experiencing the mind—even one's own—as 'object' and experiencing another as making a *claim* upon me. The problem of how to acknowledge the 'enigma' of otherness rather than seeking to 'know' and cognitively master the other is precisely how Cavell specifies the dimensions of an *ethical* negotiation with skepticism—a negotiation that is never finally at an end. The promise has to be repeatedly remade as 'acceptance' of the everyday takes on an 'eventual' character, that is, one riven by enigma rather than seeking to exclude it. And for Cavell, too, this difference might be said to have a theological dimension. For he writes: "The withdrawals and approaches of God can be looked upon as tracing the history of our attempts to overtake and absorb acknowledgement by knowledge; God would be the name of that impossibility."[20]

If the 'withdrawals and approaches of God' correspond in any way to the contemporary experience of a problem of meaning which has something of the form I have sketched above, then without being in a conventional sense 'theological' about it, it seems necessary to reject the existential hero's response to a crisis in this domain of life. For the existentialist hero derives too much from the faith that God is 'really' dead, that there is 'really' nothing there and thus that the grounds of external authority were falsely constraining grounds. In doing so he collapses acknowledgement of the inherent alterity of authority and authorization, into a knowledge of the mundane that must remain haunted by its other pole of skeptical possibility—a scenario in which not God but *we* are dead, our lives given over to the meaninglessness of the *non-eventual* everyday.

Echoing this invocation of fundamental questions of life and death, Santner writes:

The subject of psychoanalysis ... begins not with biological life but rather where biological life is amplified and disturbed by the symbolic dimension of relationality at the heart of which lie problems of authority and authorization. To borrow a term from Giorgio Agamben, we might say that the life that is of concern to psychoanalysis is *biopolitical* life, life that has been thrown by the enigma of its legitimacy, the question of its place and authorization within a meaningful order.[21]

'Biopolitical' life in the sense Santner uses it here, is life at once riven by the question of whether it is *really* alive and whether it is 'authorized' to exist at all. If this is the subject of psychoanalysis, how might it also be the concern of philosophy to speak to this moment and to this question? Running through all that I have said thus far is a challenge to the assumption sometimes made by philosophical counsellors that psychoanalysis offers a profoundly different process of engaging with a client's malaise of sense from anything that could be acceptable to philosophers. Although it is clearly the case that psychoanalysis has evolved in a number of directions, with competing schools of thought organizing different practical approaches to therapy, Santner's treatment of the unconscious and the bearing it has on problems of meaning allows us to identify a core of affinity between certain starting points of psychoanalytic thought and certain major strands of philosophy that begin in the late nineteenth century and carry their questions and problems no less ripely into the twenty-first. It would be unduly dogmatic to seek to exclude these strands of reflection from philosophy and especially their bearing on how to interpret problems of meaning as well as, perhaps, offering some recourse for them. Philosophers might well need to learn something from psychoanalytic practice if the unconscious is to become something that counselling, at a minimum, acknowledges in the life of a client. And there are indeed rich resources of thought to be tapped here. Life "thrown by the enigma of its legitimacy" seems to me a highly apt way to capture a certain experience of the loss of meaning, especially when we grasp the force of this question in relation to the question of what it means to be alive at all—to be *really* alive, not simply going through the repetitive motions, but really *living*. Again, the existentialist-heroic response to this problem would seem most readily to suggest the need to undertake some kind of adventure, to become 'heroic' through a direct confrontation with the risk of death. Yet Santner's approach allows us to delineate a different kind of response to a crisis of meaning, one which leads in a direction that engages with the problem of 'acknowledgement' that Cavell identified at once as at the heart of ethics and as forming the theological horizon of philosophical thought.

As we have seen, the implication Santner draws from his reading of the unconscious is that induction into a socio-symbolic order is not primarily a cognitive achievement and relation—it is not, for example, a matter of *mastering* a language—but is, rather, something that takes place in an important sense through an encounter with the 'enigma' of the 'otherness of the Other,' the question of one's place within their desire. "Our entire being", he writes, "is in some sense permeated by making these enigmas by which we feel ourselves addressed; these scraps of *validity in excess of any meaning* make sense."[22] Hence the importance of intervening just *here*, somehow suspending the need to make sense, to translate demand into action, by refusing to allow an interpretation to become effective as part of a repetitive pattern of response. Hence, too, the importance placed by psychoanalysis on the centrality of the inter-relational constitution of self, which however, following Lacan, I have suggested must be broadened beyond any 'family romance' of the Oedipal adventure to comprise a consideration of our place within all linguistic interaction. It is central to the task of psychoanalysis to 're-enact' the relationships in play here in the effort to 'transfer' their force in a new direction. Yet it seems clear that on the whole philosophical counselling has tried to avoid this complexity of relation, as if pretending that we spoke together of 'neutrally' accessible topics, as though our dialogue were independent of the force of what takes place between us. But if meaning and knowledge of the other's meaning never quite float freely like this—and especially not where a *crisis* of meaning is being undergone—then philosophy must reflect further upon its own communicative conditions of possibility.

A first step, perhaps, would be to set acknowledgement before knowledge as a response to encounter with the other's enigmatic words, the other's crisis, or cry, '*Why hast thou forsaken me*' or '*I am afraid*'. To set acknowledgement first would imply foreswearing any promise of 'cure' or of a 'cognitive therapy' for the anguish of existence. This surely must *not*, however, imply simply affirming the irreducibility or the value of such anguish *per se*. The question becomes, how is it possible to move at all within this space of encounter? How to begin to turn anguish towards the kind of desire for life of which Nietzsche wrote? We can perhaps begin to address these questions by considering what as philosophers and counsellors we are competent to do—what kind of resources we possess and how we *interpret* those resources. So one might perhaps ask, what is it to 'acknowledge' another and to hear what they have to say in this spirit of acknowledgement? And then, how would paying attention to this question shape philosophical counselling practice?

At the outset of any induction into counselling practice there is an important emphasis placed upon learning to listen. It is perhaps evidence of some of the claims made here about the enigmatic aspects of our inscription in language, that listening to what another person is saying, which we think of as something we do all the time, turns out to be something we are on the whole exceptionally bad at. Before having fully understood what someone else is saying we begin to argue with them. After resting our attention with the other for a couple of moments we turn the focus back to ourselves. It is as though in our ordinary interactions we did not want to be brought into a relation to exteriority though our exchanges, as though we tend naturally to seek either mastery of a communicative situation or to withdraw into ourselves. This phenomenon might be referred to the everyday attempt to 'manage' the enigmatic relation to others that takes place in language. Indeed, even if we place a certain interpretation on what we are doing in *trying* to really listen to the other we may *again* be trying to reduce enigma in the direction of knowledge and mastery rather than acknowledgment. For instance, we may suppose that at some 'deep' level the other really knows his or her own mind, and it is our task in listening to excavate and make shared that hidden sense. Or we may suppose that what we are aiming to do through listening is to make possible the exchange of fully articulated opinions which might then be subjected to a rational scrutiny. Although I do not wish to deny that there is a place for both these gestures they nevertheless carry certain risks. For in either case we are seeking to restore a circuit of mutual intelligibility to the encounter, and even if we do so with a view to *including* the other in that circuit (which otherwise risks being merely solipsistic) we must realize that we simultaneously bring to a close that interruption of the repetition of patterns of interpretation which requires a dwelling in enigma.

One wonders how much of what is commonly understood to be 'communication' takes place in this haze of indifference to the life and texture of language. For it is clearly possible to achieve a degree of understanding sufficient for what Habermas calls 'action-co-ordination,' without worrying at all about the texture of the language we exchange; we ordinarily remain quite unbothered by all the complexity that Wittgenstein sought to draw attention to in focussing on the problem of the 'meaning' of a cry. What is it, then, that one seeks to learn in 'learning to listen'? And what has it to do with going beyond the 'merely' everyday towards the 'eventual' every-day—into a space where the only chance is that something might 'happen.' My intuition would be that although it may also be important to retain some of the defensive skills we are, for the most part masters of—and perhaps, *especially* as philosophers—listening must also be thought of as a kind of undergoing, a going down into an abyssal space of encounter. In my own experience, this undergoing when another is communicating a sense of *meaninglessness* is particularly hard to enter into and particularly difficult to endure.[23] One becomes impatient to return to the ground where it is possible to ask questions at a level which presumes intelligibility: Why do you think that? Does that make sense? What is it you want to achieve? But all the time that one is *able* or *compelled* to occupy the space of listening one is forced to share the abyssal sense of the untenability of such questions, the powerlessness of reason to draw either of you up out of this abyss. The counsellor is required, then, to endure an interruption in the circuits of intelligibility on a radical level, if he or she is to learn to listen not only to the conscious interlocutory partner of a dialogue but also to the subject-with-an-unconscious of an 'undergoing.' In sharing this space with another it is at least possible that something will happen through the very openness to a 'meaning' that remains enigmatic, irreducible to what one or the other anticipated finding.

What, then, of the specifically *philosophical* counsellor? At the outset of any induction into philosophy, there is an emphasis placed upon learning to reason, or as this is sometimes transcribed, to think critically. One is taught to isolate varying and mutually contradictory opinions and to hold them up for scrutiny. One learns to examine oneself and others in this way. One learns to always ask 'Why?' and to discriminate between different kinds of questions that one might pose by asking 'Why?' and hence different orders of appropriate answer. This kind of reasoning is the sort of skill one might seek to share with a client in a counselling practice which draws upon distinctively philosophical talents, and it is indeed a very useful skill to bring to bear on certain purposes. But are there other aspects of philosophy that may do more justice to the abyss that opens where reasons seem to end? Nietzsche's commentary on the fate of philosophy in nihilistic times might be read as an engagement with this question. For Nietzsche, philosophy makes a deadly mistake when it seeks to *reduce* life to reason, as for instance he takes Socrates to have done when he 'saved' the Ancient Greeks from their pathological love of tragedy by introducing the philosophical practice of dialectics. Again, Socrates' error is characterized for Nietzsche by its adherence to a formula of closure "Reason=Virtue=Happiness."[24] This Socratic wisdom is one that any philosophical counsellor inspired by Nietzsche would have to avoid; for a 'vital' matter is not reducible to a 'Why?' question and an enigmatic problem must resist reduction to the demand of consciousness for intelligibility. Moreover, to draw also here upon the reading Cavell develops of Wittgenstein's philosophy, the alterity of the other is not something we might seek to 'know' as though it were reducible to a set of propositions or opinions. The other as subject-with-an-unconscious is not only a 'stranger' to me but a stranger to him or herself.

There is a nice image that Žižek introduces here to bring out the 'negativity' or lack we must acknowledge at the heart of relationality—a lack we are always tempted to fill out, fill in, close over. In our efforts to understand another culture, he writes,

> We should not focus on its specificity (on the peculiarity of 'their' customs etc.); we should rather endeavour to encircle that which eludes their grasp, the point at which the Other is itself dislocated, not bound by its 'specific context'... I understand the Other when I become aware of how the very problem that was bothering me (the nature of the Other's secret) is already bothering the Other itself.[25]

Philosophical counselling might sometimes be thought of as requiring an 'encircling' of what eludes our grasp, and will do so to the end. The value of such 'encircling' gestures are perhaps manifest in Wittgenstein's treatment of the 'cry' and in any attempt to 'undergo' encounter with what cannot be clearly seen or mastered in oneself or others. These 'encircling' gestures are integral to certain moments of listening. In such ways we must acknowledge a place in philosophical counselling for an openness to the enigmatic aspect which rational conversation, concerned with the exchange of points of view and cognitive mastery, by its very nature risks closing down.

The problem of acknowledgement is a problem about displacing the desire for certainty, curbing the desire for knowledge that would give one 'mastery' or would cover over the gap between speaking and understanding, commanding and obeying, force and meaning, by rationalizing the difference. Through acknowledgment of enigma, conversely, what is sought is an intervention into the problem of a life that risks being lead skeptically, given over to the meaninglessness that haunts the merely 'undead' existence. Being 'alive' requires a relation to exteriority that is foreclosed by the skeptic's desire for certainty. But equally it requires that the enigmatic excess of validity over meaning, which may come to appear as an unbearable level of demand, be transformed into a way of living that is an experience of desire—of having a goal and a way of being in time that neither refers to the radical interiority of the sovereign subject nor to the impassive exteriority of sheer repetition in the mundane everyday.

Most philosophical counsellors would quite reasonably consider a case like that of Judge Daniel Schreber to lie outside their competence. Delusions of the sort he describes would seem to imply a danger to both himself and others around him that public responsibility demands a firm institutional response to. Philosophical counselling does not possess such an institutional framework as yet, nor does it as yet have any developed account of itself that would seem to make it equal to dealing with such difficult cases. Granted then that this would be an extreme case of the crisis of meaning, it remains that a philosopher informed by some of the considerations adduced here about the place of the unconscious in our sense of authorization, of our relation to meaning and our relation to others, might yet begin to engage with what Schreber described so vividly as a sense of abandonment, as living in a way that was not really alive but merely 'undead,' as undergoing a 'soul-murder' that undid the very possibility of everyday life and its closed structure of repetition. To do so would require, however, that philosophy acknowledge its affinities not only with rational dialogue but with forms akin to what Nietzsche called the 'aesthetics of existence' and what Cavell speaks of as 'ethics,' both conceptions of philosophy that enable it to accommodate acknowledgement of our rich and richly strange unconscious lives.

Notes

[1] *The Will to Power*, Trans. Walter Kaufmann and R.J. Hollingdale, New York, Vintage1967, #22, dated 1887.

[2] *The Will to Power*, #20

[3] *Enjoy your Symptom: Jacques Lacan in Hollywood and Out*, London and New York, Routledge 1992, pp.94 -5

[4] See Nietzsche, *The Birth of Tragedy Out of the Spirit of Music*, #1-7 and *passim*.

[5] See, *The Gay Science*, Trans Walter Kaufmann, New York, Vintage, 1988, #341, but also *Thus Spake Zarathustra*.

[6] See, *The Gay Science* #354.

[7] *On the Psychotheology of Everyday Life: Between Freud and Rosenzweig*, Chicago, University of Chicago Press, 2001.

[8] Santner, Op. Cit., p. 26

[9] Santner, Op. Cit. pp.33-4.

[10] Slavoj Žižek, *The Abyss of Freedom/ Ages of the World*, trans Ann Arbor, University of Michegan Press, 1997, p.50

[11] Santner, *Psychotheology*, p.46

[12] Op. Cit, p.54.

[13] As we might gloss *Philosophical Investigations*, #2. Trans G.E.M. Anscombe, Oxford, Blackwell, 1981.

[14] Op. Cit. #91.

[15] Op. Cit. #109.

[16] See Stanley Cavell, *Must We Mean What We Say? A Book of Essays*, Cambridge: Cambridge UP, 1995 and, particularly, *The Claim of Reason: Wittgenstein, Skepticism, Morality and Tragedy*, Oxford, Oxford University Press, 1979.

[17] *Philosophical Investigations*, II p.189.

[18] Op. Cit., p.188.

[19] See, for instance, *Contesting Tears*, Chicago, University of Chicago Press, 1996, pp.104-6

[20] Cavell, *Must We Mean What We Say?* p.347.

[21] *Psychotheology*, p.30.

[22] *Psychotheology*, p.97

[23] I draw here on my experience over several years as a volunteer counsellor at a Rape Crisis Centre as well as experiences with close friends.

[24] See *Twilight of the Idols*, Trans. R.J. Hollingdale, London and New York, Penguin, 1989, 'The Problem of Socrates', and *The Birth of Tragedy, passim*.

[25] *Abyss*, p.50.

Chapter 8

The Pathologos: The Unsuspected Underlying Belief

Pierre Grimes

The intellectual life of mankind is marked by various difficulties, and chief among them is the crisis one faces in the attempt to rid oneself of a kind of ignorance that has its origin within the family. The ignorance about the false beliefs about the self does not entail they are unconscious, merely that they have not yet been articulated. These false beliefs are concluded in silence, and until they are expressed they have a life of an unacknowledged prejudice. While this kind of ignorance is the cause of repeated failures and a dissatisfaction with life, its presence is hardly suspected even though it is a false belief about oneself. These beliefs are not without an influence on our lives since they are irreconcilable with the attainment of one's most significant and meaningful goals. The continued presence of these beliefs is ruinous to many who otherwise could have fulfilled their dreams and contributed to our society.

Philosophical midwifery is a mode of philosophical counselling that addresses itself to this problem and has devised a method to surface and eliminate this kind of false belief. Philosophical midwifery as defined here is an adaptation of Socratic midwifery by Pierre Grimes, and it utilizes a dialectic as a mode of psychotherapy. As a dialectic it follows a formal course of questions[1]; the questions are designed to surface these unsuspected false beliefs; discover their origin and the reasons for its continued effect upon our lives. The method of this dialectic has been the subject of a validation study.[2] The validation study demonstrated that the purely rational approach used in philosophical midwifery was being strictly followed, and its methods "surfaces emotionalized behavior by identifying the pathologos and its underlying problematic behavior and it does so by a demonstrable specific method."[3] The use of dialectic as a mode of psychotherapy in the treatment of alcoholism was reported in 1961 and 1966.[4]

The conclusions of such dialectical sessions are always tested in one's experience because in that way it is possible to determine what aspects of the problem have been resolved and what parts are in need of further explorations. These false beliefs are of a certain kind and only manifest themselves fully when there is an attempt to pursue such goals with excellence. Thus, the more noble the goal the more likely there will be a conflict with these beliefs and, correspondingly, with secondary and practical goals it is less likely that they will have to be confronted. The avoidance of seeking excellence in a personally meaningful pursuit is the hallmark of someone being under the influence of such false beliefs.

In order to explore further we must first come to understand that the kind of beliefs we are concerned with were believed because the circumstances that led to their acceptance appeared to the believer to be justified. Even though we ourselves came to believe these beliefs others were involved in their transmission. When they transmitted them they appeared sincere and truthful. If this is the case, then there is a vicious kind of ignorance that is directed against ourselves and others that arises from what appears to have been an ethical choice, and the elimination of the belief is the consequence of judging its transmission as unethical. In that rejection a new standard of the ethical naturally emerges which restores the integrity of the individual and makes possible a new kind of moral excellence. For the individual breaking away from the old to the new morality it is no easy and simple task because the individual must successfully pass through a moral crisis. Surely, there is nothing new in declaring that the pursuit of what seems good rather than the good is the source of our problems. But to add that the solution of this problem requires a rectification of the good and the justification of names might be recognized as an adaptation of a rather ancient tradition.

In order to explain this moral crisis we must first account for the circumstances and the judgments that brought one to the acceptance of the false beliefs instead of the true. Let us then review the factors that produced this illusion. It is this we shall set forth by first describing the nature of the formidable power of the pathologos and, then, the crisis that must be faced to release oneself from it.

1. The transmission and imposition of a model that members of a family accept as true. This acceptance brings a unity to the family.

2. While the model may include aspects of culturalization of family members, it is the particular manifestation of the model that is communicated to family members.

3. This unique expression of the family's model has a core set of beliefs which are transmitted through successive generations so that one can perceive they are a part within a manyness of a whole.

4. What children believe about themselves after discovering what their parent-guardian really believes about them and the world is the pathologos.

5. The failure to resist the model successfully and the acceptance of the pathologos produces a false idea of the self, and as a consequence it supports a negative view of the way things are, or the nature of reality. Since this false image and belief of the self has such a pernicious effect upon one's life we call it a sick belief, or the pathologos.

6. The pathologos seems to function as if it has an autonomous existence and formidable power.

7. There are only a small number of fundamental learnings based upon the pathologos-model that are responsible for many of our problems.

8. The most significant aspect of these false beliefs, the pathologos, is that for the most part that they are unknown to the believer.

9. The pathologos generates a class of failures and dissatisfactions with life;

10. and these are derived from conclusions that have been made from one's own youthful past learning.

11. These failures are repeated through one's life. They go through a set of stages or scenes as if they are parts of a drama. The drama goes through a cyclical sequence of scenes.

12. The pathologos has a unique origin within the family.

13. The transmission of the learning that creates the pathologos must take place at those times when one is open and receptive, self absorbed, and engaged in one's own pursuits.

14. After the transmission there are many scenes that further refine and add a measure of precision to the transmission. This repetition often takes a symbolic form that echoes back to major features in the transmission scene. Slogans and saying echo the values of the transmission. These repeated sayings function as reminders and are called pathologos themes.

15. Events will be interpreted from the perspective of the model; favorite past scenes will be repeated as additional reminders of the model;

and those persons who exhibit similar themes will become ideals within and for the family model.

16. As a result of the transmissions of the model particular roles are accepted and assigned within the family. Some roles have more power and authority than others and therefore some can be said to be, relatively speaking, better roles.

17. There is a natural attraction to finding situations at work or play outside of the family where there is the possibility of playing one of the more authoritative roles, or a favorite role.

18. Relationships bound by these kinds of "pathologos" loyalties are as predictable as they are shallow.

19. Playing out a more favored role at home or in society against those who have inferior roles allows an interlude of authority and power over subordinates. Those perceived as being not part of a restrictive social structure become objects of suspicion, envy, and/or hate.

20. There is no evidence of any corporeal punishment in the formation of the pathologos, and it is not unusual for these pathologos learning scenes to have little or not action or drama in them. It is not a punishment scene because the presence of coercion and physical abuse can be understood, one can accept it as either just or unjust, where as the pathologos is always a particular belief one concluded about oneself for accepting that model.

In many families it is common for one of the parents to belittle the other and in so doing communicate their own private views about man and society. If these discussions are kept secret from the other party the child must come to a conclusion about the truth of discussions and the reason they are being shared. One is in words, the other is not. The silent conclusion forms the pathologos. The undermining of the child's image of the parent creates a fundamental doubt about the child's own ability to judge. However, if it is openly discussed no pathologos is born.

The acceptance of the past learning which became a model for one's behavior also set the boundary and limits on what is possible for the believer. It fixed the manner and style of one's life.

The model functions as a trap that restricts the freedom and free choice of the believer. In accepting the model one has to accept the suffering since the consequence of having made one's own choice makes it one's own. The resignation becomes painful as the realization of what has been sacrificed becomes clear. The injustice of having to live within the boundary becomes the basis for a growing bitterness and anger.

When we approach states of freedom and openness in things most significant to us we are already violating the model and our pathologos.

A pathologos can only be learned if we have become convinced of its truth, and for that condition to be met presupposes that those who do the convincing really know us and the reality that confronts us. Consequently they have to appear very convincing, as if they are possessors of a secret truth, and therefore they stand and appear as if they are true knowers. This appearance becomes the standard for judging and how to appear as a knower. It becomes the model to be imitated and it becomes the standard for how to appear before others as knowing.

The transmission of such a belief can only occur in one's youth and only in situations where the child is open and receptive. These are the times when the child is exploring his or her own world and indifferent to whatever model the family has before it. Seizing this time for the imposition of the model not only stamps in the model but the child realizes that it is dangerous to be so open and doing their own thing. Thus, this open state is no longer entered into freely and the child learns to be cautious about entering into it.

Clearly, the convincers must be people significant to us, those who played a significant role in our lives. The believer must be open and sensitive to the transmission of the model, as the persuader must appear knowing and sincere. What is learned is maintained and nurtured and through this device the guardians rule with a strange and powerful authority.

The transmission must take place under circumstances that break free from the usual course and pattern of the family's life. It is when someone shifts into playing an authority role, it is when they disclose and share some belief they hold to be fundamentally true. These unusual circumstances are the occasions when the child discovers what the parent really believes about them and what they are doing. This makes the situation memorable. At these times the persuaders must convince us that they are doing whatever they do for our own benefit, that in sharing their truth about us they are revealing what has been on their mind. The persuaders-guardians emerge from their usual way of being at these times, and they become authoritarian, certain, powerful and in control, but above all they must communicate a sincerity in their words and deeds. Thus in believing them we were accepted as a member of the believing group, the family.

To have rejected such words as false at the time would have been equivalent to rejecting their most sincere way of appearing. To reject it when they appear as caring knowers would be unthinkable for someone immature and dependent. During the imposition of the model the persuaders have to pay careful attention to the child or the message will not be believed.

It often happens that at such times the persuader appears not only most sincere and truthful but gives the best appearance of him- or herself and so he or she may seem most beautiful. The scene has a greatness to it because these qualities appear so apparent in those we respect. It is these qualities that give the sense of truth to the scene and give justification of the adult authority. These transition scenes are few, and so they gain a greater importance and significance. In accepting the pathologos we accept the appearance as real.

The content of the model and the pathologos becomes a way to explain many things that previously were puzzles about oneself and the family. The pathologos becomes the justification of the way things are. There is a deep resignation in this painful disclosure because while we have known there was something wrong we now know that's the way things must be. Once accepted, authority is accepted, roles are distributed, and the whole is defended as the necessary way of being. This imposition into our lives of the pathologos becomes the root cause of our anger.

Since we have seen those we respect and love in such ideal poses, un-knowingly, we mold ourselves to it; without this molding to be like what we perceive there would be no pathologos. As we see them exhibiting a greatness we match it with a desire to be like them, and so greatness is the condition for the pathologos. Much of the way an individual expresses him- or herself through gestures and attitudes was displayed by the persuaders and is taken on and becomes part of the self of the believer. In imitating we become like the model, striving to become accepted as someone or something, and all that is guided by an urge to become like what we accept as great.

The transmission of the model and the pathologos can be regarded as a kind of primitive social contract. It provides the condition for membership in the family, and within this condition rewards and punishments can be distributed. It defines the roles within the family, sets out protocols, and determines the kinds of relationships permitted within the family. All out-side the orbit of the family is, by contrast, diminished in significance. The skillful use of benefits, praise, love, intimidations, humiliations, coercion and exile bind the family into a whole.

An inevitable crisis occurs when one begins to see the need to separate from the pathologos because an understanding of the factors that generated the pathologos undermine the loyalty to the family model. At this stage of reflection it is not unusual for some people to turn away from further exploration of the pathologos since it challenges this primitive social contract. They may have wanted to be free of the negative side of the pathologos but when they face this crisis they see other features of the model that now seem more positive than what they saw before. They reflect that it did provide a role, a clear way of relating, a set of values, and that means it did have a certain security. To leave these behind one has to discover new ways to function which means having to trust one's own integrity and vision. Thus, some experience this crisis as a state of bitter emptiness and fear isolation. Rather than face this state, some would rather scale down their aspirations than go any further in the quest for self development. To stay within the limits of the pathologos is to have a limited existence.

In the transmission of the pathologos the authorities must convince the believer that since they couldn't achieve excellence, it couldn't be expected that their child could.

The persuaders must convince the believer that they themselves simply can't be expected to go any further because they have reached their limit.

Once the limits are accepted the child is justified for being within those limits. All that came before is devalued and loses its significance, thus the child's world of experience is diminished and forgetfulness sets in. There is no pathologos without this element of amnesia since we remember what we value and ignore what is not of value.

This is something that is concluded in silence and never discussed, and since it was never put into words, it cannot become the object of recollection. Being wordless it is unavailable to thought but it not an unconscious thing. Left wordless no judgement of it is possible; its absurdity is concealed, and exists like an unreflective prejudice. Unavailable for recollection it will not surface in reflective thought so that it remains unknown but not unconscious. Probing questions that explore the drama and the content of the pathologos can surface it and make it an object for reflection. Bringing it from silence into the light creates a crisis.

The crisis can be intensified to the degree that the believer wants to save the image of their loved ones. It often happens that the believers blame themselves or others before they can even deal with the idea of the responsibility of the parental figure.

Some believe that, when they consider the many sacrifices their family has made for their survival, it wouldn't be fair to judge them negatively.

Others may have been convinced that they themselves are incapable of making such judgements. This is often the case where the believer has been repeatedly exposed to a systematic undermining and devaluing of value judgements. When the very terms that are involved in judging become forbidden they can't be used against the parental figures of the family.

Some may retreat from further inquiry and defend the model as well as their own pathologos. It is not uncommon for them to have recourse to Protagorean arguments such as "who is say who is right or wrong, it's all relative to the way you perceive."

But for others the crisis is over the issue of blame. They wonder how they can blame their parent-guardian when the parent has sacrificed so much for the child.

As a last resort some believers review the questions being explored and insist that the questions force those kind of answers on them and that it expresses an agenda of the questioner.

In the transmission of the pathologos the authorities are only dimly aware that they are actually seeking their own benefit and are reluctant to admit they do it only for themselves. To them they may only be doing what others have done to them but one thing is certain—they are blind to the consequences on the lives of the believers. Had they known the consequences it is most certain they would never have indulged in this practice.

Many people require further reflection before they can accept that it is we, individually, who are responsible for our own pathologos. While we made the conclusions, there is no blame, because we didn't even know we concluded as we did. We are responsible, but the conditions for blame are absent. As for those who were the persuaders, they only knew that they did what they did but now why they were doing it. They continued a tradition but were blind to its implications.

But without the judgement it is impossible to name and describe how those who have played a decisive role in our lives actually were functioning. To move to the level where one must describe how someone functions is to move to a level that is divorced from merely judging appearances. When judgements are confined to how people appear then the way they function through those appearances is obscured and even lost. The willingness to judge how the persuaders functioned means that we must stand alone, without the validation and support of others. The standing alone and judging how they were functioning awakens the believer to the same crisis they experienced during the transmission of the pathologos. Since they could have made a similar judgement in the transmission scene but did not, they experience an impending sense of failure and futility.

The milieu construction of a loving, caring, and sacrificing parent or guardians can often be placed in severe jeopardy when the believer is asked to describe how the milieu functioned and, then, to judge who actually benefited from these scenes. The milieu scene can present an appearance in marked contrast to the pathologos transmission scene.

When the milieu provides the believer with the notion that their own judgement is central to their way of being, either positive or negative, then they have to face the question of whether or not they were fooled when they were led to believe they were superior when in reality they themselves were fooled. For these people the idea that they have been fooled and manipulated by someone they thought their inferior is difficult to accept. The crisis becomes more intense as they deal with the possibility that they were fooled by those who only gave an appearance of possessing those virtues and in reality didn't know and weren't sincere.

The crisis lessens as they realize that for them to reach this conclusion they themselves had to be sincere in their exploration and had to show unusual courage to go through such explorations. They gain a new sense of what it is to understand because to reach this point in their explorations they had to learn how to properly describe others and understand how they function. But, beyond these they are brought to realize that whatever conclusion they reached through dialogue must be confirmed in their own experience, so they reach a new idea of truth.

Thus, we learned from scenes that were structured to make conclusions stand as certain and indubitable. These situations were structured to produce a "silent" pathologos or belief, and it is because of this that we can say they were not taught. The situations in which the pathologos was learned are unique yet they share a general form, and questions designed to reveal that form also illuminate the conditions that gave birth to the pathologos.

The exploration of these problems through philosophical midwifery is based only upon the language and ideas of the subject so there is no need for any external interpretation. In these explorations both parties are familiar with the questions and the method. The patterns of behavior discovered provide a basis for prediction in general and are understandable in particular. The level of human behavior explored is not superficial since it reaches the depth of "emotionalized behavior" and surface ideas significant to the subject's understanding of their problems. The conclusions reached in the dialectical sessions are considered tentative, and it is expected they will be tested and verified through their own subsequent experience.

The level to which human problems can be effectively explored and resolved in philosophical midwifery is a function of the subject's willingness to face their own moral crises. Many people enter philosophical midwifery to solve their problems, and in the process they discover a new way of understanding that requires a more profound view of a morality; a morality that has its necessity in the ethical, and ethics has become an individual morality.

Notes

[1] An outline of these formal questions is available as well as a computer program has been made of some 400 questions that have been structured as a dialogue so that users can record and discover the roots to their own problems. Since the questions form the basic method for surfacing these beliefs and for their subsequent analysis then both the process and the analysis are a repeatable methodology. The resultant data provides a base line from which both changes can be distinguished and, if necessary, psychological profiles can be constructed.

[2] A validation study has been made of the Grimes adaptation of this Socratic philosophical midwifery and was presented before the 94th annual American Psychological Association in 1986 that demonstrated that "significant elements of GDRP (Grimes' Dialectic as a Rational Psychotherapy) is prescriptive and has the capacity for verification and evaluation without requiring external diagnostic criteria such as the *DSM-III*. Thus, the long held belief that a rational psychology is, in principle, incapable of either being empirically verified, or of affecting emotionalized behavior, is rejected."

[3] Grimes, P and R. Uliana., *Philosophical Midwifery: A New Paradigm for Understanding Human Problems and Its Validation*, Hyparxis Press, 1998, p 273.

Chapter 9

Critical Thinking,
Not "Head Shrinking"

Elliot D. Cohen

This paper will discuss the process of Logic-Based Therapy (LBT),[1] a form of cognitive-behavior philosophical counselling related to Rational-Emotive Behavior Therapy (REBT).[2] In this context, it will show how irrational, *suppressed* premises in enthymematic, emotional reasoning can contribute to behavioral and emotional problems, even ones stemming in part from unconscious, repressed thoughts and other psychological ego-defense mechanisms.

LBT's Theory of Emotional Reasoning

LBT holds that human actions and emotions are primarily deductions from premises, in particular from a prescriptive rule–by which one tells oneself how to act, think or feel—and a report—by which one files one's perception of particular fact or reality under the rule. Aristotle referred to such deduction as practical syllogism.[3] LBT refers to this form of reasoning as *emotional reasoning*.[4] While it is well known that Aristotle regarded actions as deductions from premises in a practical syllogism, he also appears to have regarded emotions and their physiologic concomitants as the results of prescriptive rules and descriptive reports. Thus, he stated,

> Outbursts of anger and sexual appetites and some other such passions, it is evident, actually alter our bodily condition, and in some men even produce fits of madness. It turns out that a man behaves incontinently [has such outburst of emotion] under the influence (in a sense) of a rule and an opinion [report].[5]

It is such a broad concept of "deductive logic" that is used in LBT. While some logicians would reject this broad usage, there are, in my experience, considerable practical advantages of applying concepts of deductive logic to help clients identify, refute, and disable the premises that underlie many of their self-destructive emotions and behavior.[6]

LBT's Theory of Suppression

In this regard, LBT holds that irrational emotions and actions are often the results of enthymematic practical syllogisms with false or unrealistic premises, especially where the prescriptive rule is suppressed. Herein lies a major distinction between LBT and classical theories of psychotherapy such as the psychoanalytic variety associated with Freud. While the latter attempts to uncover *re*pressed, subliminal beliefs, LBT attempts to explicate *sup*pressed premises.

These two processes of repression and suppression are distinct and, in at least one respect, opposites. A repressed premise or belief is kept at an unconscious level because of its perceived threatening nature. On the other hand, a suppressed premise is tacitly *assumed* in the client's reasoning as a condition of the validity of the reasoning.

When a repressed premise is called to a client's attention, the usual response is to immediately and emphatically reject it as false even if true. However, when a suppressed premise is called to a client's attention, the usual response is to stubbornly insist that it is true, and to overlook its irrationality. Clients often perceive suppressed premises, once called to their attention, as self-evident and, therefore, do not feel the need to adduce evidence to justify them.[7]

The suppressed premise of emotional reasoning is usually a prescriptive rule.[8] In contrast, repressed premises are usually descriptive reports, which, when called to the attention of the client, are filed under suppressed rules that prescribe intense, negative emotions. For example, asking a survivor of sexual abuse, who has repressed memories of paternal sexual molestation, whether her father ever touched her sexually, might produce anger or rage. The rule, under which the report is filed, in such a case, is often (if not always) irrational—for example, "If my father ever did something so horrible to me, then he would be a totally rotten person, and I couldn't stand it." Such a rule is itself usually *sup*pressed, but still contributes to keeping the memory of the molestation repressed.

In some cases, clients may *rationalize* a report rather than repress it. Thus, the client may be consciously aware that her father sexually molested her, but blame herself instead of her father. Here she might assume a rule of *self*-damnation as in the following emotional reasoning leading to depression and guilt: "Since my father did this to me, this must have been because I'm a bad person and therefore deserved it."

LBT holds that such rationalization would be a self-destructive attempt to overcome anger for the perpetrator spawned by enthymematic, emotional reasoning harboring an irrational rule of *other-regarding* damnation—"Since he did this to me, *he* must be a rotten, worthless person." In effect, the client would thereby turn the anger directed toward her father, inward—exchanging the rule of *other*-damnation for that of *self*-damnation.

In such a case, LBT would first help the client to address the suppressed, irrational rule of self-damnation that sustains the guilt and depression. In overcoming her self-destructive emotional reasoning, the client would finally be able to "get angry" at her father, and, in turn, to address the irrational rule of other-regarding damnation that under girds this anger. Accordingly, the client would be afforded an opportunity to "work through" her anger.

LBT therefore challenges clients to explicate and critically examine their suppressed premises. It is in this sense that it emphasizes critical thinking and not "head shrinking." While LBT does not deny that clients may harbor repressed beliefs that foster their emotional and behavioral problems, or use other psychological ego-defense mechanisms to rationalize, deny or otherwise conceal their "true" emotions, it holds that, even in these cases, by working effectively on exposing, refuting, and finding antidotes for their *suppressed,* irrational rules, clients are better able to confront and "work through" their problems. This primary emphasis on suppression, and its priority to repression and other psychological ego-defense mechanisms, is a major distinction between LBT as a brand of *philosophical* counselling and classical *psychological* theories of psychotherapy.[9]

LBT's Six Stages

While LBT is like other forms of philosophical counselling in encouraging the use of substantive philosophical theories—from Sartre to Socrates—to explore client's premises or "world views," what makes LBT different from other forms of philosophical counseling is its emphasis on *critical thinking in its own right as therapeutic*. Indeed, it holds that what makes philosophy itself so worthwhile is its essential reliance on critical thinking—that is, careful, analytical, logical thinking. The following is an overview of this process of critical thinking, which may be subsumed under a series of stages, as follows: 1. Identifying the conclusion of clients' emotional reasoning; 2. Filing a report; 3. Exposing the suppressed rule;   4. Refuting the irrational premises; 5. Finding an antidote; and 6. Exerting willpower.

Stage 1: Identifying the Conclusion

As is standard in the construction of logical arguments, one builds the argument from the ground up, so to speak. The conclusion supplies useful input from which to formulate the premises. Therefore, LBT starts with identifying the conclusion.

The conclusion of emotional reasoning is an action or emotion. When the conclusion is an action, such action is prescribed by the consequent of the major premise rule, as in the following example:

Rule: If someone does something wrong to you then you must retaliate by doing something wrong to him.

Report: George wronged me through his deliberate deceit.

Action: You do something wrong to George.

Thus, the action conclusion supplies the consequent of the major premise rule, whereas the antecedent of the rule provides the minor premise report.[10] Thus, LBT logically begins with a *description* of the self-defeating action under investigation, and then proceeds to find the premises from which the action, under this description, is deduced.[11]

When the conclusion is an emotion, it is identified according to its *intentional object.* Thus LBT accepts the phenomenological thesis that mental states, in particular emotional ones, require such objects. It also accepts the thesis of "intentional inexistence,"[12] which recognizes (and treats) emotions about false or nonexistent things—e.g. fear of ghosts. So, even if ghosts are not themselves "real," LBT still recognizes the fear itself as a reality with which to reckon.

Here are a few examples of operational definitions for ascribing emotions according to their intentional objects:

- Ascribe *anger* when the intentional object is something that someone did, wherefore the client strongly, negatively rates the action itself or the person who did it.
- Ascribe *depression* when the intentional object emotion is an

event or state of affairs that the client strongly, negatively rates, and, on the basis of which, bleakly perceives his or her own existence.

○ Ascribe *anxiety* when the intentional object is a future event or possible future event, which the client thinks will or might have serious, negative consequences.

Stage 2: Filing a Report

Notice that the above ascriptions have two components: 1. the identification of the intentional object, and 2. the rating or evaluation of this object. Each of these components is a key indicator of a premise from which the emotive conclusion is deduced.

First, when the emotional object is properly articulated, it constitutes the minor premise report from which the emotional conclusion is deduced. For example, take a case of intense anger that Frank experiences toward his date when she fails to show up for a dinner engagement. Frank is angry *about* having been deliberately stood up by his date. Notice that the intentional object in question—his having deliberately been stood up by his date—may, in fact, be non-existent, as when his date failed to arrive not due to a deliberate (premeditated) act of not showing up but rather due to an unforeseen automobile accident. Notwithstanding the falsity of the report Frank is filing, Frank's anger would still be *about* his having been deliberately stood up by his date, which would supply the purport of the minor premise report from which this anger was deduced. Thus, the enthymematic structure of Frank's reasoning would be as follows:

Report: I have been deliberately stood up by my date.

Conclusion: Anger

Notice also that this report is itself a corollary of a more primary inference embodied in the intentional object of Frank's anger, namely, *she has not shown up for our date, therefore she has deliberately stood me up.* LBT examines the validity of such inferences within report structures and the assumptions embodied therein. For example, the validity of this inference assumes the further major premise, *whenever one's date fails to show up, then she has deliberately (premeditatedly) not shown up.* Here, LBT recognizes syllogistic inferences that are not practical in the strict Aristotelian sense of having emotions or actions as their conclusions. Here the conclusion is a *proposition*, one resting on an overgeneralization embodied in the major premise.

212 Philosophical Counselling & The Unconscious

LBT accordingly looks for empirical pitfalls in reporting such as the following:

Overgeneralizing - Inductions from unrepresentative samples, stereotypical thinking, and compositional errors (e.g. "The world is a bad place because bad things happen in it.")

Black or White Thinking - Dividing up reality in terms of contraries thereby overlooking alternative, intermediate possibilities (Either you're with me or you're against me").

Magnifying Risks - Exaggerating undesirable possibilities (e.g. "If I fly, the plane will probably crash").

Concocting Explanations - Advancing unsubstantiated hypotheses to explain purported facts (e.g. "He must be having an affair because he's late coming home from work").

Wishful Thinking - Unrealistically believing what you want to be true instead of relying on evidence (e.g., "My husband will stop beating me"—despite that he has made no effort to change).

Could-a/Would-a/Should-a Thinking - Advancing contrary-to-fact conditionals that rest on false or unprovable assumptions (e.g. "If only I had been a better lover, then she wouldn't have divorced me.")

Stage 3: Exposing the Suppressed Rule

According to LBT, the filing of unrealistic reports, such as those illustrated above, is not sufficient for deduction of self-destructive emotions. Rather, such deduction requires prescriptive *rules* under which the reports are filed. These rules are ordinarily suppressed and must therefore be exposed before they can be refuted and defused.

Consider, again, the above enthymeme:

Report: I have been deliberately stood up by my date.

Conclusion: Anger

For the conclusion to be "validated," an anger-prescribing rule must be added to the premises. For example:

Rule: If someone deliberately stands me up, then this person must be a totally rotten person who deserves hell and damnation.

Report: I have been deliberately stood up by my date.

Conclusion: Anger [with damning thoughts about the date]

As noted above in brackets, the prescribed anger would include damning cognitions about the date—namely, that she is a rotten person who deserves hell and damnation. If the client does, indeed, entertain these cognitions, then the rule in question can be said to *validate* the anger.

Since there can be other evaluative cognitions entertained by the client—for example, that the date has done something terrible, horrible, and awful; that what happened must never happen—other prescriptive rules could also (simultaneously) be making deductive contributions to the anger in question. In fact, LBT recognizes *fallacy syndromes,* that is, deductive chains of two or more rules wherein one rule is a corollary of another. For example, "As people *must never* treat me unjustly, and, as being deliberately stood up is unjust treatment, it's a *terrible* thing; and, as it's a terrible thing, the perpetrator is *totally rotten.*"

LBT helps clients identify such suppressed rules and syndromes within the framework of their emotional reasoning. To this end, it provides a catalog of rules and syndromes of rules that are commonly at the roots of many self-destructive emotions.[13]

For example:

Demanding Perfection: If the world fails to conform to some state of ideality, perfection, or near-perfection, then the world is not the way it absolutely, unconditionally *must* be, and you cannot and *must not ever* have it any other way.

Catastrophizing (or "Awfulizing"): If something bad happens, then it is *totally catastrophic, terrible, horrible, and awful.*

Damnation: If there is something about yourself or about another person that you strongly dislike, then you or this other person is *totally worthless.*

Stage 4: Refuting the Irrational Premises

As stated, clients typically accept suppressed rules, once exposed, as self-evident *a priori* truth, and often continue to *feel* compelled by them even after they come to realize their irrationality. It is therefore important that these rules (as well as any unrealistic reports filed under them) are carefully and persuasively refuted.

Methods of refutation, gleaned from philosophical analysis, include checking for counter-examples, adequate evidence, self-defeating or absurd consequences, and double standards.[14] For example, consider the rule that validated Frank's reason displayed above:

Rule: If someone deliberately stands me up, then this person must be a totally rotten person who deserves hell and damnation.

This rule is easily identified as an instance of Damnation as defined above, and is subject to the following refutation:

> *Refutation of Damnation*: Doing something worthless doesn't equate to *being* (totally) worthless. Otherwise everyone or almost everyone would be worthless.

Here, the method amounts to a *reductio ad absurdum* of the idea that *doing* something bad automatically equates to *being* bad. Taking the refutation further, Frank's emotional reasoning would imply that Frank *himself* is "totally rotten" insofar as he admits to having ever behaved just as badly. Inasmuch as Frank does not think of himself as a rotten person, he would accordingly be applying one set of standards to himself and another to his date. Such a set of "double standards" would be inconsistent and hence illogical.

Stage 5: Finding an Antidote

An *antidote* to an irrational premise is another premise that corrects it.

Accordingly, refutation sets the stage for finding an antidote, since it provides a functional analysis of what needs to be corrected.

For example, in the previous example, the defect was in the assumption that doing something worthless equates to *being* worthless. Thus, one antidote would be a rational rule as follows:

You should stick to rating *actions* (yours and others) and not *persons*.

This rule provides a rational "should" that counters Frank's irrational "must" that prescribes hell and damnation for perceived wrong doers.

Antidotes also figure as premises in *antidotal reasoning*, which provides a counter-*argument* against the irrational argument it corrects. Thus, for example, the following antidotal reasoning corrects Frank's irrational reasoning:

Rule: If I think someone has done something rotten to me, I should stick to rating this person's action and not the person herself.

Report: I think my date deliberate stood me up, and, accordingly, did something rotten to me.

Action: I rate my date's action as rotten but not her person.

Notice that, in the above, Frank reports that *he thinks* his date did something "rotten" to him. This is a true statement insofar as it reflects a psychological state of his and not necessarily a defensible evaluation of his date's conduct. The main issue here is not whether his date *really* did something condemnatory. More important is that Frank *thinks* his date so acted. Whether or not Frank's rating of his date's conduct is rational, this rating should not be confused with that of the date *herself, as a person.*

It is inevitable that clients will encounter others who will treat them unjustly. A viable antidote to the tendency to rate people should not, therefore, depend on whether their acts are *truly* unjust. More generally, LBT holds that rational antidotes help clients to deal with genuine adversity, since this is an unavoidable—albeit regrettable—fact of life.

LBT also distinguishes between antidotal reasoning and the more general concept of *reframing* employed in other cognitive-behavioral forms of counseling. Whereas antidotal reasoning always aims at correcting defects in emotional reasoning, reframing a situation may merely aim at taking a different, more optimistic perspective—without trying to correct a defect. For example, according to Nietzsche, great suffering can provide an occasion for growth, an emotional triumph over adversity. Thus he states,

> When a misfortune strikes us, we can overcome it either by removing its cause or else by changing the effect it has on our feelings, that is, by reinterpreting the misfortune as a good, whose benefit may only later become clear.[15]

The misfortune may be real, and the suffering may proceed from rational premises. There may, therefore, be no corrective antidote because there may be no fallacy to correct.[16] Nonetheless, a reinterpretation may focus on other more positive aspects of the situation, and, therefore, may help quell the pain of misfortune. For instance, in tragedy and loss people may turn to religion and belief in heaven, and experience some consolation notwithstanding the loss. People who suffer from incurable physical maladies such as paralysis and blindness may reinterpret their situation in terms of what capacities they still have intact. Without denying the reality of their loss, many are able to triumph over undeniable misfortune and, in fact, lead, productive, happy lives—sometimes, even more productive than what otherwise would have been. In this respect, it is more rational to reframe the situation than to remain focused on the tragic nature of the loss.

Nevertheless, in many cases in which people suffer serious misfortune, their emotions are self-destructively driven by irrational reasoning—"It's so terrible, horrible, and awful that life is not worth living"—that they may be unnecessarily inclined to entertain suicide as their "only" option. In these (and, perhaps, in most cases where clients suffer substantial loss), it is not enough to reframe the situation. The irrational premises—the rule and/or report—in the emotional reasoning, must be refuted, corrective antidotes found, and willpower exercised to overcome the tendency toward self-de-struction.[17]

Stage 6: Exerting Willpower

Contrary to Socrates, the knowledge of right and wrong does not guarantee that one will choose the right action. The problem of weakness of will, raised by Aristotle, makes this clear.[18] LBT takes seriously the condi-tion of *cognitive dissonance* in which physiological, behavioral, and cognitive currents predispose clients toward the irrational while they are cognizant of a more rational antidote leaning in an opposing direction.

According to LBT, whether or not a client will take the antidote depends upon the cultivation of willpower. The latter is conceived on the analogy of a muscle that requires development through practice before it can carry the weight of rationally resolving cognitive dissonance.[19] LBT, in fact, defines human freedom in terms of the human's ability to harness this internal muscle to redirect behavioral and emotional currents. Phenomeno-logically, this is an internal *feeling* of power that arises in decisional contexts and especially in states of cognitive dissonance. While LBT does not claim that such a power corresponds to freedom in the metaphysical sense (in which determinism is false), it postulates that this sense of freedom is part of an evolutionary endowment that enables human beings to deal more adaptively with environmental conditions. Without this sense of freedom, we would function as mere automata. Whether such a feeling is reducible entirely to physiological processes that are completely determined by causal laws is deemed irrelevant from a practical perspective. The development of this internally perceived "muscle" helps clients to live more happily instead of being cogs functioning according to rules that they have been socialized (conditioned) to accept. Indeed, LBT holds that humans have, to a varying degree, the ability to transcend self-defeating rules of socialization, refute them, find more productive antidotes to them, and overcome them in accordance with these more rational rules.

Summary

LBT regards critical thinking as therapeutic. It distinguishes between repressed thoughts rooted in the subconscious and suppressed premises assumed in enthymematic emotional reasoning, and holds that repression and other forms of ego-defense mechanisms can be addressed without resorting to classical psychoanalytic methodologies.[20]

LBT embraces critical thinking instead of "head shrinking." It identifies emotional and behavioral disturbances deduced from irrational rules and/or reports; uncovers and exposes troublesome, suppressed premises; refutes self-destructive emotional reasoning; constructs corrective antidotal reasoning; and overcomes the inertia of cognitive dissonance through cultivation and rational exercise of willpower. Its formulation of cognitive-behavior therapy in terms of practical, syllogistic logic, and its rigorous application of logical techniques and standards to manage emotional and behavioral problems sets it apart from other popular forms of cognitive-behavior approaches such as Rational-Emotive Behavior Therapy, to which it is related.

Notes

[1] See especially Elliot D. Cohen, *What Would Aristotle Do? Self-Control Through the Power of Reason* (New York: Prometheus Books, April 2003); "Philosophical Principles of Logic-Based Therapy," *Practice Philosophy*, Vol. 6.1 (Spring 2003); "The Use of Syllogism in Rational-Emotive Therapy," *Journal of Counseling and Development*, 66 (1987); Syllogizing RET: Applying Formal Logic in Rational-Emotive Therapy," *Journal of Rational-Emotive Therapy*, 10.4 (1992).

[2] For a recent discussion of REBT, see Albert Ellis, *Overcoming Destructive Beliefs, Feelings, and Behaviors* (New York: Prometheus Books, 2001).

[3] Aristotle, *Nicomachean Ethics*, Bk. 7, Ch. 4, note 14. According to Aristotle, the conclusion of a practical syllogism does not follow automatically. Instead, given its premises, "the man who can act and is not prevented must at the same time act accordingly." Aristotle, *Nichomachean Ethics*, Book 7, Ch. 3, 1147^{a}30. Similarly, LBT accepts that there can be

internal and external conditions that prevent the conclusion of a practical syllogism from being deduced, or from continuing to be deduced. One such important condition discussed below is the construction of antidotal syllogistic reasoning that can be used to overcome the prescriptions of irrational practical syllogisms.

[3] The conclusion of emotional reasoning may be an action as well as an emotion.

[4] Aristotle, *Ethics*, Book 7, Ch. 3, 1147a15.

[5] For many case examples supporting this claim, see, Cohen, *What Would Aristotle Do?*

[6] Cohen, "Philosophical Principles of Logic-Based Therapy," p. 27.

[7] Emotional reasoning often consists of syllogistic chain arguments. There are usually several suppressed major premise rules in a chain. In addition, the edifice of reasoning that is used to justify the report also typically involves inference chains with several suppressed inference rules.

[8] The qualifier "classical" must be added here because many contemporary psychological approaches, including existential, person-centered, and cognitive-behavior approaches do not ordinarily aim at uncovering repressed thoughts.

[9] The report is actually the *motive* for performing the action and can therefore be gleaned by asking the client *why* he/she should perform it.

[10] For a more detailed discussion of actions as conclusions, see Cohen, *What would Aristotle do?* Ch. 8.

[11] See Roderick M. Chisholm, *Perceiving: A Philosophical Study* (Ithaca: Cornell University Press, 1957), Ch. 11.

[12] Cohen, *What would Aristotle do?*, Elliot D. Cohen, *Caution: Faulty Thinking Can Be Harmful to Your Happiness* (Ft. Pierce, Trace-Wilco, Inc., 1994).

[13] Cohen, *What would Aristotle do?*

[14] Nietzsche, *Human, All Too Human*, 108.

[15] This does not mean that there is no emotional reasoning juxtaposed to the emotional reasoning from which suffering is deduced. It just means that this reasoning is not antidotal in the strict sense of correcting a fallacy.

[16] However, the rational process of overcoming irrational emotions can take considerable time. In cases of loss of a loved one, for example, the grieving process generally includes a period of irrationality in which irrational rules drive emotions and conduct. The process of *working through* the grief means exposing the irrational premises, refuting them, and overcoming them with antidotes and willpower.

[17] Aristotle, *Ethics*, Book 7.

[18] Aristotelis Santas, "Willpower," International Journal of Applied Philosophy, 42 (Fall 1988), 9-16.

[19] Contrary to Freud, LBT would add that critical thinking is a "royal route" to the unconscious!

Chapter 10

Dialogue and the Unconscious

Alexander Kealey

Dialogue, especially philosophical dialogue, is clearly an activity carried out by the conscious minds of the participants. It is a mistake, however, to exclude the unconscious from it, for the unconscious contextualizes it, supplying emotional, psychological and cultural influences on the unfolding dialogue. Philosophical counselling might seek to make some of these explicit as in questioning assumptions, but even if these are not pursued or revealed, there is still a sub rosa dialogue going on between the conscious and unconscious minds of the participants. Some forms of dialogue are deliberately designed to encourage such interaction, for example, Bohmian dialogue. In Bohmian dialogue the intention is not to "make the unconscious conscious" as in Freudian psychoanalysis, but to be inspired by it, with the hope that it thus deepens dialogue.[1] When we thus compare a Freudian with a Bohmian approach to the unconscious we see that intention determines how the unconscious comes into play in dialogue. In the Freudian context the unconscious is suspect, harboring some secret force and embarrassment that we would rather not reveal, not least because we fear it might harm or act in disregard of others.

In the Bohmian context the unconscious is the womb of inspired thought and depth of insight that is optimally responsive to the situation of fellow participants. Although intending is an act of the conscious mind, it determines, to a large extent, how the unconscious interacts with the focus of the conscious mind.[2] There is no necessity that philosophical counselling deal directly with the unconscious. Nevertheless the philosophical counsellor should be mindful of its incursions in the dialogue and be prepared to respond appropriately. Very possibly, the philosophical counsellor (dialoguer) might question the client (dialoguee) about it, perhaps to analyze its logical structure. For example, if the dialoguee laughs inappropriately in response to some statement, the dialoguer could choose either to ignore it and stay focused on the conscious topic of the dialogue or divert the dialogue into exploring the reason for the laughing. The latter choice might be appropriate in a counselling situation but inappropriate in a public dialogue. The philosophical counsellor may have an intentional set about such manifestations in dialogue, even a formal methodology, as Socrates apparently had, but may also be open to respond to such manifestations with inspiration from one's own unconscious. Having a variety of methods in one's "background" (the personal historical unconscious) can give more play for one's unconscious to respond more flexibly, complementing one' conscious modus operandus with creativity and insight.[3]

A phenomenology of perspectives on the unconscious would seem almost as important for a philosophical counsellor to have knowledge of as of general philosophical worldviews. While an academic philosopher could very well carry his philosophical investigations without reference to the unconscious, a practical philosophical counsellor will be running into it all the time. A philosophical practitioner could choose not to deal with the unconscious directly, discussing it only when the dialoguee brings it up as a topic of discussion. In such a case, it is only the dialoguee's views of the unconscious that is questioned, not her unconscious itself. Many philosophical counsellors make a sharp distinction between philosophical and psychological counselling.

Whereas psychologists usually operate with some theoretical presuppositions about what the unconscious is, the philosopher is unlikely to assume the unconscious is anything apart from explanations of it, which are themselves beliefs, whatever their derivation. There is, moreover, a strong correlation between belief and the unconscious. Belief implies faith in the truth of something that goes beyond the facts. "Beyond the facts" could be equivalent to the unconscious, or, more accurately, perhaps, be about something that we are partly or wholly unconscious of. Polanyi's concept of tacit knowledge is apropos here. Whatever is the case (i.e., explicit for the conscious mind) is nested in greater orders of context that are implicit (unconscious, or relatively so). Effective living involves an interplay between the two which is dynamic. Competency involves attention to and mastering details, but such concentration is insufficient for effective action which requires the re-integration of the focus (worm's-eye view of the left brain) with the holistic, tacit understanding (bird's-eye view of the right brain).

Polanyi uses such examples as that of running a race and playing a piano. If a runner places too much attention on putting one foot in front of the other he loses the sense of the race as a whole, which is a more holistic conception held by the tacit understanding, and trips over himself. Similarly, if the musician concentrates exclusively on her fingering she loses the grasp of the musical piece as a whole and messes the rhythm. One must master the details, of course, but that becomes true mastery only when integrated into the broader vision held by what Polanyi calls the tacit understanding.[4] In contemporary neuroscience, it is the right hemisphere of the brain that is the seat of such "broader picture" abilities as grasping the pattern that holds the details. Hence, creative and/or effective action requires a dynamic gestalt of both a conscious focus and an unconscious background.

Polanyi's term, tacit understanding, is a more positive term than is the unconscious. The "unconscious" suggests a more dualistic conception of consciousness neatly divided between focal and peripheral or background awareness, whereas "tacit understanding" conveys more the idea that different functions of consciousness are complementary, a Gestalt. Conscious elements drift into the unconscious, and unconscious patterns give way to conscious focus, ever shifting in search of a "golden mean" appropriate to the situation.

Creativity is an important aspect of philosophical dialogue. The philosophical counsellor is not merely dispensing stock advice to the client. The maieutic aspect of philosophical counselling entails breaking through impasses into creative problem solving and new ways of thinking. It is not merely pedagogical in the sense of rote learning of information. Healthy thinking goes beyond the known and to do so one must be able to suspend attachment to habitual modes of thought (the set of which is conventionally understood as—or frequent inhabitant of—the conscious mind) and be open to fresh thoughts. Something is "fresh" when it breaks into your consciousness from what it is unconscious of.

To be the midwife of such breakthroughs is not just a matter of surgical intervention. The philosophical counsellor cannot just (certainly not always) engineer such a metanoia, but must await it, prodding away at the obstacles to its birth. In this waiting the counselor opens his own unconscious. It is not an abreactive unconscious, but the nurturing unconscious of the counselor that is stirred in this case. He attends to the client with an openness. Quite often, for example, the counselor is trying to bring the client's problem into a larger perspective. The larger perspective is "right brain"-ish in comparison to the more limited focus of the client's perspective and is thus "unconscious" to the client until insight occurs. Client and counsellor are both conscious and unconscious in respect to each other. The other is unconscious to one's own sphere of knowing. Philosophical dialogue thus involves one's conscious mind with one that is unconscious to it because it is not known, not familiar, not even—in most cases—similar to minds one is used to conversing with. (In the latter case it wouldn't necessarily be so dissimilar or unfamiliar if the dialoguee is also a philosopher, although in a philosophical counselling situation the dialoguer would probably be a senior philosopher and mentor, and thus still representing a depth of philosophical knowledge and wisdom that is unknown and unconscious to the dialoguee.)

The client is also unconscious to the philosophical counsellor to a significant extent. Respecting the otherness(/unconscious) of the person before him, the counsellor engages in dialogue, listening, probably, more than speaking. The ratio of consciousness to unconscious shifts through dialogue. The dialoguee becomes more conscious to the dialoguer as well as to herself. What is unconscious in the dialoguer to the dialoguee also becomes more conscious, although not altogether directly in the sense of getting to know the dialoguer. Rather the dialoguer holds back somewhat from personal self-revelation in order for the dialogue to nurture the self-revelation of the dialoguee to whom he is in service. The dialoguer thus transfers an unconscious, tacit component to the dialoguee along with what he says consciously and explicitly. Rather than filling this unconscious component with conscious content, the emptiness of what is given acts maieutically, like a magnet, to draw the dialoguee into greater self understanding. This is apparently what happens even in psychotherapy where studies have shown that the type of psychotherapy is a relatively insignificant factor in the effectiveness of the therapy compared to the compassion the therapist is able to bring to the therapy.

Compassion is a tacit force. One can fake it or muscle it in true Kantian dutifulness, but such explicitness chokes the real force of compassion which comes from the "heart," a dimension of the unconscious. Kant, after all, intended to explicate a totally rational ethic. Perhaps some philosophers may wince at the notion that "heart" has any role in philosophical counselling. I don't think it has to be a bleeding heart kind of sentimentality. In fact, just what it means to be compassionate is itself a matter of philosophical questioning. What motivates the philosopher to become a counsellor? To be philosophically compassionate is not something that can be completely conscious. Otherwise it becomes Kantian duty which may be laudable as a moral stance in many respects, but which is probably too explicit to be effective in the maieutic (nurturing) context of philosophical counselling. More so than in psychology, which has given itself to the medical model, the philosophical counsellor must question what he does and why.

Notes

[1] For information on Bohmian dialogue see "Dialogue: A Proposal" by David Bohm, Donald Foster and Peter Garrett (1991), published on the Internet at http://world.std.com/~lo/bohm/0000.html.

[2] The boldest method of direct study of the unconscious is through the use of psychedelics where researchers have determined that "set and setting" have the greatest influence on the nature of the psychedelic experience. Set refers to the intentions and motivations of both the researcher and the subject for undertaking the psychedelic journey. Researchers expecting a psychomimetic effect will likely have subjects undergo a very unpleasant psychopathological type of experience. Those who contextualize the psychedelic journey as a spiritual sacrament, on the other hand, will see subjects undergo mystical experiences. A summary of the range of experiences of the unconscious explored through psychedelic research can be found in Stan Grof's *The Realms of the Unconscious* as well as several of his other books.

[3] Even Socrates may have employed more than a purely rational method of working with his students, for he was often compared to a shaman whose affect on students often went beyond what could be attributed to his rational arguments.

[4] See Michael Polanyi's *Personal Knowledge: Towards a Post Critical Philosophy* (University of Chicago Press, 1974) and *The Tacit Dimension* (Peter Smith Pub., 1983).

Chapter 11

Hidden Kantian Full Thoughts in Modern Socratic Dialogues

Bernard R. Roy

The facilitator of a modern Socratic dialogue purports to make it possible for the participants of the dialogue to bring to their consciousness knowledge they already possess. A facilitator of dialogue is a member of a larger class of philosophical counsellors, all of whom offer various methodologies to bring to light stored away and unperceived knowledge. Socratic dialogists, therefore, work under the weak, albeit unargued, assumption that we possess knowledge of which we are not conscious. In this chapter, I want to argue for two things: for the plausibility of unperceived knowledge on the transcendental grounds that without it no form of minimally successful counselling would be possible, and for the desirability of a method aimed at retrieving such knowledge. A corollary of this result will be that there is kind of unperceived knowledge that the methodology of a modern Socratic dialogue is best at seeking out and that this knowledge, because it finds its genesis in a stage of subjective cognition that belongs to epistemology, should become the differentiating mark between philosophical counselling in general and other forms of counselling such as psychological, pastoral or spiritual. Psychologists presumably seek out knowledge retained in a posited "unconscious"; pastors and spiritual leaders seek it out of a posited "soul." I suggest that the philosophers facilitating moral or non-metaphysical Socratic dialogues seek knowledge out of a posited "reproductive imagination."

1. The Modern Socratic Dialogue

The kind of Socratic dialogue I have in mind here is the kind developed and practiced by Leonard Nelson, Jos Kessels and Dries Boele.[1] The dialogues owe their Socraticity to the emphasis they place on maieutic and elenchic processes: they enable the retrieval of latent knowledge through successive stages of consent and dissent. Although Socrates (469-399), according to Plato (426-347), demanded of his interlocutors that they share "*experienced*" knowledge, "if human beings didn't share common experiences, some sharing one, others sharing another, but one of us had some unique experience not shared by others, it wouldn't be easy for him to communicate what he experienced to the other,"[2] the level of the experience was noetic rather than empirical. So, the modern dialogue differs from its ancestral parent in paying greater attention to empirical experiences. In fact, it owes its modernity to Immanuel Kant (1724-1804); the sought-after knowledge has its source in the manifold of representations or appearances, that is to say that it is of empirical nature. According to Kant, the matrix of the understanding assigned to human beings is useless unless activated by sensory intuitions and assisted by the imagination; he argues that "Thoughts without contents are empty, intuitions without concepts are blind." (A 51 or B 75)[3] Kant, by being the first philosopher to give the faculty of the imagination some cognitive value, provides philosophical counsellors with an epistemological receptacle full of untapped "full thoughts."

Although each facilitator brings into the dialogue his or her own rules, all dialogues share a common structure and goal. The graphic representation of an hourglass is often used to represent the structure of these dialogues: through various stages of consent and dissent, as many individual stories as there are participants are condensed and funneled down to a core statement, the comprehension of which is expanded so as to yield as close to a universal definition as it is possible to reach. A critical aspect, therefore, of the modern Socratic dialogue is the metamorphosis of multifarious experiences into universality without loss of experience. The dialogue moves from the particular to the general, and the general is always conditional on the particular. As such, the goal of the dialogues is for every participant to have an intuition-based experience of the universality of concepts. The experience, therefore, is much broader than the noetic experience favored by Socrates, although it cannot entirely exclude it.

More concretely, a dialogue consists of a facilitator and at most ten participants. It begins with the selection of a question of philosophical import, preferably of the form, "What is X?"[4] The question is either of a metaphysical nature, such as, "What is a number?" or of a moral nature such as "What is friendship?", "What is integrity?" Metaphysical dialogues are not the best representatives of the modern Socratic dialogue because they begin with definitions which the participants proceed to scrutinize for universality. However, metaphysical dialogues naturally must remain within the province of philosophy, and it will be fairly unchallenging to justify them on linguistic grounds appealing to an innate generative linguistic faculty. During the process "new" bits of knowledge surface, mostly by implicature. If a participant knows that P, and is told that if P then Q, he or she will have learnt Q. Q's experience can be described as that of a comfortable fit: the new bit of knowledge nicely coheres with the existing system of beliefs, as if having been generated by it.

Moral or non-metaphysical dialogues, on the other hand, instead of beginning with definitions, begin with each participant giving an instance of what he or she considers to have been a *personal* experience of the concept under discussion. For example, if the original question is "What is friendship?" each participant describes what he or she considers a real life and personal instance of friendship. Generalities and hypotheses are excluded because they can be experienced only through particular instances; other generalities, such as underlying and unexpressed assumptions, will surface and be subject to analysis in subsequent phases of the dialogue. This gathering of personal experiences gives rise to one of the most crucial and critical movement of the dialogue, namely the narrowing down from a list of as many instances as there are participants to a single instance with which each participant sincerely relates or empathizes. The movement is crucial because the participants whose personal experience was not selected must still feel that they are very much part of the dialogue. There is no method or algorithm to follow; here, it is the facilitator's patience and perseverance that keeps everyone inside the project. By remaining "inside the project," I mean that at no time does the dialogue drift into generalities.

The instance is then anatomized into minute sequences of events by the participant, called the exemplar, whose instance was selected. The other participants are then encouraged by the facilitator to ask as many clarifying and interpretive questions to the exemplar as are needed for all of them to empathize with the exemplar's experience. The empathy must be sincere and here again the facilitator's role is key in probing each participant for his or her sincerity. Moreover, the probing may reveal unperceived or stored away information. This often arduous and grueling process, which somehow mirrors the passage in Plato's "Allegory of the Cave," where the cave dweller rebels against the philosopher's muscled "assistance" in the ascent out of the cave and in the light, eventually leads to the selection of one particular sequence of the anatomy of the experience, the "core statement." The core statement is the light, it is that which best captures the spirit of the concept in question. The participants are then asked to figure out why the core statement instantiates the topic under discussion. The responses will make up a list of premise-like statements, $Q_1, ..., Q_n$, so that the final version of the statement will have the form: $Q_1, ..., Q_n$; therefore X is P where P is the core statement. Boele calls this phase of the dialogue "regressive abstraction."

The "new" knowledge uncovered during non-metaphysical dialogues is of a much different nature from the knowledge retrieved in metaphysical dialogues. If one insists that the nature of a dialogue is to retrieve knowledge then the knowledge must somehow be preexisting. Metaphysical dialogues, therefore, need postulate a credible form of innatism. The kind of innatism I shall be suggesting refers to the simplest form of generative linguistic faculty. Because we, as human beings, are able to produce entirely original combinations of terms, we must possess a faculty (an innate ability) to do so. I reject, therefore, the "previous life" innatism of Plato or the theistic innatism of Leibniz, although the latter's account, as I shall attempt to show, is a prototype of the linguistic model.

There are good *prima facie* reasons to reject the kind of innatism argued for by Plato or Leibniz. For one, a radically innatist account of knowledge, instead of distinguishing philosophical counselling from its psychological counterpart, may very well achieve the opposite, and thus, weaken or invalidate this chapter's claim. Radical innatism, Plato's kind in particular, is not about our interaction with the external world, what he calls the "world of becoming," it is about a "world of being." If the "world of being" turns out to be a fantasy then we shall know more about our psychology than about the external world. And, most importantly, ties with innatism, be they with Plato or with Leibniz, must be severed if only because they leave too many questions unanswered. It is not that the Kantian solution that I shall later propose is any simpler—Kant's epistemology is famously complicated—it is that the Kantian solution contains less mystery.

2. Plato's innatism

Plato's innatism cannot be used in modern Socratic dialogues because it calls for a "world of being" that is too difficult to justify; second, it gives conflicting messages about women and knowledge. The difficulties of justifying a world that is only knowable through the understanding are obvious, and the payoff is mixed. The benefit of having objective moral values would be offset by the awkwardness of explaining changes in permanence. So much for the world of being. What about the conflicting message about women and knowledge?

Modern practical philosophy has gotten much hay out of Plato's analogy of the philosopher with the midwife. However, the analogy says a lot more than it appears to say; so, let me add my slightly opprobrious reading of the analogy to the fray of its admirers. In the *Theaetetus*, Socrates explains (and/or argues) the role of the philosopher by comparing it to that of a midwife. A midwife, herself not pregnant, but having in the past experienced childbirth, helps the body of a pregnant woman gives birth to another body. As crude as it may sound, this, to Plato, is the essence of childbirth because the result, Socrates tells Theaetetus, is either a healthy baby or a stillborn. And here the disjunction needs be understood exclusively and exhaustively. As such, it cannot matter that the infant be mentally or physically handicapped; all that matter is that it be a living body. Thus, the barren body of a woman with previous childbirth experience assists the body of a pregnant woman give birth to either a living or a dead body. The process is clearly exalted as purely physical and feminine.

Analogically, the mind of the male philosopher, himself void of any knowledge, but having experienced knowledge in the past, assists the mind of his male interlocutor deliver truth or falsity (a true or a false definition). The process is here clearly exalted as purely mental and masculine.

How seriously should we take Plato's analogy? Let us begin with the knowledge that the philosopher does not possess, but yet has experienced. We know from the *Phaedo* (63-69) that after death the soul, separated and delivered from the distracting and tomb-like body, can best realize its potential: "And indeed the soul reasons best when none of these senses troubles it [the soul], neither hearing nor sight, nor pain, nor pleasure, but when it is most by itself, taking leave of the body and as far as possible having no contact or association with it in its search for reality." (65c) We also learn in the *Phaedo* that it travels to "other" worlds where the gods are "very good masters" (63c), that is to say where the soul partakes of the gods' knowledge. This acquisition of knowledge in other worlds is again confirmed in the *Meno* when Socrates explains to Meno that the slave has learned certain things "at some other time" when "he was not a human being." (86a) What the *Meno* attempts to demonstrate is that the learning of the truth is a recollection "stirred by questioning." When a soul enters some body it is "pregnant" with the acquired knowledge and the new body/soul unit needs a philosopher to assist him in experiencing the innate knowledge. It is in this sense that Plato characterizes knowledge as recollection in the *Meno*. To say that the knowledge that is brought to consciousness was stored in the soul is to say that the knowledge is recollected from the memory.

One advantage to Plato's account is that, were it tenable, it would argue that this knowledge is infallible; a characteristic which Plato thought was so inseparable from knowledge that it steered him into a quagmire for which nearly two thousand years of western philosophy would attempt to find a foundation. I grant that the coherence and power of Plato's account make it intriguing, but the account itself is in need of so much justification that only blind faith can legitimize its use. It may be defensible to argue that the mind is a sort of exposed photographic paper in need of chemical solutions (a philosopher) so that that which it is a picture of can be made visible, as long as the exposition of the photographic paper occurred in justifiable circumstances. The circumstances described by Plato are not justifiable.

The price that Plato pays for infallibility is obvious in the number of unanswered questions he leaves. How exactly are we to understand the passage of the soul from the "other world" to a body? Why do souls so get punished if they best function free from the body? Do souls occupy bodies other than human bodies? If no, why not? Granted that a pregnant midwife may be faced with a conflict of interest, should she have to give birth at the same time she is helping another pregnant woman give birth, how precisely would Plato explain the conflict of interest between the philosopher and his interlocutor? Does Plato really mean to say that it is as impossible for the body of a man to be pregnant as it is for the mind of a woman to have knowledge? If neither the mind of a woman nor the body of a man can be "pregnant"—since the analogy cannot be pushed in the direction that if the mind of a woman can be "pregnant" with knowledge, *mutatis mutandi*, the body of a man should be able to be "pregnant" with another body—does that mean that women are entirely deprived of knowledge?

Although Socrates, in the *Apology*, claims that he holds dialogues with "anyone" he "happen[s] to meet, young and old, citizens and strangers," (30a) the list conspicuously omits gender divisions. Yet, other references to women unambiguously state that women have the use of reason and hence access to knowledge. Furthermore, Plato never suggests that women have bodies or body functions so drastically different from that of men that they present insurmountable obstacles to the search for knowledge. On the contrary, he argues that the bodies of men and women have enough in common that they can share physical training and both aspire to guardianship, as he has Socrates argue in the *Republic*, "men and women are by nature the same with respect to guarding the city, except to the extent that one is weaker and the other stronger." (456a) What is this common "nature" if it is not physical? In fact, in the *Laws*, the Athenian bemoans the fact that no laws in the states of Clinias and of Megillus apply to women, "half the human race—the female sex, the half which in any case is inclined to be secretive and crafty, because of its weakness—has been left to its own devices because of the misguided indulgence of the legislator," (781a) suggesting, here and at 805a, that women can be guided by laws. If women can be guided by laws, and laws are rational products, as is argued in the *Crito*, then clearly women must be rational. The superficial character traits that Plato imputes to women—women are secretive, crafty or weak(*Laws*, 781e); women cry and cannot control their emotions (*Phaedo*, 117d-e)—are not enough to justify the claim that women's bodies are such as to make them impervious to knowledge. The analogy, therefore, cannot be taken so seriously as to exclude the possibility of a source of knowledge other than the "pregnancy" suggested by Plato.

The quagmire, which Plato steered himself into in order to preserve the infallibility of knowledge, was bequeathed to and wholeheartedly adopted by western medieval and classical philosophers. The story was modified so as to accommodate a Judaeo-Christiano-Islamic God; the consequences of the emendation provided no clearer justification and left as many unanswered questions. It is to Locke that we are indebted for offering a systematically justifiable account of knowledge that makes innatism unnecessary. If all knowledge, including certainty, can be explained without bringing in innatism, so much the better for our explanations. Locke, however, unwittingly began a tumultuous era that led to Berkeley's idealism and to Hume's skepticism, and ended with Kant's transcendental idealism.

3. Locke and Leibniz on innatism

John Locke (1632-1704), in his *An Essay Concerning Human Understanding*, made an attempt to argue that it was "near a Contradiction, to say, that there are Truths imprinted on the Soul, which it perceives or understands not," (I,II, 30-32) thus suggesting that there could be no knowledge of which one was not conscious. In Locke's mind the "near contradiction" originated in his observation that the term 'imprint,' as applied to the soul, implied perception. Nothing imprinted on the soul could fail to be perceived. Locke's argument is aimed at Descartes' concept of the soul as *res cogitans*: thought cannot be, as Descartes maintained, the essence of mind because the mind is not always conscious of having knowledge. The view that the mind is capable of not being conscious of knowledge excludes a doctrine of innate ideas, but overlooks the function of the memory. This overlook forced Philalethes, Locke's mouthpiece in the *New Essays on Human Understanding,* written by G.W. Leibniz (1646-1716), to abandon Locke's argument, conceding that it was an assertion he had "let slip without having thought enough about it."[5] Theophilus, Leibniz' mouthpiece and Philalethes' interlocutor, convinces Philalethes that since we cannot be conscious of everything we "know" at the same time, some of our beliefs must be stored in the memory. It follows that some knowledge must be unconscious, and that some device or "assistance" must be found to *re*collect it: "Well might this be called *souvenir* (*subvenire*), for recollection needs assistance. Something must make us revive one rather than another of the multitude of items of knowledge, since it is impossible to think distinctly, all at once about everything we know."[6] Leibniz explicitly states the kind of assistance and the kind of knowledge he has in mind: it is the guidance that Socrates gave the slave boy in the *Meno* to "recollect" some truths of geometry. Locke and Leibniz, thus, come to side with Socrates with regard to some help being needed to retrieve a specific kind of knowledge from the memory and to bring it to consciousness. But although they agree as to the presence of unconscious knowledge, they disagree as to its origin: for Locke all of it must be derived from the senses; for Leibniz some (or all?) of it will be innate.

The dialogue that Leibniz imagined and wrote between Philalethes, the eponymous lover of truth, and Theophilus, the eponymous lover of God, makes no attempt to hide the fact that God (of Abraham and Jesus) occupies the central position in his metaphysics and epistemology. The world consists of an infinity of entirely independent and self-sufficient monads which differ from each other by how much knowledge (how many clear or obscure representations of the world) they are conscious of. God, conceived as the only monad conscious of all truths, provided the best possible distribution of representations and their qualities among monads, so that all would be in harmony without having to interact, and he instilled in them a desire or tendency to pass from one representation to another, hence a desire to bring truths to consciousness. Thus, the human mind is a monad which, like any other monad, possesses all truths, many of which, called *petites perceptions*, it is not conscious of; as a monad it also continuously strives to pass from one representation to another. Leibniz' monadology prompted the German historian of philosophy, Wilhem Windelbrand, to compare Leibniz' *petites perceptions* with modern psychoanalytic unconscious mental states.[7]

Leibniz' weightiest point in his favor is that innatism grounded in God guarantees certainty: "The senses can hint at, justify and confirm these truths [necessary truths], but can never demonstrate their infallible and perpetual certainty;" (80) Leibniz' lightest point in his favor is that the coherence of a system, like that displayed in the monadology, does not guarantee its truth. For Leibniz, the truth of the system does not lie in its coherence but in what we "know" and "understand" of the Christian God. As in Plato's case, certainty is bought at a price that may be higher than truth itself; if God is believed to be the truth, there is no motivation to search further. Pascal (1629-1662) was wrong in the formulation of his wager, which supposed that nothing was lost by believing in a God who did not exist. It is as if, for the sake of authenticity, a pianist insisted on having his or her right arm amputated in order to play Ravel's *Concerto for the Left Hand*.

Locke, as a more sophisticated empiricist than Thomas Hobbes (1588-1679), but less so than David Hume (1711-1776), is not quite ready to give up certainty. So, the debate between him and Leibniz is really about how each goes about justifying certainty and collapses into two different ways of looking at the world: for Locke the particular is a guide to the general, and for Leibniz the general is a guide to the particular. This difference is most conspicuous in the two philosophers' accounts of necessary truths. For both philosophers, no one can deny that some propositions are necessarily true. For Leibniz, "truths of reason," which include the idea of God, general principles (metaphysical and moral), necessary truths (arithmetic and geometry), and "pure" ideas are examples of certainty because they "come only from what is within us," and it is in the nature of souls to recognize the idea of God, because, "they [necessary truths] are accepted as soon as they are heard." (76) Locke, on the other hand, attempted to explain everything Leibniz explained by tracing its origin back to sensation or reflection; with regard to necessary truths he turned to a nominalist account grounded in the doctrine of predicables. All truths are rooted in empirical experiences: from particular experiences we induce general principles. Genera are general names arbitrarily given to ideas from which certain attributes have been substracted. The ideas of mathematics find their origin in reflection and numbers, and numbers find their justification in empirical ground. The idea of God, or of any seemingly inconceivable idea, is arrived at by aggrandizing existing legitimate ideas. Since Locke, the philosophical community has favored, often tendentiously, the empiricist program assiduously working, borrowing Neurath's vivid image, at stopping a myriad of leaks while remaining afloat.

However, Leibniz' fictitious face-off with Locke on the topic of innate ideas does not make specific use of his monadology. His argument seems to rely a lot more on the notion of containment of concepts than on unity in a plurality of monads. A containment at the level of concepts is what contemporary philosophers of language call intensional containment, and much has been written on Leibniz' insights on intensional interpretations of propositions.[8] An argument for innatism, primarily based in Leibniz' philosophy of logic and language and only secondarily in God, is hinted at in the *New Essays* and cannot be so readily dismissed as the argument solely based in God in view of the recent writings by contemporary linguists. Linguists and philosophers, such as Noam Chomsky, attempt to bridge the enormous gap between the richness of our propositions and/or theories and the poverty of available empirical data, by constructing accounts that rely on innate linguistic knowledge. I want to argue that Leibniz' account contains a proto-version of innate linguistic knowledge and that it is the kind of knowledge that brings us the idea of God to our consciousness.

Theophilus tells Philalethes that "truths of reason" potentially contain all particular instances, "truths of fact," represented to us with the help of the senses. For example the principles of mathematics potentially contain the laws of physics; the principle of inertia contains the potential movement of all bodies; the laws of morality contain all human actions; the most general idea contains all other ideas. Some truths of reason are readily "legible," expressible in language and reducible to identities, others are more like dispositions or instincts that guide our actions or reasoning. The dispositions are only "read" and articulated by philosophers and logicians; they are, using Leibniz' metaphor, like the veins in a marble block. They let the future sculptor know the best form or figure the block will yield. Likewise, dispositions and instincts let us know what the best conduct in life is. Leibniz' taxonomy of innate truths exhibit a certain hierarchy grounded in the scholastic doctrine of predicables: "Thus *innate* truths can be distinguished from the *natural light* (which contains only what is distinctly knowable) as a genus should be distinguished from its species, since innate truths comprise instincts as well as the natural light" (94), and innate truths are "contained" in specific truths: "Innate truths, considered as the natural light of reason, bear their distinguishing marks with them, as in geometry for instance, since they are contained in immediate principles." (98) How are we to understand the notion of containment here? A genus is metaphysically prior to its species; semantically, this means that its extension contains its species and species contain it in their 'intension' (meaning): the genus *animal* contains in its extension the species *cat, dog, etc.*, and each species contains animality in its intension. Arnauld and Nicole, in their influential *Logic or the Art of Thinking* (1662-1683), which Leibniz had read and favorably commented on, pointed out to an interesting relation between extension and intension: the higher the genus the greater its extension and the smaller its meaning. The highest genus is the idea of *being* which contains every idea and is contained by every idea, but itself has no expressible intension. But all ideas have intension and extension; an intensionless idea, therefore, finds its intension in its cause, namely God who himself placed the idea in us. The same presumably holds between general principles (necessary truths) and specific truths (contingent truths); the latter are contained in the extension of the former, and contained the former in their intension. The most obvious necessary truths are the truths of mathematics and geometry, which happen to govern the universe, and, at least and at most to the human mind, they are entirely devoid of intension. Since they are implicit in every function the mind performs, they must be innate.

Leibniz' justification of necessary truths and the revival of atheistic innatism by some contemporary linguists are two fruitful paths to follow in order to understand how the retrieval of knowledge in metaphysical dialogues proceeds. Since they begin with definitions, a semantic concept, and proceed through the further semantic analyses of the concepts contained in the definitions, the "discovery" of new concepts can be attributed to some generative innate faculty. This is a bit like what Descartes (1596-1650) does in the *Meditations* with the assistance of the method of doubt; the meditating process can be seen as an internal dialogue with the method of doubt as the facilitator. The meditator begins with what he or she habitually believes, checks it against the method of doubt, rejects whatever does not check, and finally reaches knowledge of the self as a thinking thing, that is a thing which affirms, denies, imagines, etc. Thus, the linguistic version of Leibniz' innatism, is helpful in justifying the source of the retrieved knowledge in metaphysical dialogues. However, the innate approach, without Plato's experiences in previous lives, a view we were earlier forced to abandon on account of the number of unanswered questions, is fruitless in non-metaphysical dialogues. In order to account for the nature of the knowledge retrieved in these dialogues, I now turn to Kant.

4. Kant's "reproductive imagination"

In what follows, I pretty much take what I like out of Kant's transcendental deduction of his first edition of the *Critique of Pure Reason* and ignore all the difficulties that Kant himself and later Kantian scholars found in the special use he made of the imagination. What matters is that Kant posits a stage of cognition that is justifiable on transcendental ground (without it something else would have to be posited in order to give an account of knowledge) and that this stage of cognition can be fitted into a slightly different overall scheme of apprehension.

The experience of empirical data is possible, Kant argues, through a threefold synthesis: "namely, the *apprehension* of representations as modifications of the mind in intuition, their *reproduction* in imagination, and their *recognition* in a concept. These point to three subjective sources of knowledge which make possible the understanding itself—and consequently all experience as its empirical product." (A 97-98) The manifold of appearances, the various sensory inputs, are unified by the unity of apperception, the self, held in continuance by the imagination, and mapped onto a concept of the understanding (substance, causality, existence, etc.). The reproduction in the imagination is necessary, for without it each new representation would destroy its predecessor. Without a reproductive imagination, Kant argues, we could never imagine drawing a line since each new point would erase the previous one. The intermediary stage of the imagination thus becomes a "transcendental act of the mind," an act without which no experience would be possible. Why does this reproductive imagination make such a compelling case for philosophical counseling?

The answer to the last question lies in the nature of the imagination as conceived by Kant and in the various phases of the Socratic dialogue. In Kant's account of perception there are no *prima facie* reasons to suppose that the stage of reproductive imagination cannot be re-reproduced or revisited, as frequently as one wills, for hidden thoughts. Particular frames of perceptions are like the postcards of strange places that we send to friends: we generally choose them with the help of our cultural trousseau. Each new perception is a new perception and, like new places, the data is overwhelming; so, at first, we choose what looks familiar.

Another advantage to the postulating of such a stage of cognition is that it is not overly psychological, meaning that, although it rests on some "objective" concept of human psychology, it argues for a stage of cognition that captures, synthetizes and retains a manifold of representations caused by something outside of us. The stage of retention is in part the result of a subjective unification of mental apprehension and in part the result of an objective organization by means of law-like rules of the understanding (the psychological part). All the while, what is simultaneously apprehended, retained and organized is caused by empirical data (the physical part). The retention of the subjective apprehension of the manifold of appearances is that part which should be targeted by philosophical counsellors and which should concern the facilitator of a modern Socratic dialogue because the essence of a non-metaphysical dialogue is the recollection of details of *particular* empirical experiences. Although, according to Kant, this is not the kind of process we are conscious of when it takes place, because it is spatio-temporal there is no inherent contradiction in supposing that this spatio-temporal stage of cognition cannot be revisited. It is, after all, always accompanied by the pure intuitions of time and space, without which, according to Kant, no experience is possible. There is abundant evidence of an active faculty of imagination, which brings to consciousness past and present perceptions. Consequently, it is not hard to suppose that whatever we ever perceived is and remains recorded in the imagination, and access to the cache is granted to whoever utters the right abracadabra.

Some objections can be raised. One difficulty lies in the veridicality of the reports of the imagination. Could the imagination combine bits and pieces of various perceptions and reproduce an "event" that never took place? Of course! But that is not a serious objection because the analysis of the perceptual frame takes place, so to speak, under supervision, that is under constant probing and questioning by fellow participants, facilitators or counselors. The questions allow the making of certain adjustments and the correcting of an imagination that was given too much of a free rein; our free imagination is creative and often fictitious, but our supervised imagination is a fountain of useful hidden insights because its content is traceable to perceptual experiences.

Another difficulty may be that the pictures of old memory are so faded with time that they cannot be "read." In truth, however, as long as one is capable of recalling particular frames, the forces at work in the dialogue will bring them back in focus. This is what a dialogue is best at doing. The focusing process begins at the time the participants select the example and continues all the way into the stage of regressive abstraction. The selection of the example is the phase when the exemplar contemplates his or her experience or when participants compare their personal example to that of the other participants; they search their memory with the help of the imagination either to know more about their own example or to recover an instance of their life that looks like the examples of the other participants. This means revisiting familiar places, but revisiting them with a more focused attention to it and its surroundings. The totality of the dialogue is precisely about paying numerous visits to the same places, but each time with some better understanding of them. A better understanding that is attained thanks to the unceasing questions and comments with which *everyone* is expected and directed to relate. Each question and each comment acts like a guide pointing to a detail of a tableau that each participant scrutinizes in his or her imagination. Each question contains words that act as keys capable of unleashing vaults of hidden treasured information. While, at first, participants all see different things, because there is so much to see, by the end of the dialogue they should all see the whole picture. The experience is like that of driving back to a familiar neighborhood after having studied a map of the area, or revisiting a monument you have done research on and understood a lot more about, or rereading a book. Anyone who rereads for a profession knows how stingy a text is on a first reading; why should our perceptual experiences be any different? We *need* to revisit them. The new theoretical or practical knowledge that you bring to the experience forces you to "see" details that you would normally not have been able to see given the overwhelming quantity of information available. The reproductive imagination is like a library stack of images; questions and comments are but catalogue numbers, authors' names or titles. The recalling and *re*viewing of images is credible and possible with a function like that performed by the reproductive imagination.

Since the examination of the reproductive imagination is essential to the philosophical counsellor and only incidental to the psychological, pastoral or spiritual counsellor, the positing of such a stage of cognition, as opposed to the "unconscious" or the soul, is what should help in singling out philosophical counselling from other forms of counselling. Philosophical counselling stands out *sui generis* because it stresses the role of a reproductive imagination in the acquisition of knowledge.

So, while metaphysical dialogues can appeal to a non-theistic linguistic account of recollection, non-metaphysical dialogues can appeal to the reproductive imagination. Neither the linguistic generative faculty nor the reproductive imagination are special concerns of the psychologist, the pastor or the spiritualist, but they are concerns particular to the philosopher. They are two accounts that have been examined and justified by philosophical methodologies and that should be the earmark of a type of counselling that is qualified as philosophical.

Notes

[1] "The Socratic Method," by Leonard Nelson in *Socratic Method and Critical Philosophy: Selected Essays*, by Leonard Nelson. Translated by Thomas K. Brown III. New York: Dover Publications, 1949; "The Training of a Philosophical Counselor," by Dries Boele in *Essays on Philosophical Counseling*, edited by Ron Lahav and Maria da Venza Tillmans. New York: University Press of America, 1995. Jos Kessels has published works in the Dutch language.

[2] Plato's Gorgias, 481c-d. All quotes from Plato are from Plato: Complete works, edited by John M. Cooper. Indianapolis: Hackett, 1997.

[3] All quotes from Kant are from Immanuel Kant, Critique of Pure Reason, tr. Norman Kemp Smith. New York: St. Martin's Press, 1965.

[4] On the nature of questions for Socratic dialogues, see my article, "Fecund Questions," published in *Elenchus*, the SPI newsletter, December 1997.

[5] G.W. Leibniz, *New Essays on Human Understanding*, tr. and ed. by Peter Remnant and Jonathan Bennett. Cambridge: CUP, 1985, p. 77.

[6] *Ibid.*, p.77. In this quote, the translators leave the French word '*souvenir*' and the Latin word '*subvenire*' for 'recollect' in order to stress that the etymology of the French and Latin words indicate help or assistance. Of course, as the French reflexive use of the verb suggests, the assistance can come from the self.

[7] Wilhem Windelbrand, *A History of Philosophy*, vol. II, p.424. New York: Harper & Brothers, 1958.

[8] Most important are: Bertrand Russell, *A Critical Exposition of the Philosophy of Leibniz*, London: Allen & Unwin, 1900; Louis Couturat, *La Logique de Leibniz d'après des documents inédits*, Paris: Aubin, 1901; Nicholas Rescher, "Leibniz' Interpretation of his Logical Calculi," in *The Journal of Symboic Logic*, 19, 1954; G.H.R. Parkinson, *Logic and Reality in Leibniz' Metaphysics*, Oxford: Oxford University Press, 1965; Gottfried Martin, *Leibniz: Logique et métaphysique*, tr. by M. Régnier, Paris: Beauchesne, 1966; *Philosophy of Logic and Language*, Ithaca: Cornell University Press, 1972; Benson Mates, *The Philosophy of Leibniz: Metaphysics and Language*, Oxford: Oxford University Press, 1986.

Chapter 12

The Unconscious and Philosophical Counselling

Dennis F. Polis

A projection is a mapping in which dimensionality is lost. A simple example is found in mechanical drawings as illustrated below. There two-dimensional drawings, or 'projections' represent a three-dimensional object. Note that, while each projection is different, they are all objective and true.

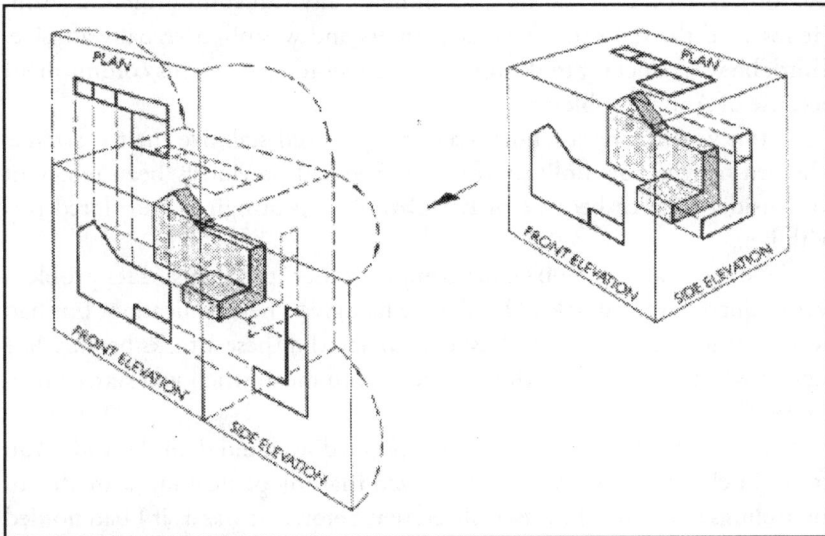

The philosophical application of the 'projection paradigm' is in the thesis that all human knowledge consists of true, but incomplete projections of reality. We attempt to understand wholes by constructing a model incorporating all of the projections that we have encountered. Obviously, the more projections we have available, the better our model.

In the context of philosophical counselling this paradigm allows us to accept our dialog partner's view of reality as possibly objective and true, even if it differs from our own. This supports an openness and moral equality that allows both partners to grow in light of each other's insight.

In this chapter I wish to apply the projection paradigm to the unconscious. I have two purposes: to explore the boundaries of philosophical counselling and to present a philosophical model of the unconscious.

Let me outline a recent counselling session. "Ann" approached me not as a counsellor, but in my capacity of volunteer catechist. Ann and her boyfriend, "Bob" had a civil marriage after she had their child. Recently, they had approached a priest about being married in Church. After administering a screening test, the priest had told them that he would not marry them unless they undertook extensive counselling.

Pursuing this, a troubling picture emerged. First, Bob had no commitment to the proposed ceremony beyond being willing to show up at the appointed day and hour. Second, their marriage had never involved any real love. In fact, Bob had never even made any real commitment to Ann. He reserved the right to have casual affairs and was often verbally abusive. Third, he was reluctant to do anything that would deepen his commitment because of Ann's "problems."

Ann was hoping a Church ceremony would stabilize their marriage. I helped her see how unlikely this was. She had previously been reluctant to consider divorce because of her Catholic up-bringing. I explored this with her.

We then came to Bob's chief complaint, her "problems." Her problem was frequent panic attacks. Her doctor had given her medication, but had done nothing further. When I asked, "When did these attacks begin?" She replied when she started dating. I asked, "You mean when you started having sex?" She said, yes.

We chatted a bit further in a non-pointed way, and then she said, "You know, in chatting with you I just realized that my panic attacks are due to my feelings about sex. I never realized that before." It was as if I had not led her to that with my earlier pointed questions.

I have not encountered Ann since, so I can only say that she left with some new insight into herself and her marriage. I left with questions about the boundaries of philosophical counselling. I was uneasy dealing with the unconscious intentionality of Ann's panic attacks. Even though I had helped her understand herself, I felt I might have overstepped my self-definition as a philosophical counsellor in dealing with her unconscious.

Some *prima facie* reasons why I thought the unconscious might be at or beyond the boundary of philosophical counselling are:

1. It seems the special province of psychoanalytic theory.

2. Philosophical counselling is often seen as the application of critical thinking to individual problems, and what is unconscious is not open to critical thinking.

3. Doubts about the reality or coherence of the notion of the "unconscious mind." John Searle, for example, argues that since the defining characteristic of mind is consciousness, an unconscious mind would be an oxymoron.

In the style of the Scholastics, let me oppose these objections with a *sed contra*: Isn't the whole point of philosophical counselling to make the client aware of realities that had previously been unconscious?

There is a lot here, certainly too much to be resolved here. The topics range from Victor White's thesis, in *God and the Unconscious*, that the unconscious includes God, to a consideration of the neural net characteristics that might be associated with unconscious contents. In light of the complexities, I have decided to make this chapter more a springboard for discussion than the defense of any particular thesis.

The notion of the mind as restricted to clear and distinct contents is a Cartesian conceit. From the earliest recorded philosophical reflection in the Upanishads to the beginning of the modern era we find a broader conception of mind. The Upanishads direct a great deal of philosophical attention at *avidya*, often rendered "delusion," but more properly translated as "not-seeing." *Avidya* is knowledge which misses important realities. Then, as now, *avidya*, lack of awareness, was seen as an explanation of personal human bondage.

If we are to deal with *avidya*, it helps to have a model that places the unconscious in a larger philosophical context. Let me outline how I have come to understand Ann's and similar cases philosophically.

An excellent projection of the human mind for philosophical counselling is Augustine's explication of the *imago dei* (the image of God) in which *Genesis* says that we are created. While Augustine was engaged in theological reflection on the Christian doctrine of the Trinity, the resulting understanding of mind warrants open consideration. I note in passing that Augustine's

Trinitarian prototype is not provincially Christian. Buddhist author D. T. Suzuki, in *Mysticism: Christian and Buddhist*, finds a similar trinity well documented in Buddhist mystical experience.

In Augustine's model the mind has three components—*memoria*, intellect and will—corresponding to the three Persons of the Trinity. *Memoria* is not to be confused with our English "memory." It reflects the Father as Source, and is that upon which we reflect in coming to know our self. As such it deals not only without past, but also with our present reality, and intentionality toward the future. Intellect is our awareness of truth, and images the Son or Word (*Logos*) which is the Father's Self-understanding. Will is our conative faculty, our intellectual desire and power of love, and reflects the Father's love of the Son, or Self-acceptance.

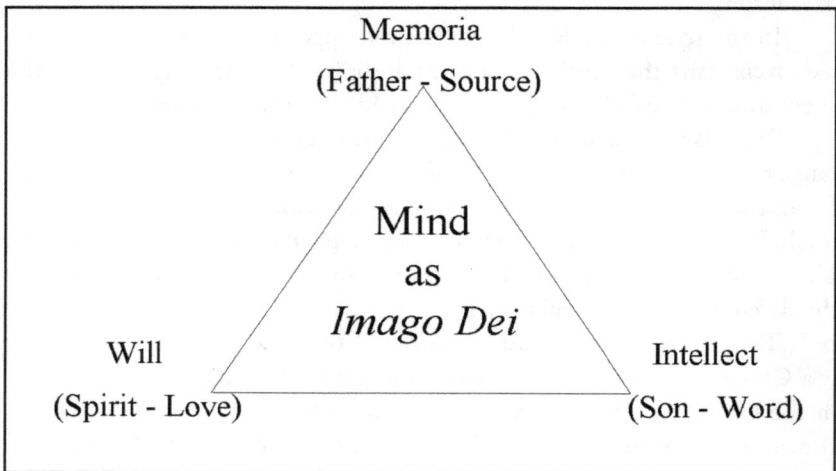

It should be clear that much of philosophical counselling can be explicated as a realization of the *imago dei*. Personal integration involves directing attention at our true reality (*memoria*), making it explicit in word, and accepting who and what we are.

In terms of the *imago dei*, the unconscious mind is those elements of *memoria* that our intellect has not illuminated. Since these elements are not available to awareness, they remain errant and divisive. We can not bring them into any conscious integration of our lives. If we intend to facilitate human integrity, we need to understand why certain elements fail to be projected into consciousness.

It is here that Augustine's psychological insight shows its strength.

Augustine does not see the intellect lighting on its objects randomly, but as being drawn to them by their inherent weight (*pondus*) or attractiveness. In other words, will, the faculty of love, directs intellectual attention to the beloved. By the same token, what we find repulsive or abhorrent is avoided by the will and receives little or no attention.

Now, let's change projections. When we have suffered a trauma, anything that brings our trauma to mind can become painful. The same can happen with acts we find morally repugnant. Thoughts of the trauma or of our repugnant acts evoke pain and become loathed and hated. Similarly, any evidence or logic leading us to consider the trauma or act is equally painful.

In the projection of classical psychoanalysis the result is *repression*. In the neural net projection failing to exercise certain links leads to their atrophying. In time, the corresponding associations become difficult or impossible to make, and what was an affective repulsion becomes embodied in a lack of connectivity in the brain. The result is an *avidya* that is no longer merely intentional, but physical.

Once these neural net links are broken, we become cognitively blind to select contents. No evidence or association that could give weight to them is activated (neural net projection). The data are repressed (psychoanalytic projection). Associations are not made (cognitive psychological projection). Consequently, the client might honestly not see evidence that is obvious to us.

That was Ann's case. Even after she told me that her panic attacks began when she started dating, it took her some time to realize that there might be a causal connection between her moral stance on sexuality and her physical reactions.

I want to conclude with a brief consideration of the relationship between morality and physical reactions. If we are able to set aside our dualistic tendencies and see ourselves as integral beings with both intentional and material projections, I think we can begin to understand how reactions such as Ann's are simply exaggerated examples of normal human functions.

I see morality as addressing the means of human self-realization. This is a view that many could subscribe to, although we might have significant differences as to what self-realization might involve. On this premise, human rights are the necessary conditions for self-realization, sins inhibit or preclude self-realization, and virtues are habits conducive to self-realization. In such an ethics, the realization of Augustine's *imago dei* plays a vital role, for we can't fully realize ourselves until we understand and accept who and what we are, our place in the cosmos, and our potential.

Our potential as human beings is in some deep sense biological and involves an integration of intentional and material factors. As Anthony Damasio points out in *Descartes' Error*, we represent the world through modifications of our bodily state. For Aquinas our knowledge of good and evil is by connatuality, *i.e.* by reflecting on our deep biological and intentional reactions of attraction and repulsion. Certainly these reactions can be obscured by acculturation and by the formation of areas of *avidya*. Still, we cannot avoid our biology, and biological systems tend toward maturation or self-realization.

While we may fail to consciously acknowledge or accept our reality, we cannot fail to manifest it. If this manifestation is not intentional, it will be physical. That is what happened to Ann. She was repulsed by the lack of self-realization in her loveless sexuality, but refused to allow that repulsion to become conscious. The result was mindless panic attacks.

Chapter 13

Can Philosophers Deal with the Unconscious?

Ora Gruengard

There are apparently three good reasons for the expulsion of the very notion of the unconscious from philosophical counselling:

The first reason is retributive: The alleged "discovery of the unconscious" by psychologists, and the claim that psychologists know how to identify its interventions in mental life and deal with them, while philosophers do not, was until recently the main excuse for the of the psychotherapists' attempts to expel philosophers and philosophy from "their" territory.

The second reason is epistemological: Philosophy has always tried to expose unjustified claims to knowledge and criticize rather than encourage them. From the point of view of contemporary critical philosophers the possibility that a great part of our mental life and much of our knowledge is not conscious is undeniable. However, much of what is said by *psychotherapists* about our "unconscious" thoughts and thinking and their presumed intervention in our life is not something that *they* really *know*, nor something that *can* be known. Some of their claims sound factual but are no more than indirectly testable hypotheses, while others are improvable and irrefutable and not always sensible speculations. Moreover, many "truths" that are supposed to be unconscious do not belong to the *category* of things that may be *known* or *unknown*. They are not discoverable *internal contents* "in the mind" of the patient. Despite their descriptive style, they are not descriptions of observable states or events, but rather *ascription*s of preferences and values to the patient, which reflect the normative map of the psychotherapist himself or those embedded in his psychotherapeutic orientation rather than that the patient's world.

The third reason is moral: Many psychotherapists maintain that the scientific validity of their claims about the "unconscious" may indeed be "somewhat dubious," but those claims may nevertheless be "justified from a practical point of view," *i.e.*, "as long as they help to improve the condition of the patient." That approach raises two unsettled moral questions: Is it right to deceive people with false claims to knowledge in order to improve their condition? Do not rational philosophers condemn healers for using the dubious *charisma* of an esoteric knower? Is it, furthermore, morally permissible to try to help people by telling them that they have unconscious *flaws, shortcomings, defects* or *horrible wishes*? Do not we criticize preachers for their pretense to lead us to salvation from the sinful wishes that they ascribe to us? Philosophers, for whom the avoidance of falsity is as important as the avoidance of other evils, may indeed use sometimes philosophical "fictions" or "myths" *as if they were true*; but they do not tend to justify deceptions, however beneficial they might be, by tribal magicians, religious gurus, political propagandists or charismatic psychotherapists. They cannot morally afford to use the problematic unconscious in their practice.

There are, however, at least three counter-reasons for the reconsideration of such a verdict:

The first counter-reason is involved with fact that the possibility of non-conscious mental contents and processes was *not* discovered by the psychotherapists. What the latter say about them was *in some way or another* inspired by philosophers. Philosophers in fact evoke non-conscious material no less than psychotherapists do. But Marx, Nietzsche etc. notwithstanding, they do it in a different way.

The second counter-reason is based on the opinion that some *hypotheses* about the non-conscious realm *are* epistemologically valid, and some *interpretations* of life experiences and dilemmas in terms of the less certain "unconscious" seem to make some sense.

The third counter-reason follows from the conviction that there are ways to relate to some *assumed* non-conscious contents and processes without deception, and with no pretension to *know* the "secrets of the mind" in general, and those of another mind—the "patient" or rather "counselee" —in particular. Those ways may be free of the condemnation of having *unconsciously* an immature mind, impaired capacity for reality judgment, malignant envy, incestual or patricide wishes, weak ego and alienated self, bad habits, moral rigidity.

In the following I purport to elaborate those counter-reasons and claim for the non-conscious its *due* place in philosophical discourse and counselling.

"The discovery of the unconscious"

"The discovery of the unconscious" is a title of a fascinating book (El-lenberger, 1970), whose conceptually somewhat confused author has com-mitted a major category mistake: The "unconscious" is not a discoverable thing: It is neither an entity nor a process, neither a law nor a principle. It is not even a kind of thought. It is not a thought just as the "natural" is not a tree. Just like the "natural," it is a label that different authors (and often one and the same author) attach to very different objects, or rather very different *categories* of objects. Some of those authors distinguish between the "unconscious" things and other things that are equally non-conscious, but are not properly "unconscious": They may call them "preconscious" or "subcon-scious," "subliminal" or "latent," "implicit" or "tacit," or indeed "conscious" but "non-thematized" or at least "not-articulated," being in the "penumbra" or the "background" of our intentional field. Among those objects we can also find those that were in fact noticed by us but were not subject to aware-ness at that time of their "real" impact, power or "true" meaning, although we theoretically could or even should have been aware of it. Indeed, we ourselves may be such objects and thus lack "self-consciousness".

Among the "unconscious" or otherwise non-conscious things we can therefore find thoughts or "ideas" and "affects" (which are supposed to pro-duce together "associations" or "complexes" of "ideas," "wishes," "emotions", "intentions," "expectations" or "fantasies") as well as semantic entities like "meanings" and "embedded messages")— all of which are mental "contents." But besides "contents" we find there other kinds of mental things: data processing (or thinking processes, associative, logical, and, according to some, also hybrid process such as the psychoanalytic "defense mechanisms"). Over and above "thought contents" and "thinking processes" we find there also innate rules, algorithms, schemes, blue prints or "archetypes" for data processing—both for "realistic-rational-secondary" thinking (Millian "rules of association," Kantian "forms of intuitions" and "categories," Chomskian "depth grammar," "Gestalts" etc.) and for "fantastic-mythical" imagining —whether Oedipal or not). To that list we have to add biological and bio-spiritual "forces" or "sources of energy" ("drives," "instincts," "Selves" and "souls") and somatic phenomena (including behavioral tendencies such as "habits" and "psychosomatic conversions"). Some would include also causal relations between thought contents and somatic phenomena ("motivation"), whose proper place is perhaps not the non-conscious part of the observed person's mind, but rather the very conscious mind of the observer. It includes, most importantly, the curious mental *absences* with which "the discovery of the unconscious" is most easily associated: We should notice in particular the unnoticed aspects of experienced reality, which are however present to the mind of the wiser: Leibniz' God, Goethe the poet, Hegel the interpreter of History, Marx the social theorist, Wundt the experimental psychologist, Lévy-Strauss the anthropologist, etc.) as well as the forgotten experiences (which are somehow "in the memory," perhaps in "memory traces" in the brain, but "out of the mind," although they have been "in" it, could still be or reappear there, and as some, e.g., Plato, Nietzsche and Freud maintain, should be retrieved). We should, finally, mention the (assumed) impact of internal "drives" and/or "internalized" norms and conventions on our life, of which (according to Spinoza, Schopenhauer, Nietzsche, Freud, Heidegger, Sartre, Wittgenstein or Lacan) most of us "fail" to be aware.

The variety of "unconscious" things is therefore not smaller than that of "natural" things, where one can find, besides trees, molecular processes and other events, behaviors, laws, causations, medicaments, abortions and death. The last mentioned "natural" item may remind us of the "repressed" and therefore "unconscious" item: the death-anxiety that is supposed to "be there" in the existential field where mind, body and environment are inseparable, side by side with "unconscious" items in the inter-subjective space, where the "Self" is involved with "projective identifications," by the mediation of "internal objects" with external natural "objects"...

It is also not clear *where* the "discovered unconscious" was precisely "located": We sometime hear that an "unconscious" thinking activity or thought content must be, or take place, beyond the "horizon of consciousness" or beneath its "threshold." On other occasions it is claimed that the "unconscious" idea is really "within" consciousness but "at the back of the mind," "pushed aside" or "pressed down." It may also be "there," but "dissociated" from the main stream of thought, and some find it "in the subtext" of a "text." Some insist that it is neither in the mind nor in linguistic texts but in the brain. Few, finally, insist that it should be intuited in the spiritual realm.

The variety of those metaphors suggests that the "unconscious" is not a discoverable object but rather a theoretical concept that has different meanings and functions in different theories. All those theories presuppose that introspective experiences and observations of overt behavior are insufficient for the understanding of human behavior, and the existence of additional levels, where non-conscious "data" and "data-processing," which do not appear on the "monitor" of consciousness, must be assumed. Ellenberg's book, written from a psychiatric perspective, does not take into account the great variety of the assumed non-conscious objects and processes, and concentrates on theories that are supposed to explain psychiatric "disturbances" or support psychopathological treatment. He therefore ignores its uses meanings and uses at other domains.

Who "discovered" it, where and when?

The title of Ellenberg's book reflects therefore an historical error: The *idea* that the mind "contains" contents of which we are not aware did not wait to be "discovered" by psychotherapists. It was already conceived by Plato, in one of its many senses, under the description of "forgotten prenatal knowledge." It was later assimilated as such into the three monotheistic traditions and adapted, respectively, to their religious worlds. Freud, loyal to the positivistic rejection of the Platonic notion of intellectually intuited essences, and Jung, adherent to the anti-intellectualistic trends within the German-idealistic philosophy, replaced the Platonic version by creating new *combinations* of already existent modern variations on the ancient theme. In the 17th century Hobbes, followed by Locke, has elaborated the idea of non-conscious associative processes, which would later have a central role in psychoanalysis and analytical psychology as well as behaviorist psychology. Somewhat later Berkley has spoken of the "notions" that we have of spirits, the unperceived perceivers, an idea which would be elaborated by Schopenhauer and would be the basis of Jung's claims about the "non-conscious and the non-intellectual Self." Leibnitz suggested the idea of "petites perceptions," i.e., unperceived sensations, which would later be the first psychological assumption to be tested experimentally. Kant investigated the mental processing that should enable some of the "blind" sensations to become "objects of perceptions" in time and space and some of the latter to become "objects of experience," subjects of intellectual judgments. In the 19th century we find, besides the development of Leibniz' idea of unperceived sensations of material objects, the development of his idea of inadequate understanding of spiritual truths, which, under the influence of Schelling, Hegel and other German Idealists, was the basis for the idea that dreams, myths and fairy-tales convey, unconsciously, spiritual messages. Schopenhauer and his followers spoke of the non-conscious "Will" whose "energy" finds its expressions in material as well as spiritual phenomena that is at the basis of our unconscious "drives" and their conscious expressions in our desires, feelings and deeds. Materialist social thinkers, like Comte and Marx, replaced "spiritual" by "social." Comte was the founding father of the positivistic approach that attributed to the members of so-called primitive societies a dream-like way of thinking even when they were wide awake. The anthropologists that would impress Freud shared that view. Marx, who had adopted Hegel's dialectical approach, claimed that the "unconscious" messages of mythical as well as intellectual texts were about hidden social conflicts in a society that was not as yet ready to confront them. Nietzsche has given a psychological interpretation to the same idea and spoke about a wishful forgetfulness, when pride, denying the deeds that memory acknowledges, wins. Maine de Biran, under the influence of biological inquiries has suggested that consciousness, which is involved with attention and intentionality, was just the "peak of the iceberg" of our mental life. Bergson, a contemporary of Freud, argued that not only latent memory-traces but also their re-activation in goal-directed bodily-movements could be non-conscious. Husserl, another contemporary and a student of the same teacher as Freud—Brentano—has turned our attention, like the Gestalt psychologists, to the background of our experiences, of which we are normally unaware: present sensations, "retentions" from the past, "protentions" to the future, and pre-given schemes or concepts according to which we "give sense" to what seems to be our raw immediate experience.

Freud, who had adopted many of the above mentioned ideas, had never pretended to have discovered that there is non-conscious mental life. He never said that it was a psychiatric or psychotherapeutic discovery. Jung, whose admiration for Goethe, Schopenhauer and Nietzsche was not a secret, pretended to be philosophical himself.

That does not mean that Freud or Jung did not say something new about our non-conscious life. It also does not mean that the behaviorists, who would prefer to talk about the mind as "the black box" rather than mention the terms 'conscious' and 'unconscious,' did not assume that processes of which we are totally unaware occur in us while we are "operating," "reacting," "learning" and "unlearning." Moreover, they share with Freud, Jung and their followers the views that our consciousness deceives us. They share, however, with most philosophers the view that what Freud, Jung and the followers pretend to know about the unconscious contents in "the black box" is even more deceptive.

For how can one know what is the "forgotten prenatal knowledge" that consists of the "memory traces" of the traumatic (or pleasant) experiences of prehistoric humans? Or, for that matter, who can know what the memory traces of "forgotten post-natal traumas" of babies are? How can one know that one has discovered the forgotten childhood memories of the fantasies that the patient "represses," i.e., refuses to remember? Or decipher the messages of the "unconscious Self"? How can one know when the patient's denial is a refutation of the psychologist's hypotheses and when it is just a "resistance" that thereby confirms the denied? How can one, finally, know that the philosophical "resistance" to such pretensions to know is a matter of bias due over-intellectualism and not to a right measure of rational criticism?

Why were the philosophers expelled?

Until the appearance of psychotherapy nobody doubted that philosophical conversations (or solitary meditations) could be of use to people in confusion, conflict, doubt, stress, distress, desolation and despair. There was, of course, disagreement whether specific philosophical *world-views* could be helpful and whether they were too logical, dogmatic and abstract (e.g., Aristotle against Plato), too detached from daily realities (e.g., Voltaire against Leibniz), too general and impersonal (e.g., Pascal against Descartes or Kierkegaard against Hegel), too subjective (e.g., Hegel against Kant), too one-sided and "metaphysical" (Nietzsche against the whole mainstream of Western philosophical tradition), too defensive (Marx against "idealist" and "utopian" approaches), too resigned (Jankelevitch against Spinoza), etc.

There were furthermore disagreements about the proper method of such conversations: Socratic questioning, rational dialogues or shocking provocations, monitored introspections or behavioral training, increasing self-awareness or reducing egocentrism, stressing common factors or fighting social conformism, commonsensical or paradoxical arguments, proofs or reductions *ad absurdum*, fighting habits creation or creating better habits; constructive or deconstructive approaches, and so on.

There were, finally, disagreements about the purpose or orientation of such conversations: Happiness? Peace of Mind? Eternal life? Understanding? Wisdom? Self-awareness? Self-knowledge, Self-control? Social awareness? Taking-responsibility? Better functioning? Moral improvement?

But despite all those differences, and despite doubts whether talks in general, in contrast to deeds, physical exercises, meditation, esthetic enjoyment, artistic creation, faith, Divine or physiological intervention, could really help, the role philosophical talks could fulfill was not contested until the appearance of the claims that real change could take place only by affecting non-conscious levels of mental life.

The first kind of claims were made by the associanists, according to whom all our mental life consists of the formation of associations of ideas, affects and behaviors, for they had realized that association can be made unconsciously, and in any case, we are very often unaware of associations that we make automatically as a matter of habit. Some of the associanists, notably Locke, thought indeed that the proper treatment for such unawareness and automatism was introspective analysis (which should liberate us from our existing "unnatural associations") and work (which could draw our attention to the world and thereby prevent further "unnatural associations").

Their "mind-analyses" were, in many respects, the forerunner of psyco-analysis." Most associanists, followers of Hobbes rather than Locke, believed however that the formation of associations is totally automatic, and no conscious reflection can change the laws of associations that they believed to have discovered. Their followers, Pavlovians and operational behaviorists alike, claimed that any behavioral, ideational or affective change is the result or formation of specific kinds of associations ("learning") or their breaking down ("unlearning"). They insisted that treatments (and education) should be done systematically by professionals according to the basic laws of associations and the regularities that are discoverable by observation of human and animal reactive behavior and the study of "conditioning" by experimental methods.

Though associationism has raised violent philosophical reactions, its conception is not less philosophical than the contrary conception, according to which we have "innate ideas," innate rules or innate capacity to develop rules for non-associative thinking. From philosophical as well as psychological—and computational—point of view there is no doubt that some of the thinking processes are associative, but there is a disagreement about the possibility to reduce other mental processes to associative ones. It seems however that all the materialist philosophers, at least some of the great dualists such as Descartes, Spinoza or Kant), would agree that in the cases in which "re-conditioning" works and reduces suffering, while logical arguments seem futile (as it is probably the case in post-traumatic anxieties and phobias), it would be cruel to insist instead on philosophical treatment by introspection, analysis or dialogue. It would be in fact as cruel as to insist that the mind alone without medical physiological intervention should fight cancer, ulcer or so-called endogenous depression. As in the case of medical care, philosophical counselling may be relevant to the discussion of the personal, moral, political and social aspects of such interventions, but they should not pretend to know that a philosophical conversation must always do a better job. Nor should philosophical counsellors try to do amateurish conditioning.

While unconscious associations of ideas are supposed to be tacit forms of acquired beliefs and affective and behavioral dispositions, alleged "Platonic," Gnostic or Nietzschean "forgotten knowledge" seem to support the other kinds of anti-philosophical claims. All those claims are based on the assumption that the "forgotten knowledge" unconsciously interferes with our conscious thoughts, feelings and behavior, but neither intellectual introspection nor rational conversations can help us to "retrieve" it and bring it to light: Whether it is supposed to be non-intellectual wisdom and whether its is supposed to be irrational, it is supposed to appear only in symbolical forms, and the deciphering of those hints are a matter of professional expertise, beyond the scope of philosophical reflections. The professionals —psychiatric hypnotists, psychoanalysts, Jungian analysts and lay "dynamic" therapists—pretend to understand why and how the encoding occurs and how to decode them. Moreover, they are supposed to know how to induce in their patients states of mind that accelerate the mental processes that are necessary both for more intensive emitting of encoded hints and for insightful change of attitude and behavior. Philosophical conversations are supposed moreover to have a counter-effect: to suppress such processes, to prevent insights and change.

It is also assumed that a change of a problematic thought, emotion or behavior can occur only if one is led back to the state of mind in which it was first acquired (or "got stuck"). This assumption is common to behaviorists (one is supposed to be able to change somebody's habits only by creating in him, or rather "conditioning him to," counter-habits) and hypnotists (a past hypnotic "suggestion" can allegedly be later cancelled only by a new hypnotic "suggestion") as well as "depth" psychologists. The latter share however an additional assumption. They assume, over and above the common belief that suppressed or repressed traumatic experiences should be re-enacted "affectively" rather than discussed rationally in order to get rid of its unconscious disturbing impact, the assumption that the natural process under which the problematic complex of beliefs, desires, emotions and behavioral tendencies were formed or acquired is a *developmental* process. That process is supposed to be involved with contents and ways of thinking that are different than the contents and processes of conscious and rational thinking, i.e., the contents and processes that philosophers pretend to have studied, by logical, transcendental, phenomenological, or semantic analyses of introspective findings. They do not agree about the meaning of that development: Some psychotherapists assume that the non-conscious contents are important "vital" or "spiritual" or "self-ish," but in any case, wise, messages that the intellectualist bias of Western societies leads us to ignore and suppress, and others, closer to the positivist tradition, assume that they are residues of primitive, indeed silly, ways of thinking and crises that are specific to "immature" minds. But they all agree that those non-rational factors—whether they emit "messages" and whether they create "symptoms" —intervene unconsciously in the adult's life and are involved, *inter alia*, with mental and behavioral "disturbances." "Depth" psychotherapists are supposed to understand those contents and processes and know moreover how to read the overt signs that allegedly symbolize, by non-intellectual ways of thinking, the non-conscious contents. They are also supposed to know how to enable the patients to pass into the non-intellectual's states of mind which are allegedly necessary for insightful self-understanding as well as overcoming, mentally and behaviorally, the mental problems. Philosophers, on the other hand, do not know how to identify, attend to or read the "symbols," and are certainly not the right persons for the inducement and treatment of non-intellectual mood in other persons. Their intellectualist perspective must finally render them intolerant to alternative ways of thinking. They tend therefore to be "judgmental" and criticize the "irrationality" or "immorality" of the patients rather than "neutral" or "empathic" listeners and interpreters of the patients' mental worlds.

The expelled philosophers do not pretend to have such abilities. Some contemporary philosophers appreciate Freud's or Jung's contributions to the growing conviction that we are not as transparent and intelligible to ourselves as some philosophers think we should be; but they do not pretend more than other philosophers (Schopenhauer and Nietzsche not withstanding) to *know* what is hidden beyond the opaque front. Other philosophers might be better aware of the fact that Freud and Jung were inspired by Schopenhauer's and Nietzsche's rebellion against the hope that science—whether in the positivistic sense and whether in the German Idealist one—will enable our full reflective self knowledge ("self consciousness"). They might also remember that the so-called rationalist philosophers—the ancient Plato and Aristotle, as well as the modern Descartes, Pascal, Spinoza, Leibniz or Kant —never shared the opinion that all our ideas of ourselves are, can or will be "adequate" or "*clara et distincta.*" Nor did they share the conception that our psychology is that of a self-transparent *homo economicus, i.e.,* reducible to utilitarian calculations with no inner conflicts, ambivalence or ambiguity, and with no unintelligible "weakness of the will."

Why are the philosophers still there?

Actually, philosophers were expelled from the field of understanding people and helping them to cope with their confusion, distress etc. for anti-Cartesian reasons: Descartes, following Saint Augustine, believed that introspection was the way to investigate our mental world, and behaviorism as well as the Freudians and the Jungians do not believe in introspection. The behaviorists do not care about it, the Jungians distrust Cartesian introspection, because the introspecting Cartesian "I" is allegedly both intellectually-biased and conventionally-conditioned, and the Freudians follow Freud. Freud, whose admired teacher of philosophy was Brentano, had latter disagreed with Brentano's approach in his study "Psychology from an Empirical Point of View." By 'empirical' Brentano meant introspective, in contradistinction to the conceptual analyses of the British empiricists, which reflected to his mind their mechanical preconceptions. Freud owed a great deal to Brentano, but he thought that even his approach could not lead to Freud's own "discoveries" about the unconscious. Typically, Freud did not mention Brentano's name but said "empirical psychology," but by that term he referred to Brentano's well-known book and not to the beginnings of experimental psychology, which he explicitly despised.

Philosophers are still in that field because for some or other reason many of them disagree with the behaviorist assumptions that all our beliefs are just a matter of acquired habits and our being conscious of them is irrelevant to our behavior or to the attempts to change it. Even the believers in objective automatism are aware of the subjective relevance of beliefs and affects, and therefore not a few among them believe that dealing with beliefs and affects from a philosophical point of view can be helpful.

Many philosophers disagree furthermore with Jungian anti-rational ism. Among those who agree with Schopenhauer and Nietzsche that much of what we are doing is motivated non-rationally and unconsciously by biological drives or instincts and accept the idea that we are aware of only a selected part of our sensations, affects and their processes of their elaboration and interpretation, many do not tend to agree that we have, beside the "perceptive" and "intellectual" capacities also "emotive" and "intuitive" ways of knowing the world. They prefer to see emotions as the outcome of judgments that are biased by wishes, and they interpret "intuitions" as guesses that are based on inexplicit processes, such as subliminal perceptions, associations, analogies and inferences. Most of them reject the idea of an inner "Self" that knows better than the "I" what is proper for the specific individual, because they doubt the possibility of an inner perfect knower, because they believe that we choose our aims and actions in light of refutable beliefs, and/or also because the ideal of obeying the orders of an inner perfect knower is based on illusions: The illusion that the religious duty to obey to a Divine call (in which most of them do not believe) is replaceable by a kind of a vital "duty" to obey the whispers of "the Self"; and the illusion that the latter "duty" is a better, mentally "healthier" and "existentially" more important alternative to the Kantian moral duty to obey the dictates of practical reason. Moreover, even those who tend to prefer the ideals of "self-realization" and "authenticity" to that of rational autonomy do not tend to believe that the Jungian theoretical speculations about symbols and their roles in the "unconscious" and the "collective sub-conscious" of human "races" and in their myths, and Jungian practical interpretations of peoples' associations and dreams, enhance those ideals. They have good reasons to prefer Rogerian phenomenological analyses—though they too assume an inner perfect knower—and suspect that the Jungian interpreter suggests choices rather than helps the patient to find what his "inner Self" really whispers. Those who are aware of Jung's ideological sympathies might see in them, under the guise of a theory about mental health and a treatment for mental illness, an attempt to propagate values that are, morally, a matter of debate.

Many philosophers disagree, finally, with the psychoanalytic approach. Even those who, unlike most research psychologists and many psychotherapists, find it interesting, insightful and useful claim, just like the latter, that it has no scientific status. Indeed many psychoanalysts admit that they offer interpretations rather than scientifically dig out from the patients' unconscious minds and explain mental "archeological" facts. Philosophers tend therefore to reject the assumption of the active though unconscious "forgotten knowledge" that is allegedly inherited from our prehistoric ancestors and re-invoked in infantile "unconscious fantasies" and adult's unconscious neurotic thoughts: It is not only untestable myth; it does not make much sense. We cannot really imagine what it could mean for a three years old child to have Freudian Oedipal wishes. Moreover, they cast in doubt the claim that psychoanalytic techniques enable the retrieval of personal defensively "forgotten knowledge, i.e., "repressed" or "disguised" thoughts and affects. Indeed, if Freud's theory about the formation of the defensive repressions and disguises is correct, and there are infinite ways by which an anxiety raising thought item can be replaced by a less dangerous association, it is unreasonable to assume that one can rediscover the repressed or disguised. It is therefore not surprising that psychoanalysis fails to offer any criterion for the distinction between the patient's "defensive resistance" to the psychoanalyst's "discoveries" about his unconscious world and his reasonable objections to being the victim of imaginary and unjustified ascription of opinions, wishes and anxieties. They therefore identify there a circle that is as vicious as the circle of the religious claim that the unbeliever refuses to see the light, and suspect that the patient's way to "insights," like the unbeliever's conversion, is due to persuasive methods that under other circumstances are condemned as brain-washing. One of the criteria for that belief is the fact that different schools of psychoanalysis, with different assumption about the contents of the "forgotten" ideas and affects, have more of less the same percentage of success in persuading the patients...

There are, of course, philosophers that accept psychoanalytic claims as metaphors about the human condition and the conflicts with which it is involved. It is therefore relevant to stress that the different conceptions of the human condition that are presupposed by different psychoanalytic schools existed independently of psychoanalysis and its assumption that the conflicts with which it is involved must be unconscious, i.e., repressed or otherwise disguised. The psychoanalytic versions are all variations on a theme that has sociological as well as psychological interpretations, inspired by ancient religious myths that have latter received secular political translation: They all presuppose a struggle between nature and culture, self-love and love of the other, individualism and adaptation to social demands, pleasure seeking and rational realism etc. and believe that the process by which such conflicts are overcome is involved with resistance and disturbances. The philosophers who accept the metaphorical interpretation accept the world view that it expresses, and accordingly different philosophers prefer different —and sometimes incompatible—psychoanalytic versions. In other words, they are aware that the question which version is preferable is a matter of debate, a philosophical debate about meanings, values and ideals, rather than about unconscious mental facts.

Philosophers that are well acquainted with the history of ideas can identify the philosophical sources of inspiration of the various versions. Freud, for example, was inspired by the Hobbes, Locke and Mill, Brentano's critique of them and the Augustinian principles in his epistemology, and Nietzsche's inversion of the Augustinian theory of love. Those philosophers are, of course, not responsible for his interpretation of the Oedipal myth and the infantile anxieties that he attributes to us, but they are the sources of the Freudian ideals to which the patient's unconscious mind allegedly "fails" to adhere: the ability to distinguish between fantasy and reality, between the desirable and the possible, between associative connections and logical ones, between thinking and assenting, wishing and willing, and willing and doing, and between social heteronomy and moral autonomy. Klein, one of his rebellious disciples, does not seem to be impressed (or acquainted) with Brentano's ideals. She is an admirer of Hegel (whom Brentano despised) and applies his theory of the "unhappy conscious-ness," which attributes thoughts that are typical to Shakespearean rascals to the unconscious mind of "immature" persons and cultures, to small children, whose unconscious thought she can only imagine. Her ideals are accordingly related to the "mature" ability to make "syntheses" (or, in her vernacular, "integrations") and recognize that the oppositions that should be "integrated" are "immanent," or, in her language, are between "parts" of "self" and "object" within the patient's own mind. She believes furthermore that the important thing is acquiring the ability of "taking responsibility." Many Kleinians do not know that that is a (dubious) application of Hegel's wish that humanity as a whole takes responsibility of its destiny and stop passing it to imaginary forces like transcendent Gods and Devils to the life of individuals. It is, therefore, not surprising to find psychoanalysts, like Kohut, Laing or Lacan, with existentialist counter-conceptions, for whom the criterion for "maturity" is the individual's recognition of the fact that the things and the others "in the world" transcend our minds, and his realiza-tion that he is neither omnipotent nor comprehensive and all inclusive as "humanity as a whole" and not as omniscient as Hegel. Winnicott, to take another example, is inspired by Rousseau, and his ideal is a kind of fostering the noble savage (identified as the "true self") and liberating him from social coercion (which forces us to disguise ourselves with "false selves"). Kohut, once more, was also inspired by Husserl and Sartre, and his ideal is to foster self-awareness in terms of an active "I can" rather than seeing oneself in the eyes of someone who takes him for a passive and determined object.

Such ideals, which are not always compatible with each other, deserve to be discussed rather than imposed as pseudo-scientific criteria for "normal," "healthy," "mature" or "well-adapted" personality. Psychoanalysis presupposes that we are neurotic, with all the "disturbances" that might go with it, because underneath our more or less "mature" conscious declarations, our "immature" unconscious mind fails to live up to those criteria. The philosophers are still there because those criteria—or ideals—are a matter of debate, and there is no proof that "failing" to live according any of them is a symptom of mental "immaturity." The philosophers are still there because they believed that an interested counsellee should choose between them explicitly and deliberately rather than be led under the emotional impact of the psychoanalytic encounter to comply unreflectively with the analyst's wish to foster in him readiness to think, feel or behave according to the specific ideals that are embedded as criteria for "maturity" etc. in the therapeutic conception of the specific school to which the analyst happens to belong.

What is morally wrong with the use of the unconscious in psychotherapy?

It would be certainly wrong to deny that many people are helped by psychotherapy. Various studies indicate that psychotherapy of each orientation is considered by about one third of its clients as helpful. No philosophical counsellor, who has neither statistics nor anecdotic information, can rightly claim that according to the opinions of counsellees philosophers are more successful. Indeed, if subjective impressions are the criteria, we might reasonably assume that the impact of magicians and spiritual leaders on those who believe in their charismatic abilities is much stronger. But philosophical counsellors do not pretend to offer more effective methods; they pretend to offer methods that are philosophically acceptable. Philosophers are not supposed to be truthful and do not pretend to have abilities or knowledge that they have not. Their philosophical conscious does not allow them, *qua* philosophers, to apply magical and mystical tricks nor create the illusion that they know what they do not know, even if such an illusion may be helpful. From a philosophical point of view the very use of pretended knowledge about the unconscious is immoral.

Psychotherapists that are aware of the epistemological status of their claim to knowledge maintain, sometimes, that not only they, but also those who apply magic and mystification, are acting morally if they help thereby those who believe in them. From a philosophical point of view, however, they not only pretend to be wiser than they are, they also pretend to know that the patients are, at least on the unconscious level, sillier than they really are. They also pretend to know that according to prevalent criteria their unconscious wishes and thoughts are immoral; and they go even further and claim that their wishes and thoughts on that level manifest an incapacity to make any moral judgment, or at least a "mature" one. The Freudian patient allegedly entertains incestual and patricide fantasies, is unable to distinguish between an intention and a deed, and his criteria were adopted blindly by "identification with the aggressor." The Kleinian patient is an envious rascal; that of Winnicott is false, and that of Kohut is a reckless megalomaniac etc.

Psychotherapists do not have evidence for their allegation. They follow Freud, who has adopted the philosophical and sociological conviction that cognitive and moral capacities are evolving through phases. In each new phase, a problem that could not be resolved by the old ways of thinking is solved by a new way of thinking, under conditions of emotional turmoil. But the process is incomplete, and residues of former phases continue to operate unconsciously and disturbingly interfere with the more advanced thinking.

The theory is debatable. But even if it were not it would not have been reasonable to assume that we get stuck in our life because older, primitive, ways of thinking interfere. We may get stuck because we cannot overcome a problem with our prevailing assumptions, but have not realized that we have to change them, and have no idea what to change. Telling people that they get stuck because they think in primitive ways is morally wrong:

While specific assumptions about unconscious *processing* of information, attitudes or projects are replaceable by alternative assumptions, the allegations of "unconscious" *contents*—thoughts, intentions, fears, emotions etc.—are sticky allegations. Alternative "knowers" attribute, as we have seen, alternative contents but once the pretending "knower," a magician or a priest, a psychologist or a sociologist, has made the respective attribution, the target or victim, at which the attribution is directed has no means to convince the "knower" (and his hearers) that he might be wrong. Whether the victim of such allegations does not know the unconscious "truth" and whether he just "defensively" or "self-deceptively" denies it, whatever he may say will never count as a proof for the "knower" mistaken or false attribution. Sticky allegations, whether by an Indian Guru or a Cabalistic persuader, a Bolshevik police investigator or a anti-communist brain-washer, and whether by a psychoanalyst or a Jungian therapist, a mind-reading parent or spouse, or the neighbor who "knows" it from the Reader's Digest, are not only ir-refutable theories. They are often experienced as irrefutable malevolent and malignant accusations. They are involved, moreover, with a denial of the victim's ability to form an independent view or have a reliable self-concep-tion, and though he is still "entitled to have his own opinion" about himself, his right to claim his freedom of thought is actually cast in doubt.

It would be misleading to say that such allegations are "unphilosophi-cal." Some philosophers participate in such activities; in fact, philosophers were among the initiators of such tricks. Theories about knowledge and meaning gave birth to pretensions to know better than the non-enlightened subject himself what he unknowingly think or mean. But such activities seem to be incompatible with critical approaches to philosophy, approaches that condemn unjustified claims to *knowledge* and abusive speech acts.

Philosophers pretend to know more than they actually do, and like other people, make sometimes false ascriptions. But philosophy is discursive. It presupposes that a philosopher has to *give good reasons* for any ascription of non-conscious motives, emotions, memories or ways of thinking to an-other person. It also presupposes that everybody, including Menon's slave (in Plato's dialogue *Menon*) as well as all the other "non-initiated" persons, whatever is the sect of "knowers" to which that they "fail" to belong, may refute by a good argument unjustified claims to knowledge, and therefore is entitled to participate in the debate. The failure of psychotherapists, despite their inter-and intra-school controversies, to accept the "patient" as a par-ticipant in the debate about himself, their resistance to his "resistance," their aggressive profession-defensive rhetoric against his "aggressive-defensive" disagreements with their methods and interpretations, is itself a sufficient reason to "regress" in the case of indecision, confusion, doubt or despair to the old tradition of philosophical conversation.

May philosophical counselors use the concept of the unconscious nevertheless?

The answer is "of course," provided they interpret the Platonic idea of "forgotten knowledge" as presuppositions or implications of which we are unaware. We need sometimes to realize that problems that seem insoluble could be solved from a new perspective. Philosophers may sometimes propose a new way of seeing, but their major contribution consist in the critic of presuppositions that prevent us from seeing that our prevailing assumptions are false, or at least, not necessarily or exclusively true. The philosopher is not a mind-reader and does not know what the counselee tacitly presupposes or what he unconsciously implies. He assumes a logical connection between an explicit thought and an assumed implicit belief. And he has to examine it with the counsellee.

Chapter 14

Causal Nets and the Disappearance of the Unconscious

Martin Hunt and Peter B. Raabe

The definition and description of the unconscious has undergone enormous changes from the time of its early articulation by, among others, Pierre Janet, Sigmund Freud, and Carl Jung. Much of the critical focus on the unconscious has been directed at its questionable ontological status, often resulting in the denial of its existence by means of reference to the most recent neurological research. This is because the preeminent proponent of the unconscious, Sigmund Freud, long ago insisted that all discussion of mental problems should be distanced from superstition and religious references—such as that they are caused by evil demons inhabiting the soul—and instead be carried out in the functionalist discourse of medical science: that of the causal interactions of inner states.[1] Freud was, after all, a trained physician and neurologist. Neurology deals with the physiological functioning and malfunctions of the 'electrical wiring' in the human body. When Freud treated people whose minds were not functioning according to what was considered the norm in his day he took a medical science approach, conceptually reducing a person's emotional distress or existential crisis to what he believed to be its internally hidden cause, and then redefining it in medical terminology as 'mental illness' requiring a treatment procedure compatible with established medical protocol. Unfortunately, by labeling mental or emotional distress as pathology or illness, Freud defined the *source* of the problem as being endogenous, or located within the distressed individual, rather than in the external environments of family, church, and society. His medical approach thereby led him to view both psychological and existential problems as the consequences of fairly clear-cut endogenous causes in his patients.[2] Professor of psychology, Laurence Simon writes that Freud reified many of his own concepts, making non-conscious mental processes into "the unconscious," containing the conflicted activities of the id, ego, and super ego, which psychoanalysts claim are "the real source of mental illnesses."[3]

Freud, his contemporaries, and his followers treated what they called mental illnesses the same way a medical doctor treats a patient with an organic or physical illness: there is a penetration into the ailing mind of the patient that will "unearth the primary cause,"[4] and treatment is administered that is aimed at eliminating that cause. Treatment, whether it is medication or analysis, are administered by the doctor to the patient in the form of prescriptions. The prescriptions need not be understood by the patient; recovery simply depends on the patient obeying the doctor. Freud held that, in the same way that a medical doctor diagnoses a patient by examining the patient's body, he would diagnose his patient by analyzing the patient's unconscious. The unconscious, according to Freud, was where the root cause of a patient's ills were located; it is where the unfulfilled desires and wishes of infantile sexuality are stored in a disguised form.[5] He wanted his 'psychoanalysis' to be seen as a scientific means for diagnosing and treating the root causes of problems endogenous to his patients. While from a natural science perspective Freud's model of the unconscious had substantial explanatory power, this very same scientific perspective is a serious flaw in Freud's approach to human problems.[6]

The problem with Freud's medical/natural science model of treatment lies in the fact that it is reductionist: it reduces people to something like cause and effect machines. In other words, his conception of the unconscious reduces the description of a person's emotional distress or existential crisis to a simple 'effect of an internal stimulus.'[7] Freud wrote, "the moment a man questions the meaning of life and value of life he is sick…. By asking this question he is merely admitting to a store of unsatisfied libido to which something else must have happened, a kind of fermentation leading to sadness and depression."[8] In other words, it is simply the unsatisfied libido that, according to Freud, is the cause of the 'sickness.' When the ramifications of Freud's conception of an unconscious—an inaccessible area of the mind overflowing with the unfulfilled wishes and desires of infantile sexuality that rule each individual—were understood, many professionals as well as lay people in his day were incensed that such an eminent scholar and medical practitioner could reduce human distress, not to mention desire, intention, and motivation, down to such a simple mechanistic explanation. But because this model seemed to explain a lot of 'abnormal' behaviour it quickly became part of cultural lore and folk wisdom, and the technical words Freud had devised to articulate the functioning of the human mind—such as libido, ego, repression, projection, paranoia, neurosis, fixation, hysteria, and even the word 'unconscious' itself—soon became common currency within the vernacular of pop culture. Today many people still hold Freud's theories and ideas as part of their basic assumptions about the human mind.[9]

This so-called scientific conception of the unconscious, as the place where the root cause of any metal illness is located, has been rigorously criticized over the past century.[10] The academic and medical worlds have challenged Freud's model of the tripartite mind by questioning the very examples Freud gave to support what he considered his scientific evidence for the unconscious, such as hypnotism, slips of the tongue, hysteria, and so on.[11] And many of the techniques which clinical psychologists use to supposedly access the unconscious—such as dream analysis and Rorschach tests—have been scientifically proven to do nothing of the sort.[12] Over the years medical science has discovered other explanations for the phenomena Freud attributed to hidden causes in the unconscious and other ways to interpret dreams, so that the mysterious and multi-leveled unconscious, full of disguised desires and wishes from the past, is no longer necessary as an explanatory element in a discussion of the causes of human distress and the motivation underlying human thinking and behaviour.[13]

While present-day medical explanations of human brain pathology in terms of organic malfunctions[14] have significantly reduced the need to diagnose human suffering with the problematic term 'mental illness,' Freud's attempt to reduce human distress and behaviour to single *psychological* causes (typically a desire or an unfulfilled wish from the distant past) has also proved to be problematic. This problem has persisted down to our day in the fact that many troubled individuals—and indeed their therapists—are convinced that their emotional or existential problem will disappear once '*the* cause' has been found in the unconscious: the hidden desire, the unfulfilled wish, or as is currently popular in North America, the forgotten trauma.[15] There is still a pervasive belief in a one-to-one causal relationship which holds that for every symptom there is a single cause, usually located in a person's past history.[16] But can the distress felt by an individual really be explained so easily? Can the complexities of a person's mental pain and suffering be ultimately attributable to a single cause?

This reductionist one-to-one causal relationship has been an extremely powerful explanatory paradigm in the field of mental health until very recently. It has only been in the last decade or so that mental healthcare professionals have been making an effort to promote the idea of 'comorbidity,' which is explained as "the coexistence of two or more psychiatric diagnoses in the same individual."[17] This modern 'comorbidity' initiative appears at first glance to be a shift in the psychotherapeutic community away from Freud's mechanistic, simple-cause-and-effect, explanation of human behaviour. But while it acknowledges multiple disorders within one individual, comorbidity is still based on the assumption that an individual's distress can be reduced to separate disorders, and that each disorder has one underlying cause. Comorbidity is an explanation of human distress in terms of multiple, parallel, *but still simple*, cause-and-effect relationships. What is lacking in this perspective is a shift away from the classical Freudian, natural science view of linear causality and a recognition of the fact that a person's mental pain may not only have a multitude of interconnected psychological causes but that mental distress may originate from a multitude of interrelated existential reasons. Some medical scientists have in recent years become much more accepting of a holistic approach to human beings, that is they have come to recognize the interconnectedness of not only the various physical systems within the human body, but of the interaction between mind and body, and, perhaps more importantly, between the person's well-being and his or her ongoing physical and social environment. And while much of modern biopsychiatry busies itself with trying to find the biological causes behind both suffering and behavior,[18] other mental healthcare professionals are abandoning and even denouncing the medical/natural science paradigm of mental illness in favor of a more humanistic approach.[19] But what is still lacking is an unambiguous and coherent articulation within psychotherapy that a patient's so-called diagnosed mental illness may not simply have a single internal cause.

Take for example the case of an individual who is afraid to speak in public. The classical Freudian approach, and the one which still seems to be predominant in biopsychiatry, in much of psychotherapy, and in popular culture, is to diagnose this 'condition' as anxiety disorder, specifically 'social phobia.'[20] If pharmacotherapy (medication) is avoided then treatment is based on the assumption that there must have been an event in that person's early childhood which had such an acute impact on that child's unconscious that it literally determines that person to feel fear any time he or she is required to speak in public. Treatment therefore calls for the analyst to root out that causal event. But is it reasonable to assume that a fear of public speaking is caused by a single life event? The following diagram illustrates how a great many interconnecting factors—a 'causal net'— may be responsible for a person's fear of speaking in public.

Notice that causality cannot be depicted as linear, that is, as A causes B which in turn causes C, and so on. There is a significant amount of overlap, and many factors are not directly connected to the fear of speaking itself but instead act on other factors which in turn act on a number of other factors. Furthermore, while some causal elements are in the past, many are in the present, and some are even 'located' in an imagined or anticipated future. Some causal factors are endogenous—internally generated values, beliefs, and assumptions (some of which are unfounded)—while others are

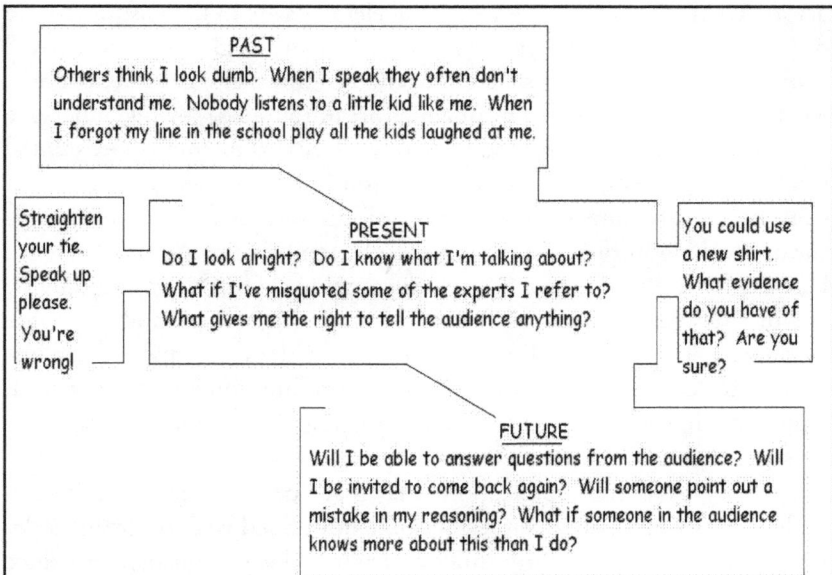

PAST
Others think I look dumb. When I speak they often don't understand me. Nobody listens to a little kid like me. When I forgot my line in the school play all the kids laughed at me.

Straighten your tie. Speak up please. You're wrong!

PRESENT
Do I look alright? Do I know what I'm talking about? What if I've misquoted some of the experts I refer to? What gives me the right to tell the audience anything?

You could use a new shirt. What evidence do you have of that? Are you sure?

FUTURE
Will I be able to answer questions from the audience? Will I be invited to come back again? Will someone point out a mistake in my reasoning? What if someone in the audience knows more about this than I do?

Problem as stated by the patient: "I'm terrified when asked to speak up in a group of people."
Standard psychotherapeutic diagnosis: 'anxiety disorder' or 'social phobia'
Typical prognosis and popular conception: There is something in his unconscious from his childhood that's causing him to be this way.
Standard approach to treatment: Find the cause in his unconscious, and/or anti-anxiety medication.

270 Philosophical Counselling & The Unconscious

exogenous—the result of external, contextual, environmental, or existential influences and events. Of course the person in the middle of the diagram is not necessarily immediately aware of all the various factors creating the fear of speaking in public. It might even be tempting to say that many of these factors are in this individual's 'unconscious,' but this would only be true in the sense that not all beliefs, assumptions, values, and so on are continually in the form of active thoughts. It does not make these un-thought-of factors some sort of sinister controlling force stemming from 'repressed' childhood wishes, desires, or trauma as is commonly associated with the term 'unconscious.'

Notice that causality cannot be depicted as linear, that is, as A causes B which in turn causes C, and so on. There is a significant amount of overlap, and many factors are not directly connected to the fear of speaking itself but instead act on other factors which in turn act on a number of other factors. Furthermore, while some causal elements are in the past, many are in the present, and some are even 'located' in an imagined or anticipated future. Some causal factors are endogenous—internally generated values, beliefs, and assumptions (some of which are unfounded)—while others are exogenous—the result of external, contextual, environmental, or existential influences and events. Of course the person in the middle of the diagram is not necessarily immediately aware of all the various factors creating the fear of speaking in public. It might even be tempting to say that many of these factors are in this individual's 'unconscious,' but this would only be true in the sense that not all beliefs, assumptions, values, and so on are continually in the form of active thoughts. It does not make these un-thought-of factors some sort of sinister controlling force stemming from 'repressed' childhood wishes, desires, or trauma as is commonly associated with the term 'unconscious.'

It is a gross over-simplification to say that a person's fear of speaking in public is probably 'caused' either by some unfulfilled wish or dream or by some traumatic event in early childhood.[21] It is always a mistake to reduce human emotions and behaviour to linear or sequential cause-and-effect explanations. But such simple causal explanations serve medical science well in that they are convenient and useful in the production of uncomplicated hypotheses.[22] These scientific hypotheses become the medical diagnoses which allow for clear-cut prognosis and treatment recommendations that make good methodological sense within the medical science paradigm (and good financial sense in a managed healthcare system), but which are in fact inadequate in dealing with the real-world complexity of a person's mental health. Yet science and medicine have, until very recently, so conditioned us to think of ourselves in linear cause-and-effect terms—in which some thing from the past in the unconscious 'determines' what we think and how we act—that it is difficult to imagine mental distress and motivation in any other way. But if a so-called mental illness is not a clearly biological malfunction of the brain, and it can't be explained as being caused by some unfulfilled wish, desire or past trauma hidden in the unconscious, how then can mental distress and anguish be explained? A reasonable alternative to scientific reductionism is not to discard the concept of causation but to make the description of causality more complete. In fact if causality is explained more fully, in terms of a causal web or net, the unconscious disappears on its own accord.

Causality and the Causal Net

At this point is might be helpful to briefly summarize what is meant by the term 'cause.'

1. To speak of '*the* cause' of an event is to over-simplify causality either for convenience or understanding.
2. What is claimed to be 'the cause' of an event is rarely the only causal factor. An event—meaning anything from a natural disaster to emotional distress—is almost universally the result of many causal factors, not all of which are visible from only one perspective.
3. Causes are not only material or physical. They may be psychological, spiritual, circumstantial, etc., or a combination of several of these.
4. Causes in social and personal dynamics are propositionally multi-layered. That is, a cause may be expressed in various, yet equally valid, propositions or statements.
5. Causes are contextually multi-layered. That is the context or situation within which causes arise are subject to various, yet equally valid, interpretations.
6. The causes behind human events are temporally multi-layered. That is, they originate in the past, present, and envisioned future.
7. The causes of suffering in human beings may be either endogenous (internal to the individual) or exogenous (external to the individual).
8. Medical science recognizes that some of a patient's suffering may be iatrogenic (caused by the treatment itself).

9.   Causes in human affairs are often conceived as consisting of a hierarchy of factors, where some factors are more important, more influential, more relevant than others.

10. Causes rarely actually function in a hierarchical or linear fashion. Instead they are more analogous to a web or net in four dimensions. But what does it mean to speak of a causal web or net?

A causal net is a kind of causality where each 'cause' has many 'effects' and each 'effect' has many 'causes.' It is called a net to distinguish it from the linear, sequential type of cause and effect that we consider 'normal.' Causal nets are probably very much more common than we realize. Causal nets are probably common enough that sequential causality is actually quite rare in proportion. But sequential causality seems very common to us. Why is that?

It is at the level of material objects that sequential cause and effect are most important. Sequential causality is important to humans because it provides an easy-to-comprehend way of relating objects to each other. But then not everything in the world is an object. For example, groups of objects are not themselves objects. Rolling a bowling ball at a single bowling pin produces sequential cause and effect. This is predictable and boring. But when a bowling ball is rolled at a bunch of pins the behaviour of the group is different enough from the behaviour of the individual pins that it makes an entertaining game. Now maybe bowling pins don't quite make a causal net as distinct from a sequence of events, but they mark a boundary. Natural science, especially physics, chemistry and biology, left behind long ago the description of the world in terms of objects and sequential causality. But the human sciences—psychology, sociology, anthropology—still describe human behaviour in terms of sequential cause and effect, perhaps because these disciplines are tied to spoken and written language, which is by nature sequential and linear.

The visualization of a causal net can start with the idea of a sequence of cause and effect. This can be seen as a line of points, with earlier points being causes of later points, which are effects. Note that being a 'cause' or being an 'effect' is not an intrinsic characteristic of a point, rather, it is a characteristic that is relative, depending on the relative (i.e., early or late) position of points on the line. Each point on the line is therefore both a cause (of later points) and an effect (of earlier points). A point that is both a cause and an effect might be called an event. So a sequential type of cause and effect implies a sequence, or line, of events.

It is easy to extend our visualization of a sequence of events as a string with a series of knots in it by making a net of events, where each event has more than two connections to other events. One simple form would be like a fishing net—say a square one where each event is connected to four others or a triangular one where each point is connected to six others.

In a linear causality we move along the line at a constant rate. We might identify time with the distance between events. With even a simple causal net these temporal and spatial relationships no longer hold. It is possible for an event to be influenced by two or more events in the past. It is possible for an event to be influenced by events in the present. And in human affairs it is possible for an event to be influenced by imagined or anticipated events in the future. So with even a simple causal net, the identity between time and the distance between events breaks down. With sequential causality, the thing that defines the place in the sequence is time. With a causal net there are other factors besides time that define the place in the net. And because of this, events that appear sequentially in time may in fact not be causally connected.

The sketch provides an illustration of various conceptions of causality. On the left is a linear sequence of cause and effect—the arrow of time runs parallel to it, and the perpendicular to the arrow hits the points on the line in the same order by which they are connected. The two sketches to the right illustrate different causal nets. Notice how the perpendicular still strikes points in an order in time, but that order no longer reflects the links of cause and effect in the nets. With a causal net, sequential events need not be causally connected.

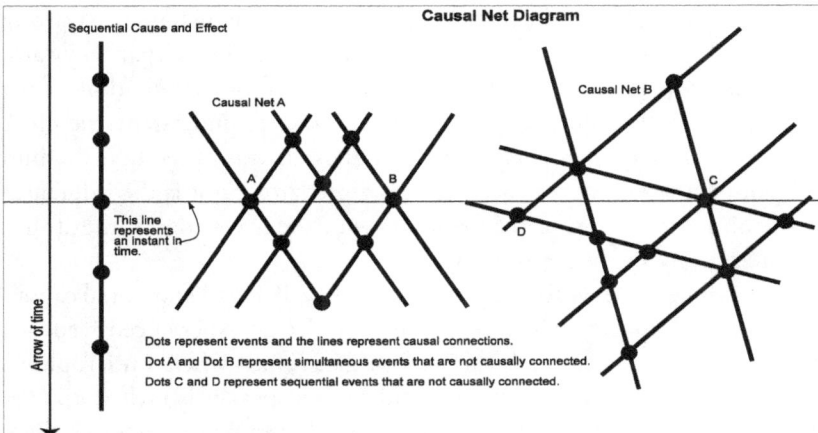

Dots represent events and the lines represent causal connections.
Dot A and Dot B represent simultaneous events that are not causally connected.
Dots C and D represent sequential events that are not causally connected.

So far only very simple examples of causal nets have been considered. Even a simple, regular net has properties that are quite different from sequential causality. A more realistic causal net would not look anything like a fishing net and is probably not visualizable at all. There is no reason for a causal net to be limited to two or three dimensions. A dimension is, after all, just a way of indicating an independent parameter. For example—space has three dimensions. All this means is that it takes only three numbers to specify any point in space. Among dimensions, one is special: time. Time is important when one thinks about causality. In linear causality a cause must precede its effect. But as we've already seen, causal nets mean that sequential events need not be causally connected. And while even in a causal net all effects always come after their causes, some of the causal reasons why people think and act as they do come from what they believe the future will bring.

By increasing the density of nodes in a causal net we may approach a situation where the net is continuos. If we were looking at a two dimensional net, the holes in the net would get smaller and smaller until they disappeared. A three dimensional net would then be like a solid—the nodes would define a volume. It seems reasonable to identify such continuous nets with the idea of an environment. An environment is a space where very many events mutually interact with each other continuously.

One of the claims of scientific reductionism is to say that the perspective of subatomic particles and fields, etc, is the fundamental one. All other levels of reality are therefore just manifestations of the activity at that 'fundamental' level. But this view is too simplistic. Imagine one of the atoms among the many atoms of a living bird. By philosophical magic, that atom is fixed in space. Now, if the bird flies away from the branch it's been sitting on all of the atoms, and all their interactions, suddenly depart skyward. Could this departure be understood by means of an examination of the interactions of the visible atoms? Hardly. In order to understand the bird's flight it would require a perspective that allowed you to see that the bird has spotted a worm, or was fleeing from a predator. So it is the influences on the bird—the worm or the predator—not the necessities of the atoms, that are causing the bird atoms to move.

Causal nets allow properties that are not available to sequential causality. A feedback loop provides an example. We've all experienced feedback loops. A common example is the screech that results when a microphone is connected to a speaker. First, a sound from a speaker is picked up by a microphone. If that speaker is connected to that same microphone then, obviously, it repeats the sound that it just emitted. This process is reiterated again and again. Examples of feedback loops in human terms are addictive behaviour, compulsive behaviours such as repetitive hand washing, and eating disorders. While a feedback loop is produced by a constant causality, causal nets are things whose properties are continually changing from moment to moment according to the waves of self-reinforcing stimulation that sweep through them.

The brain forms an easy-to-visualize causal net. This is because we are all familiar with the idea of the brain being made of neurons connected by long string-like axons. Each neuron is connected to thousands of others via these axons. In 1949 Donald Hebb at McGill proposed that a simple idea might account for much of the development of neuronal structures in the brain.[23] Hebb's idea was that when one neuron stimulates another into firing through a synapse, that synapse will more readily stimulate the firing the next time. The vast network of connections among neurons in the brain where this phenomenon takes place mean that circuits of neurons become distinct from their fellows and join to form semi-permanent associations—associations that have structural internal relations and perform external functions. The linkage between many of those functions and mental facilities has been made. Now just as all things can be reduced to atoms, all brain structures can be reduced to neurons. But it is not always useful to do so. And from the perspective that brings those brain structures into view, one can see that they too seem to be linked in a causal net of their own.

The unconscious in the Freudian sense disappears in light of complex causality, but this is not to say that we don't have underlying mental capacities we are not aware of, upon which our higher capacities, like awareness, depend. One might think of those low-level capacities as a kind of 'unconscious.' It is not too much of a conceptual leap to identify those low level mental capacities with the brain structures discussed above. And if those brain-structures are linked as a causal net, then it follows that what has been defined as the 'unconscious' is in fact nothing more mysterious than complex mental functioning at the level of a causal net.

Causal Nets and Philosophical Counselling

Early in the twentieth century Carl Jung summed up the accepted medical model of the unconscious that was, and still is, the predominant perspective in our society. He wrote of the 'infectious' nature of the evils within the unconscious.

Our patients suffer from bondage to neurosis; they are prisoners of the
unconscious.... Like doctors who treat epidemic diseases, we expose
ourselves to powers that threaten our conscious equilibrium, and we
have to take every possible precaution if we want to rescue not only
our own humanity but that of the patient from the clutches of the
unconscious.[24]

He went on to explain that everyone "harbours his 'statistical criminal' in himself, just as he has his own private madman or saint."[25] In other
words, Jung, like Freud, believed that the cause of human behaviour was
located in the dark unconscious, even to the point that this cause could be a
second personality with an intentionality all its own.[26] While the notion of
a second personality may seem complex, it is in fact a simple, linear causal
explanation. It answers the question, "Why did he do that?" with, "Because
a second person inside him caused him to do it." This, of course, leads to an
infinite regress beginning with the next logical question, "And what caused
that second person to cause the first person do it?" Amazingly this conception of multiple personalities within a malfunctioning mind is today still
accepted as a fact about 'mental illness' within the 'common knowledge' of
most western societies.

Philosophical counselling questions common knowledge. It approaches
the issue of human distress and behaviour from the perspective of reason,
intention, and motivation. Philosophical counsellors understand the difference between medical disorders that are pathologies caused by a physical
malfunction of the brain and the suffering and mental distress (often mistakenly diagnosed by psychotherapists as mental illnesses) for which there
are reasons stemming from the individual's beliefs, world view, or social
environment.[27] It is the relief of mental suffering of the latter sort for which
philosophical counselling is particularly well suited. Philosophical counselling begins with a presupposition of shared rationality between counsellor
and client. Because of this, philosophical counselling has been criticized as
either being unable or failing to deal with the wishes, desires, and traumas
hidden in the unconscious, in the psychoanalytic understanding of that term.
Philosophy, it is argued, can't deal with causes that lie in the depths of the
mind beyond the reach of rational philosophical discussion.

This argument would be valid if the classical Freudian description of
the mind were accurate, if there exists the sort of unconscious in which a
childhood wish, desire, or trauma is hidden that is in fact the single 'key'

cause behind a person's distress, or if, as is commonly believed, the unconscious of each individual harbours some other personality that is the cause of
unwelcome behaviour. But the Freudian conception of the unconscious has
been abandoned by almost all mental healthcare practitioners and theorists,
except for Freud's most devoted followers; and Jung's theory of 'a person
within the person' has been professionally debunked. Unfortunately Freud's
and Jung's theories are still held to be factual by a great many individuals in
our culture, including some who call themselves philosophical counsellors.
In fact, as Jeffrey Schwartz and others have demonstrated, the depths of the
mind may be as reachable by rational philosophical discussion as they are
by drugs or surgery. Schwartz's work with what psychiatry calls 'Obsessive
Compulsive Disorder' revealed that a purely cognitive therapy—consciously
directed thoughts and feelings—actually changed the brain structures that
were associated with the problem.[28]

What both philosophical counsellors and their clients need to understand is that two of the main differentiating features between philosophical
counselling and the many other forms of therapy that identify themselves
as part of medical science is, first, that philosophical counselling does not
need to accept the existence of an unconscious to be an effective therapy
for the relief of human suffering, and second, that an individual's problem
is never the result of a single, underlying, causal factor from the past such
as an unfulfilled wish, desire, or trauma.

A limited understanding of causality can easily lead to the assumption
that the world is predictable because cause and effect make it determined.
But the lesson of chaos theory is that it is possible to have a system that
is materially deterministic yet fundamentally unpredictable. In nature, it
takes very few interacting components to create a system whose behaviour
is unpredictable. Certainly, the causal net of the brain and mind would be
expected to have a chaotic way of relating behaviour to experience and the
environment—sometimes you can predict it, sometimes not. One of the
problems with reductionism, as it occurs in psychotherapy, is the assumption
that all materially deterministic systems are predictable. In fact, predictable
systems are very rare.

In psychotherapy the issue of predictability often gets swept under
the rug. Mental illnesses are correlated with what are believed to be their
causes, and yet, while no causal links are proposed for the correlation, the
correlation is regarded as if it were causal. A correlation then becomes the
standard basis of treatment. This may be the most serious problem in accept-

ing linear causality: therapists who have the mistaken idea of the reliability and usefulness of such knowledge will take it for granted that a patient's symptoms and response to treatment are largely predictable. This can lead to the not-uncommon scenario of the patient being blamed for a treatment regime which fails to cure!

The acknowledgement of *unpredictability* in therapy and counseling is very important. What is the proper way of functioning in an unpredictable 'environment'? Obviously, therapists and counselors need to be both cautious and exploratory. Philosophical counselling is both a cautious and an exploratory form of therapy which takes into account the unpredictability of causal nets. If causality were in fact linear then so-called psychodynamic or depth analysis, which follows the single thread of causes and effects backwards to the hidden wishes, disguised desires, and traumatic memories in an assumed unconscious, would then be the best therapy. But research has repeatedly shown that in actual fact the best therapies, those with the best long-term outcomes, are those which fall under the general heading of cognitive therapies.[29] These are a variety of open-ended, client-centered discursive approaches in which the therapist works with the troubled client in discovering not only incidents from the past, but both the explicit and implicit assumptions, values, beliefs, wishes, desires, and so on, as well as the client's physical and social environment, that have combined to form the complex root of the problem. This type of therapy does not need the explanatory power of a theory of the unconscious. It is this approach that is found in philosophical counselling.

In philosophical counselling, the treatment result, or the 'cause' of improvement, in the suffering individual—for example, the person who has a fear of speaking in public—is not psychotropic medication which supposedly eliminates the 'cause' of the 'illness,' and it is not some magical Freudian "catharsis" or internal remission of the illness by means of rooting out repressed desires, wishes, or trauma in the unconscious, as is claimed for psychoanalysis. In fact improvement is not due to any single factor, but is instead due to, again, a sort of causal net of inter-connected factors. Through philosophical investigation and discussion improvement results because the individual who has a fear of public speaking comes to understand the following:

1. that she is not suffering from a biological mental illness (despite the fact that she may have been diagnosed as such by a previous therapist)
2. that she is not the *victim* of an internal affliction
3. that her fear of speaking in public is not unique, that it is a common

fear experienced by many individuals and therefor quite 'normal'

4. that her fear is not somehow her fault

5. that her feelings are not spontaneous or random, but do have causes behind them

6. that her problem is not internal (endogenous) but relational and social (exogenous)

7. that there are external factors in the past, present, and imagined future that have created her fear

8. that the philosophical counsellor cares about her as a person and is not merely focused on 'curing' the 'illness'

9. that she does not need to be dependent on an authority figure to administer a prescribed treatment

10. that she has the ability to 'treat' herself by means of (a) improved understanding, and (b) intentional activities that will diminish her fear (such as participating at group meetings)

11. that the past has been influencing her and, while she can't change what's happened in the past, she has the power to choose whether or not to allow its influence to continue

12. that she is a worthy person despite her fear (improvement in self-esteem and self-confidence)

13. that she can resolve many of her future problems with this same philosophical approach

Philosophical counsellors don't need to yield to the pseudo-scientific diagnoses and classifications of mental pathology that have been devised for use in psychoanalysis and psychotherapy. In fact philosophical counselling sees the clinical psychological practices—of classifying human distress as 'mental illness,' diagnosing it with medical-sounding terminology, assuming it can be reduced to a single causal factor in the unconscious, and even the more recent innovation of labeling a 'comorbidity' of mental illnesses within one individual—as falling far short of a complete picture of human mental suffering. Philosophical counsellors recognize that the reasons for human distress are not at all hidden in some dark and mysterious corner of the mind called the unconscious, and that these reasons almost always come in a complex form that may be referred to as causal nets.

Notes

[1] Freud often insisted that his work in psychoanalysis was both medical and scientific. For example, he wrote, "I treated my discoveries as ordinary contributions to science and hoped that others would treat them in the same way." He called it "our branch of science," and spoke of it as "medical psychoanalysis" among other fields of science, in his essay, "History of the Psychoanalytic Movement" (first published in 1913) in *The Basic Writings of Freud*, New York: Random House, 1995. p. 911, 921, 924.

[2] Carl Jung also promoted an organic model of the unconscious. For example he wrote, "We have known for a long time that there is a biological relationship between the unconscious processes and the activity of the conscious mind." *Essays on Contemporary Events.* New Jersey: Princeton UP, 1989 ed. p. 1.

[3] Simon, Laurence. *Psychology, Psychotherapy, Psychoanalysis, and the Politics of Human Relationships.* Westport, Conn.: Praeger, 2003. p. 124.

[4] Webster, Denise. "Somatoform and Pain Disorders" in *Rethinking Mental Health and Disorder.* Mary Ballou and Laura S. Brown eds. New York: Guilford Press, 2002. p. 145.

[5] Freud wrote, "It was proved that psychoanalysis could not clear up anything actual, except by going back to something in the past" in "History of the Psychoanalytic Movement" in *The Basic Writings of Freud*, New York: Random House, 1995. p. 903.

[6] Many psychoanalysts themselves are uncomfortable with the claim that their field is a science. See for example Stefan de Schill's scathing critique in *Crucial Choices Crucial Changes: The Resurrection of Psychotherapy* (Amherst, NY: Prometheus, 2000. p. 62), and Laurence Simon's *Psychology, Psychotherapy, Psychoanalysis, and the Politics of Human Relationships* (Westport, Conn.: Praeger, 2003).

[7] This is how reductionist 'behaviorists' defined humanity in the mid-twentieth century.

[8] In *Letter of Sigmund Freud.* James Stern and Tania Stern, trans. E. L. Freud, ed. New York: Harcourt, 1960. p. 436.

[9] For example the 2001 *Family Desk Reference to Psychology* talks about disturbing memories or emotions "repressed" in the "unconscious mind" that have "great power over us" in familiar Freudian language (Chuck Falcon. Lafayette, La: Sensible Psychology Press. p. 30).

[10] See, for example, the book *The Challenges to Psychoanalysis and Psychotherapy* edited by psychiatrists Stefan de Schill and Serge Lebovici (London: Jessica Kingsley Publishers, 1999) and philosopher John Searle's book *The Rediscovery of the Mind* (Cambridge, Mass.: MIT Press, 1998) especially Chapter 7, "The Unconscious and its Relation to Consciousness."

[11] For example, in *The Seven Sins of Memory* (New York: Houghton Mifflin, 2001) Daniel L. Schacter writes, "Hypnotic procedures frequently elicit inaccurate reports, and sometimes amplify the suggestive effects of misleading information. Recent reviews of the scientific literature have turned up little or no evidence [of the effectiveness of] hypnosis." (p.118)

[12] See for example Ernest Hartman's *Dreams and Nightmares* (Cambridge, Mass.: Perseus, 2001) and "The Rorschach Inkblot Test, Fortune Tellers, and Cold Reading" by Wood et al, (*Skeptical Inquirer* Vol. 27, No. 4, July/August, 2003)

[13] Defenders of Freud argue that his description of the unconscious—as being composed of id, ego, and super ego—is only metaphorical. But this raises the question, For what is 'the unconscious' a metaphor? Explanations are typically either question begging ("The unconscious consists of unconscious things") or circular ("Proof of the existence of the unconscious can be found in the unconscious").

[14] For example, conditions such as syphilitic dementia, Alzheimer's disease and Tourette syndrome were at one time believed to be mental illnesses. They are now known to be organic diseases of the brain.

[15] While it is popularly believed that the unconscious is a storehouse of repressed memories of past trauma, research has revealed that traumatic memories are in fact highly memorable. See K. K. Shobe and J. E. Kihlstrom's essay "Is traumatic memory special?" (*Current Directions in Psychological Science.* 6: 1997. pp. 70–74.)

[16] See for example the *Introductory Textbook of Psychiatry*, in which the authors say that in the search for the cause of schizophrenia, "In the absence of visible lesions and known pathogens, investigators have turned to the exploration of models that could explain the diversity of symptoms through a single cognitive mechanism." (Nancy Andreasen and Donald Black. Washington: American Psychiatric Publishing, 2001. p. 231)

[17] *Psychiatric Diagnosis and Classification.* Maj et al eds. New York: John Wiley and Sons, 2002. Preface. p. ix.

[18] T. Bedirhan Üstün, Somnath Chatterji and Gavin Andrews write, "The determinism of psychoanalysis and early behaviorism has been superseded by the logical empiricism of biological psychiatry that is searching for the underpinnings of human behavior in the brain in particular, and in human biology in general." "International Classification and Diagnosis of Mental Disorders: Strengths, Limitations, and Future Perspectives" in *Psychiatric Diagnosis and Classification.* Maj et al eds. New York: John Wiley and Sons, 2002. p. 27.

[19] For example, in *Psychology, Psychotherapy, Psychoanalysis, and the Politics of Human Relationships* (Westport, Conn.: Praeger, 2003) professor of psychology Laurence Simon writes, "Two destructive forces have been unleashed by the field's insistence that it is a natural science. First, it has produced numerous (if competing) visions of humanity that conceive of us as either some form of robot or machine behaving at the mercy of forces external to us or as a primitive animal controlled by impulses or drives within...." (p. 6).

[20] More recently called 'social anxiety disorder.' For diagnostic criteria and a discussion of treatment see Chapter 22, "Phenomenology of Social Phobia," in *Textbook of Anxiety Disorders.* Washington: American Psychiatric Publishing, 2002.

[21] Or some "chemical imbalance" in the brain.

[22] One of the uses (misuses?) of the word 'cause' in medical science is to identify as a cause whatever in a situation lends itself to manipulation. If I have a cold, which I caught because I spent time with a sick friend—the visit isn't seen as the cause of the cold—the cause is seen to be an infection I picked up from my friend. The infection is seen as a cause because the doctor can do something about it: the doctor can cure the infection. For the doctor, it is not useful to say that my cold is caused by a visit. So the practitioner, when faced with a problem, tends to identify as the cause of the problem whatever circumstance is associated with the problem that the practitioner can do something about. This effective cause is different from reductionism, which says that low level causes are more fundamental or 'real' than high level causes. In reductionism, the goal is to reach a level where the complexity of the world is seen to be the result of the interaction of simple components. An effective cause is also a simplification—but for a different purpose and with different philosophical implications.

[23] Hebb, Donald. *The Organization of Behaviour*, monograph, 1949.

[24] Jung. *Essays on Contemporary Events*. New Jersey: Princeton UP, 1989 ed. p. 45.

[25] Ibid. p. 55.

[26] Freud wrote that the ego "is not even master of its own house, but must contend itself with scanty information of what is going on unconsciously in the mind." Quoted by Frank Tallis in *Hidden Minds: A History of the Unconscious*. London: Profile Books, 2002. p. 171.

[27] One study concluded that between 41 and 83% of people given psychiatric diagnoses, including schizophrenia, are later determined to have neurological or other physical disorders. Cited in *Rethinking Mental Health and Disorder*. Edited by Mary Ballou and Laura S. Brown. New York: Guilford Press, 2002. p. 157.

[28] Schwartz, Jeffrey M. and Sharon Begley, *The Mind and The Brain*. New York: Harper Collins, 2002.

[29] Documented evidence for this claim is pervasive in the psychotherapeutic literature. See, for example, pages 86, 99, 144, and 275 in *Textbook of Anxiety Disorders*. Washington: American Psychiatric Publishing, 2002.

Chapter 15

Transcending the Unconscious: Philosophical Counselling Sessions with Arthur Schopenhauer

Eli Eilon and Ran Lahav

Philosophical counselling, by its very nature, centers around philosophizing: philosophical conversations between the counsellor and the counsellee. Although there are different approaches to philosophical counselling, we believe that any reasonable approach would agree that philosophizing is a critical investigation aimed at developing a better or deeper understanding of relevant ideas (concepts, presuppositions, theories, etc.). In the context of counselling, philosophizing is used to investigate those ideas that are relevant to the counsellee's predicaments—for example, the concept of guilt in the case of guilt feelings—with the aim of making a positive change in the counsellee.

However, it is commonly believed nowadays that a person's behavior and mental states are influenced to a considerable extent by psychological factors that are not conscious or are not under conscious control. The question is then how philosophizing, specifically philosophical counselling, can possibly make a significant impact upon the counsellee if it focuses on conscious understanding, thus giving up, so it seems, psychological techniques of influencing unconscious factors.

In what follows we will propose a way for philosophical counselling to address this issue. Using Schopenhauer's philosophy, we will suggest that philosophizing can help the counsellee go beyond rather than directly address the unconscious psychological factors that underlie his or her predicament.

The unconscious

In order to sharpen the issue, let us first clarify the notion of the un-conscious. According to most contemporary approaches to psychotherapy, many aspects of our human psychology exert a significant influence on our behavior and on our mental life, even though we are not aware or conscious of their existence. Various forms of depth psychology, for example, speak of unconscious inner conflicts, repressions, or traces of past experiences which presumably influence the way we feel and behave.[1] Cognitive therapies may speak of automatic thoughts or belief patterns, of which we are often not aware, that affect our emotions and behavior.[2] Humanistically oriented therapies may speak of false selves and facades or disowned parts of ourselves;[3] and so on. In some cases the person is said to be conscious or aware of the existence of such factors, but not of the influence which these factors exert upon her behavior and emotional life. For example, she may be aware of needing her mother's approval but without being aware of how this desperate need is making her an ambitious achiever thirsty of success.

Different psychotherapies construe differently the psychological reality that underlies the person's consciousness and unconsciousness. Freud, for example, sometimes describes the unconscious as psychological processes which are kept apart from conscious ones by a barrier.[4] Rogers uses the no-tion of a "conceptual filter" which screens out or rejects certain parts of one's experiences, thus leaving them out of one's awareness (which can be taken as equivalent to 'consciousness').[5] Perls speaks of lack of awareness of ongo-ing experience, a state which he describes as "illusion, or fantasy… a kind of dream, a kind of trance."[6] For our present purpose we need not resort to any of these theoretical explanations of the psychology of the unconscious (or lack of awareness). We can remain on the more directly observable sur-face and say, as most psychotherapies would agree, that some aspects of the person's psychology—be they emotions, thought patterns, traces of child-hood experiences, causal interactions between them, etc.—are not available to the person's consciousness (awareness). They are not available at least in the sense that the person is currently unable to report them directly or to integrate them with the rest of his or her reportable self-understanding. Such psychological states or events can be said to be not conscious or unconscious (we will use these two terms interchangeably).

Since unconscious psychological factors are beyond the horizon of our consciousness, they are beyond our conscious control. Furthermore, even those aspects of our mental lives that are conscious are often not under our conscious control. One may be conscious of, say, being depressed, while not being able to directly influence this depression through any conscious desire. It can be said, therefore, that such inner states are not under conscious control in the sense that we are unable to directly influence them through any conscious desire to change them.

We can now formulate the challenge for philosophical counselling: If philosophical counselling's major tool is philosophizing, and if philosophizing is directed primarily at the person's conscious understanding, how then can it hope to deal with the powerful psychological factors that are not under conscious control, or are not even conscious at all?

Note that psychological types of counselling and therapy do not face this challenge. Conversations in psychotherapy are not based on philosophizing and are not aimed primarily at achieving conscious understandings of ideas. Since they are not bound by the standards of philosophical investigations, they can employ a variety of tools to tap into the person's non-conscious psychological factors and modify them.

Case study: Counseling Schopenhauer

We will try to answer this question by means of a fictional case study, after which we will summarize our proposed answer. We chose Arthur Schopenhauer as our imaginary counsellee because we believe that an interesting avenue of addressing the issue of the unconscious can be found in his philosophy, his life, and their mutual influence. It should be noted, however, that our intention is not to present a full and detailed interpretation of Schopenhauer's writings, but rather to use his ideas as a starting point for presenting our own view on philosophical counselling.[7]

1. Mr. Suffering recounts his suffering

It must have been his impressive presence—or was it his obstinacy?—which made me invite my insistent visitor into my house at such a late hour. His German accent, his gray hair, and his weary expression suggested that he had just concluded a long and painful voyage from afar. I offered him a chair and a glass of water. He stared at me and then, still standing, started speaking in fluent English, which, I later learned, he had acquired during his long visit to the British Isles.[8]

"My name is Schopenhauer; Arthur Schopenhauer. If you read my writings, you probably know that I have been experiencing a tremendous amount of constant suffering which nobody has succeeded to alleviate so far." He examined me and then added, "I came to you as my last resort. I have been literally everywhere, from Vienna to Rishikesh; I have tried every therapeutic technique, save, off course, philosophical counseling. That is what you do, isn't it, philosophical counseling?"

I begged him to sit down and asked him to tell me about the suffering that made him cross the Atlantic in order to come and see me. I soon came to learn that although the external circumstances of his life seemed quite comfortable—a nice steady income from a company inherited from his father, plenty of free time, reasonable health—virtually every stage in his life brought him much pain. His adolescent longing for the presence of his father, who had taken his own life when Arthur was only 17 year old, was merely the first painful part of his story. A long and tedious list of his unsuccessful relations with women came next, followed by his self-depreciatory comments, and then again more descriptions of more pain. Finally he depicted at great length the frustrations he had suffered during the time he had served as a lecturer in Berlin, when not a single soul appeared in his classes. Everybody explicitly favored his rival, Hegel.

It was long past midnight now. I excused myself, asking him to come again the next day.

2. From personal suffering to suffering as such

Schopenhauer spent our second session telling me about his unfortunate relations with his mother, neighbors and colleagues, until I managed to take advantage of a pause in his endless, doleful speech, and to squeeze in a question: "I see that you suffer so much, Herr Doctor Professor Schopenhauer. Tell me please, how do you understand the meaning of this suffering?"

This question marked a new stage in our conversation, for we now moved from a factual description of his particular life to an examination of the meaning of suffering in general.

"I understand it philosophically, of course," he answered. "To my mind one must start philosophizing by acknowledging the facts of existence. And the most fundamental fact about human life is suffering."

"Is this," I asked, "an assumption about humanity in general, or just about your own life?"

"About life in a most general sense, my friend. But this is not an assumption at all. It is a fact, one which can serve as a starting point for philosophizing and on which we can safely base our ideas. You see, people suffer throughout their entire lives. Suffering is an immediate feeling, while happiness—so rare and vague—is only a secondary feeling, the negation of suffering. Happiness is mostly an unrealized ideal, and even when it is briefly realized, it is always under the shadow of the approaching death."[9]

"Is it really a fact?"

"Indeed," he replied with confidence. "Look at the Greek tragedies; look at folk songs. 'You were born to suffer, my child,' as the old rhyme goes. Life is short and burdensome. Christianity invented hell as an otherworldly possibility—but hell is right here in this very world. The world may be nice to look at, but not to live in." He fell silent. Then he added, murmuring as if conversing with himself, "Can you imagine? People say that life is a gift. To my mind it is more like a debt: You pay the interest—suffering—throughout your life, until, at the end of the term, it is time to return the principal: your death."

3. Rising to the philosophical perspective

Following our second session I spent some time thinking about my client's predicament. After some deliberation I decided that it was time to take a step towards a philosophical examination of his worldview. This is an important stage in philosophical counseling, because in order to overcome one's predicament, one must rely on the resources found in one's own worldview. For this purpose a careful philosophical examination of the foundations of one's worldview is needed. Most of my counselees are not professional philosophers, and with them this is a complicated task. With Schopenhauer, of course, the task was very simple. He already had a full-fledged philosophy.

"So far in our two counseling sessions," I said to him at the beginning of our third meeting, "we have been doing a lot of description. First you described your personal suffering, and then the suffering that rules over human life as such. Having laid out the facts—or rather, I should say, the facts as you see them—it seems reasonable now to proceed to some deeper analysis."

"Listen," he replied almost agitated, "if you intend to search for the unconscious roots of my conscious experiences, spare me the time and the money. The unconscious, when it comes to human suffering, will lead you nowhere. In fact, it will only lead you to more and more despair, as it did to me."

"Alright," I said, "explain to me why the unconscious route is hopeless." Of course, my intention was not psychological—to insist on analyzing his unconsciousness, but rather purely philosophical: to encourage him to further develop his conscious worldview and explore its personal implications, hoping that this would eventually supply him with the resources to go beyond his predicament.

"What is the unconscious source of our suffering?" he said. "Why is it that we suffer so much throughout our lifetime? I have spent much time on these questions, thinking that revealing the sources of suffering could help us to overcome it."

"And your conclusions, Professor Schopenhauer?"

"Well, I came to realize that the will that you or I have, the personal will which each of us has and knows so intimately is only a fragment of something greater. Personal wills are in fact only manifestations of one undivided will, which is the essence of the world. This universal will is, in fact, what Kant called 'the thing in itself.' This one and only will lies beyond the horizons of our human understanding. Yet, Kant was wrong when he said that we can say nothing about the thing in itself. The one and undivided will has one important characteristic: It strives to escape its blindness and to represent itself to itself. But as long as it is one undivided unity, it cannot grasp itself."[10]

"You mean," I suggested, "like a baby who must acquire the notion of 'the other' in order to come to grasp itself as itself?"

"Precisely. The will needs to represent itself as an object in order to be its own subject. And while trying to present itself to itself, it must therefore objectify itself. It must manifest itself no longer as an undivided unity, but as many; no longer as a blind monad, but as a knowing subject. And so the will started manifesting itself to itself gradually: first as inorganic things, then as plants, then as animals, and finally as humans. At each of these levels, the one blind and undivided will, which contains the entire world, objectified itself through gradually higher manifestations, that is, in terms of higher levels of individuality and of knowledge. The animal's knowledge and individuality are higher than those of a plant, which, in turn, are higher than those of inorganic things."

Had I been a psychologist I would have regarded his philosophical musings as an irrelevant dribble, a diversion from the real thing, an escape from concrete personal material. But being a philosophical counsellor, my strategy was not to take him away from his conscious worldview but rather to urge him to delve in it in search of a possible source of insights and inspiration. "I suppose," I interrupted him, "that human beings are the highest manifestations of the will."

"Correct," he said, encouraged by my understanding. "Our individuality is of the highest level. Each person is a universe different from that of his fellow person. Humans have the highest form of knowledge: self-knowledge. They self-reflect. But keep in mind that any human being is nothing but a manifestation of the one will. The undivided will perceives itself through its highest manifestation: through the human being looking at his own self."

"Mmm."

"Here, my friend, we are entering humanity's innermost nature. Humans are the most individual creatures, so individual that each one sees his own will as if it were the entire world of will. Each of us knows his own will directly, while seeing other people as objects. Hence each one of us thinks of his individual will as if it was an ultimate will, the final arbiter, the only thing to be considered. And since your will has no importance to me, it is only natural that people are involved in a constant struggle. The natural state of the human species is strife between personal wills, which results in an everlasting suffering."

"Hold on, Professor Schopenhauer. If I understand you correctly, when your will and mine are fighting one another and asserting their own individuality, our duality is only apparent, right?"

"Of course," he said, reassured by my observation. "We are nothing but the one will that has fragmented itself in its manifestations. The world as will never fights itself. Only the world as representation is divided. Its particulars always fight each other. The representation of this strife is our—and every creature's—will to live. That will is the unconscious drive which is responsible for our suffering. Suffering goes on, therefore, as long as we live, since it stems from the will's basic desire to present itself to itself."

"Sounds pretty grim," I remarked.

He nodded. "You can now see where delving into the unconscious has led me," he said with a bitter smile. "As long as I focused on my—or humanity's—conscious suffering, I had a bit of hope of overcoming it. Once

I delved into the unconscious roots of our suffering, I arrived at my notorious pessimistic attitude. I ended up with fundamental despair."

Arthur left my room at a very late hour at night. I could not sleep after such a depressing meeting. I knew I had to help my counsellee find within his own worldview the resources—concepts, assumptions, ideas, etc.—with which he would be able to overcome his suffering. How could I do that?

The clue to the answer appeared in my mind when I tried to formulate the task in his own terminology. In terms of his philosophy, the goal was to enable him to go beyond those conditions which had led him to his suffering. Those conditions, according to him, were the narrowness of his perspective on life, or of what he called his individual 'will.' In his philosophy, a person suffers because he or she experiences only a fragmented portion of the universal will. This meant that I had to encourage him to somehow transcend the boundaries of his individual will, to go beyond his personal attitude to life towards a broader perspective. But how can a person go beyond his individual will in the context of Schopenhauer's philosophy?

I found on my bookshelf a copy of his *The World as Will and Representation* and spent much of the night reading it. In the morning I called my counsellee in his room at the Paradise Hotel. I asked him to come over right away.

4. Going beyond the counsellee's worldview

"You were right," I told him when he arrived. "As your analysis of the source of suffering suggests, uncovering your unconsciousness would probably lead us to a dead end. My suggestion is that we try to go beyond your analysis."[11]

He threw at me an indignant glance.

"Of course," I added quickly, "you will be the one who will construct our new analysis."

He examined my face suspiciously. "Explain yourself."

"You yourself," I explained, "have always done what I am suggesting. Whenever you reached a dead end in your inquiries, you always tried to go beyond your previous narrow perspective in order to reach a broader one. This is evident in your books. For instance, you have always attempted to broaden the modern western thought wherever it reaches its limits. You tried to bring together Kant, Plato and the Hindu tradition. You yourself have written a philosophy that integrates aesthetic, metaphysical and ethical considerations in a remarkably organic way. You have tried to bridge gaps between traditions in order to find the common and most universal element in them."

He nodded, satisfied. "Please go ahead."

"In fact," I continued, " this has been your own strategy in tackling your suffering; in your books in any case. Because in dealing with your pain in your writings you have tried to go beyond your particular suffering to a broader perspective: to human suffering in general. Then you went further and analyzed the unconscious dimension of suffering. That last move has led you to your deepest despair."

"That is certainly one way of looking at what I have done," he agreed.

"However," I said, "although your analysis of the contribution of the unconscious to human suffering is of considerable importance, you haven't gone with it far enough."

"Not far enough?" he looked at me incredulously.

"Well, let me explain," I said quickly. "In your own writings you made it clear that every person—yourself included—is a fragment of the overall will, and that once we overcome our individual point of view we will understand the folly of our individual concerns."

"True," he said. "Overcoming our individual perspective means realizing that the world is one and that there is a deeper reality underlying our personal conscious and unconscious life. So why is this philosophy not enough for you? What more can you add to it that I haven't?"

"I didn't say that your philosophy is not enough," I said. "I meant that you haven't gone far enough in applying it to your personal life." This was a crucial point, and I wondered how he would take it. Many theoreticians feel that applying their philosophy to everyday life somehow debases it from the lofty realm of ideas to the vulgar domain of concrete life.

"Applying my philosophy to my life?"

"Let me explain," I said. "If I got it right, you are recommending that each of us make a crucial move towards a trans-individual perspective. What you (and the Hindus) call 'breaking through the veil of Maya' means transcending our individual mode of existence. It means trying to be in touch with the more essential reality of one undivided world. The basic idea here, I take it, is to rise beyond your current psychic quagmire, instead of trying to understand it or solve its problems. Your writings therefore suggest a way of overcoming your obsessive preoccupation with the causes of your conscious life. The way to relieve your suffering is not to delve in it and its causes, but to go beyond them."

"Interesting," he said pensively. "You want me not only to think my philosophy, but to live it as well, don't you?"

I felt relieved that he did not reject my move right away. "Precisely, Arthur," I said to him cheerfully. "That is why I am a philosophical counsellor, not a theoretician like you."

"Alright. I can see your point. But I can't see how I can possibly apply my theory to my actual suffering."

I felt on the homerun now. "Good question. We will have to figure this out together. But at least we know what our goal is: to transcend your narrow, individual way of being."

"That is our goal," he agreed. "But how do we get there?"

"Well, we can use some of your own methods and develop a way to reach—or at least get closer to—our target. By ever-broadening our perspective of analysis, by ever-deepening our point of view, we may be able to pave our path from your individual attitude to a universal perspective that would place human suffering—and your specific daily suffering—in its proper perspective."

It was marvelous to see Mr. Suffering smile. But I wasn't going to bask in this feeling of success. It was now time for the difficult task of translating the idea of overcoming his individual perspective into actual practice.

5. Applying the counsellee's philosophy to his life

Tell me, Arthur," I opened our next session, "what do you make of the concept of 'Egoism'?"[12]

"Egoism is an utter mistake," he said dismissively. "The most foolish metaphysical misconception one can exhibit is acting in an egocentric way."

"How is that?"

"If you have followed my philosophy so far," said Schopenhauer, "you must know by now that different individuals are nothing but different manifestations of one and the same will."

I nodded in agreement.

"And if so," he continued, "then you must also agree that an egocentric act is nothing but an overemphasis of one manifestation of the will at the expense of others. You must realize that whoever acts egoistically not only ignores that understanding, but also exacerbates the pointless suffering in the world, which is caused, after all, by inner struggle among the different manifestations of the will."

"Very well, Arthur," I said. "And what is your opinion about altruistic behavior?"

"Altruism is the only way one can act reasonably. My one self is always less than the many other selves. Others comprise, after all, of a greater share of the manifested will than oneself. If anything, one should always annul oneself in the face of one's surroundings."

"You seem to say," I said, "that whoever acts this way is already half way to transcending his individuality."

"Quite so."

"Arthur, let us look at one of your painful memories. In retrospect, what do you think of the days you taught at the university?"

"I can hardly recall these days without feeling a pang of pain," he said sadly. "I have a lot of anger."

"Can you be more specific?"

"I was humiliated. Not a single student found it proper to come to my lessons. Everybody went to hear Hegel. As I said, I held my course at the same hour as his course."

"Have you done it on purpose?" I asked him quietly.

"I have already told you I scheduled it intentionally, haven't I?" he snapped. "I wanted to prove to myself that I could beat that megalomaniac. I lost, of course, but that doesn't prove anything. If only I could... Can you understand it? They preferred that speculative thinker to a real philosopher like me, a philosopher who philosophizes from the heart... They didn't take me seriously..."

"Arthur, your metaphysics is brilliant. And indeed, it originates from your heart. Yet it seems to me that it is you who don't take your own philosophy seriously."

He looked at me surprised. "What's that?"

"Why don't you try to apply your conception of egoism to your attempt to compete with Hegel?"

For the first time there was a long silence. "I see what you mean," he finally said dryly. "I played the role of the foolish self-centered egoist." He closed his eyes and pondered. I did not interrupt. He was clearly moved by a new insight.

6. Broadening insights and deepening their applications

Schopenhauer came to our next session much more relaxed than I had ever seen him. He started with a confession. Something had changed deep inside him since our last meeting.

"Your observation that my self-centeredness was inconsistent with my philosophy," he explained, "shook me up. Since our last meeting I am no longer in touch with that self-indulgent Schopenhauer who used to compare himself with Hegel. It is as if I can no longer look at myself from the minuscule perspective I once had on myself. My competition with Hegel now seems absolutely incomprehensible."

The dramatic change he reported seemed genuine. I was somewhat surprised at its abruptness, although not altogether astonished. Virtually every type of therapy relies on the fact that new insights have a considerable efficacy. Their effect is sometimes dramatic, resembling cases of religious or ideological conversions, when they inspire a refocusing of one's attitude to life. However, while some insights influence the person instantaneously as if triggering an avalanche, many others take a long time to gradually seep into the person's way of being and have their effect. It is, of course, hard to tell in advance how dramatic an impact an insight is going to have if any at all. In this sense, philosophical counseling operates not only in the domain of abstract thought, for it also relies on the capacity of life to respond to new understandings: to be inspired, moved by new visions, stirred by the power of new ideas, which is a power that works in us in an unpredictable way like—to borrow Schopenhauer's semi-religious notion—grace.

I was lucky with Schopenhauer: His first major insight happened to stir him dramatically. I told him that I was glad for his change of perspective, and even more glad that it involved not just his abstract thoughts but his entire attitude towards his encounter with Hegel. "This is precisely the challenge in philosophical counselling," I explained. "It is the challenge to transcend our narrow worldview—not just theoretically but in practice. You have just done it. You have gone beyond yourself, beyond your previous attitude towards the unfortunate competition with Hegel, and now you are relating to it from a broader perspective. But this competition was only one incident in your life. We need to go much further than that."

He nodded. "Where do we go, then?"

"Let us look again at the nature of suffering," I continued. "According to your philosophy, does the universal will suffer?"

"Of course not. Only the fragmented manifestations of the universal will suffer. I have already told you that."

"In other words, Arthur, when you suffer, whose point of view are you adopting?"

Schopenhauer looked at me agape. "Aha," he said and nodded. "I see what you mean. Only as long as I limit myself to Schopenhauer's perspective do I feel suffering. But if I manage to go beyond my self-centered point of view..."

"Exactly," I said. "At least, according to your own philosophy. Perhaps there is a way to go beyond your present attitude to suffering, just as you did regarding the unfortunate Hegel incident."

"You know," he said, "it strikes me that I already have a broader perspective on myself, on human beings, on suffering—my philosophy. I have had it for years, but I have never managed to live according to it."

"In a way you have had it all along," I agreed. "And that is what elevated your life and made it bearable."

He sighed. "But not bearable enough. It should have taken me long ago beyond my narrow self-preoccupation. It should have released me from my pitiful state."

"Indeed. The challenge is to turn your broad philosophical perspective from theory to practice; from thought to real life. That would be, of course, a considerable task. But this is precisely what philosophical counselling is all about."

"I can now see how to proceed," he said with undisguised enthusiasm. "With your help I will examine each and every incident of suffering in my life. And just like in the Hegel case, we will unravel the narrowness of my previous attitude. We will place my suffering in a broader perspective. I will rise above the suffering Schopenhauer to a broader, different Schopenhauer—a Schopenhauer who lives his philosophical perspective, a man who acknowledges pain but is not preoccupied with it!"

"Amen," I said cautiously. "But this is not as easy as it sounds. In order to go beyond mere intellectual understanding, we will need what your philosophy calls 'grace': a heart-felt realization, a break-through insight, a deep inspiration to change. You will have to go beyond the realm of theoretical ideas and start thinking from your heart."

"Anything you say, doc, as long as we don't start psychologizing my unconscious; as long as we stay with philosophical investigations. Let us do what you suggest, not only in order to liberate me from my suffering, but also because the purpose of life is, to my mind, transcending my individual point of view and attaining wisdom."

Philosophical Counselling: Transcending our individual perspective

The above case study demonstrates how Schopenhauer's views may be taken to suggest that philosophizing can be used to help individuals transcend their predicaments. Within his philosophy, this move is described as going beyond the perspective of one's individual will towards the broader perspective of the universal will, of which it is a limited and even distorted fragment. However, in the context of philosophical counselling we need not be committed to the specific details of his philosophy. Abstracting from these specific details, the basic idea is that philosophizing can help counsellees go beyond the limited boundaries of their current way of being. In this sense Schopenhauer's views provide us with a conceptual framework for addressing the problem of the unconscious in philosophical counselling. It suggests that philosophizing can help the counsellee go beyond the psychological forces underlying the predicament at hand, even though they may be unconscious or not consciously controllable. More specifically, the kind of counselling suggested by Schopenhauer's case study can be viewed as based upon the following four major principles:

First, regarding the aim of the counselling process, Schopenhauer can be viewed as suggesting that counsellees can deal with their suffering by forsaking and transcending their narrow, individual concerns and self-regarding needs and by adopting a broader attitude towards life. Acquiring a broader attitude to life is certainly part of wisdom. Hence, in accordance with the original meaning of philosophy—love of wisdom—the aim of philosophizing in philosophical counselling can be seen as wisdom.

Second, regarding the process of the counselling, Schopenhauer can be understood as suggesting that the desired change can best be achieved not by working to mend and adjust the person's current psychological states, particularly his unconscious forces, but by transcending the person's current psychology, specifically the unconscious, and move towards a new way of being. In other words, the process of philosophical counselling is that of overcoming personal predicaments by opening up to wisdom.

Third, regarding the content of the counselling conversations, Schopenhauer can be seen as saying that there is no need—indeed no use—in discussing in a psychological fashion the person's current conscious and unconscious states. There is no need to dig into, expose, analyze, re-experience etc. the hidden psychological forces that underlie the predicament at hand. Instead, the counselling conversations can be philosophical in nature. They can, in other words, focus on a way of being which is possible but not yet actual, namely on the redeeming, broader perspective on life which the person strives to achieve.

Fourth, Schopenhauer's notion of 'grace' can be used to remind the counsellor that a motivating power is necessary for turning an insight from a theoretical understanding to a personal transformation. If we go beyond Schopenhauer's particular understanding of the notion of grace, we can say that his idea expresses the insight that a radical inner transformation requires a special kind of inspiration.

Needless to say, all this is only a rough sketch of an approach to philosophical counselling which still awaits many further details and development. It is, in other words, more like a conceptual framework for further studies than a solution to the problem of the unconscious in philosophical counselling.[13] But the basic idea seems to us worth stating even in this preliminary state: that the role of philosophical counselling is to inspire counsellees to go beyond their current narrow, self-preoccupied psychological states, specifically beyond their unconscious states, and implement in their lives a broader approach to their world.

One might object that although the process of transcending envisioned here is appealing as an ideal, it is impossible to utilize it in practice. How can the idea of going beyond one's predicament be reconciled with to the framework of our contemporary view of the psyche?

The clue to answering this question can be found in an often neglected everyday life phenomenon. It is a commonplace observation that people are often inspired, for shorter or longer periods, to go beyond their current personal concerns and embark upon various projects or missions that are broader than their previous horizons. Thus, a person who normally leads a rather trite life may one day join an urgent social cause. She may now start devoting herself to social activities with great enthusiasm and perseverance, read articles and books, socialize with a different kind of people, etc. Such a person is often no longer weighed down by her previous concerns, but receives a new life: new kinds of energy, a new goal in life, new hopes. Similarly, another person may undergo an internal spiritual change, join a church, and start devoting himself to church activity. Still another person may become enchanted with art, or with archeology, or with the preserva-

298 Philosophical Counselling & The Unconscious

tion of wildlife, and sometimes abandon her previous occupations and even career for the sake of her values.

In such cases the landscape, as it were, of the person's inner world undergoes a dramatic transformation. What had previously occupied a peripheral place in the person's life if any at all, now becomes a central source of inspiration. Conversely, what had previously served as a central concern—one's salary, influence at the workplace, clothing, fun and entertainment—now becomes peripheral in the person's life. Furthermore, that transformation often happens in a specific direction: from being self-centered around personal satisfaction to broader concerns directed at a topic or cause that goes beyond the narrow boundaries of the individual.

William James describes a certain sub-type of this phenomenon at great length in his book *Varieties of Religious Experience*.[14] There he quotes numerous personal accounts of individuals who have undergone religious conversion, often abruptly and unexpectedly. As a consequence of their conversion they have been radically transformed, coming to center their lives around a new spiritual ideal which now started serving as a new and powerful source of inspiration and of meaning. Following their transformation, they were easily able to overcome the predicaments which had previously occupied them. William James analyzes these dramatic transformations in terms of a field of psychological powers, often fragmented, which rearranges itself around a new center. We regard the religious conversion described by James as a subclass of a more general type of transformation in which a person acquires a new perspective on life, focused on a new center of interest which serves as a source of inspiration. In contrast, Schopenhauer's specific philosophy represents what can be called an atheistic metaphysical subclass of the same general type.

What is interesting about this type of transformation, whether religious, ideological, artistic, or other, is that it does not occur as a consequence of psychological treatment of any kind. At no time prior to the transformation does the person need to analyze the psychological factors inside her, expose them, manipulate them, give them vent, or in short, address them in any way. Without delving into the psychological forces which underlie her current state, the person manages to bypass them, to go beyond them and be transformed into a new way of being with a broader attitude to life, a new center and a new source of inspiration.

This is precisely the vision of philosophical counselling that emerges out of Schopenhauer's ideas as described above. This vision suggests that philosophizing in philosophical counselling can inspire counsellees to transcend their current psychological state into a broader attitude to life, which is to say, wisdom.

Notes

[1] See for example Sigmund Freud, "A Note on the Unconscious," in Brian Farrell (ed.), *Philosophy and Psychoanalysis*, New York: MacMillan, 1994, pp. 3-8.

[2] Beck, A.T., Rush, A., Shaw, B., and Emery, G., *Cognitive Therapy of Depression*, New York: Guilford Press, 1979.

[3] Perls, F.S., *Gestalt Therapy Verbatim*, Lafayette, CA: Real People Press, 1969. See especially chapter 3, pp. 41-54.

[4] Ibid.

[5] Rogers, C.R., On Becoming a Person, Boston: Houghton Mifflin, 1961, pp. 104-105.

[6] Ibid., pp. 46-47

[7] In this chapter we focus particularly on specific aspects of philosophical counseling, namely, those relevant to the problem of the unconscious. For other aspects of our approach see Lahav, R. "Philosophical Counseling as a Quest for Wisdom," *Practical Philosophy*, 1: 2001; "The Efficacy of Philosophical Counseling: A First Outcome Study," *Practical Philosophy*, 4: 2001.

[8] While the opening paragraphs are based mainly on biographical details, the rest of this imaginary case with Arthur Schopenhauer is based on his principal work: *The World as Will and Representation*, (Translated by E.F.J. Payne), New York: Dover Publications, 1958.

[9] Ibid, vol. II, Ch. 46: "On the Vanity and Suffering of Life."

[10] Ibid, vol. I, Books 2-4.

[11] Ibid, vol. I, Book 4.

[12] Ibid, vol. I, Book 4.

[13] But see Lahav (2001), Ibid for more details.

[14] James, W., Cambridge: Harvard University Press, 1985

www.ingramcontent.com/pod-product-compliance
Lightning Source LLC
Chambersburg PA
CBHW031501270326
41930CB00006B/194